The Studio Musician's
JARGONBUSTER

A Glossary of
Music Technology and Recording
by
Godric Wilkie

• Musonix Publishing •

To the memory of my father, Clarence, and for my mother, Margaret.

Other titles from Musonix Publishing:

Music in Sequence – A complete guide to MIDI sequencing
Classics in Sequence – A source book for MIDI sequencing
Composing in Sequence *(in preparation)*

First published in 1993   ISBN Number 0 9517214 2 9

Published by Musonix Publishing, 2 Avenue Gardens, London SW14 8BP.

Exclusive distributors: Music Sales Limited   Music Sales Corporation   Music Sales Pty. Limited
8/9 Frith Street   225 Park Avenue South   4th Floor, 72 Bathurst Street
London W1V 5TZ   New York NY 10003 USA   Sydney N.S.W. 2000 Australia

Order Number: MX 30045

Cover design by Bob Linney

Photo-typeset in 10-point Times Roman by Musonix Typesetting.

Printed and bound in England.

Dictionaries are like watches, the worst is better than none,
and the best cannot be expected to go quite true.

Boswell's Life of Samuel Johnson (1791)

Introduction

If any single quality characterizes world culture in the late twentieth century, it is most probably communication. Not just people talking on a 'phone line between Sydney and San Diego, but the diffusion and sharing of ideas and concepts from previously separate disciplines.

Twenty years ago music, technology and recording had only limited points of contact. As we approach the millennial flip-over they have, like many other areas of human endeavour, expanded to the point where their edges now overlap, creating the complex boundary known as Music Technology. In the wake of this process comes a need for a boundary book.

This is intended to be such a book. It is not a glossary of music, nor is it a glossary of technology or recording. It is a guide to the twisting pathways through the territory where these three disciplines meet.

I have tried to write a book that will give the studio musician a clearer understanding of the fast-evolving language of Music Technology. It is becoming increasingly necessary for musicians to understand MIDI and mixing desks, for computer users to understand the principles of musical performance and sampling, and for sound engineers to understand microprocessors and musical notation. If you are entering this territory, then this book is aimed at you.

When it first occurred to me to write a glossary, I undertook a little market research. There was nothing then that covered all three areas. Without producing a book the size of a telephone directory, it would be impossible to give comprehensive coverage of all the terms encompassed by the individual disciplines of music, technology and recording. My criterion for selection has been to define those terms most likely to be encountered by the studio musician. Thus, you will not find biographies of composers, descriptions of acoustic instruments, wiring diagrams of computer circuits or the layout of outside broadcast vans. Information on all of these may be found in separate, more specialized publications.

In picking up this book, you will have noticed that it is cast in paper not in stone. Words change their precise meaning and usage and, although I have tried to reflect "state-of-the-art" thinking at the time of writing, there are bound to be divergences and omissions which I would hope to remedy in future editions.

I would like to take this opportunity to thank the many friends and professional colleagues who have helped and encouraged this endeavour and, in particular, Dr Roger Beeson, Andy Smith, Eric and John Welch, and Elizabeth Wolton. Thanks are also due to Paul Terry and William Lloyd for having been brave enough to take on the editing and publishing of this book and, above all, to my wife, Helen, for her indulgence and support.

May all beings communicate peace.

Godric Wilkie
London, 1993

Using this book

The definitions are arranged in strict alphabetical order, ignoring spaces and the capitalization of letters. Thus, **PA Version** will be found after **Pause**, not after **Pa**.

Entries that include the words "Italian for" invariably refer to terms found in musical notation. Those that mention the word "message" are terms which form part of the MIDI Specification. Readers who are new to MIDI may be relieved to know that software, such as sequencer programs, will generally shield the user from much of this highly technical information, at least for more basic work. However, byte values for the various messages do sometimes need to be input by the user. These have been given in decimal numbers, rather than hexadecimal notation – a conversion chart is included on page 109.

When additional information may be found under some different heading, entries include a reference to *see also* the topic concerned. Within each entry, words that have been capitalized are generally terms that may be looked up elsewhere in the book. If there is more than one definition for a particular term, these cross references may be followed by a superscript (e.g. Screen[2]) to indicate the particular meaning intended.

Current trade names have generally been omitted, except where they are used in a wider sense, such as ADAT or Portastudio.

A very small number of definitions are not intended to be taken too seriously, but are there to break the monotony for those who insist on reading glossaries from cover to cover.

For readers who would like to use the book to explore a certain area, a "route map" is printed on pages 110–111. This shows key entries for a number of important topics, many of which have further cross-references in the text. Although the coverage of the chart cannot be comprehensive, it may help the reader to navigate more effectively than could be offered by random plunging into the complete alphabetical listing.

A

The left-hand part of a stereo signal.

A & R

Abbreviation of Artists and Repertoire. The department within a record company whose job is to find new musicians and new music for the company to exploit. A & R departments will ensure that their discoveries match the desired image or style of the company.

A/B

A comparison between two recordings of the same material; pre- and post-equalisation, or pre- and post-effects, or any other two conditions.

Absolute Pitch

See Perfect Pitch.

Absorption

Loss due to the conversion of the kinetic energy of sound into heat during its transmission through the air or other material.

AC

See Alternating Current.

A Cappella

Unaccompanied choral singing. *Cappella* is Italian for chapel: the term is thought to originate from the practice of singing without instrumental backing, which was favoured by the church authorities at the Sistine Chapel. The term is now used to indicate unaccompanied singing, irrespective of the function of the music or the building in which it is performed.

Accelerando

An indication that the tempo of a piece of music should gradually be increased.

Accent

1. The emphasis of a sound in relation to others. This stress is achieved variously by playing the note louder, leaving a short silence before it, slightly lengthening it, or by anticipating its expected position through the use of Syncopation. A slight accent (usually on the first beat of each bar) is part of normal performance technique in many styles of music. The distribution of accents gives a piece of music its particular rhythmic character, especially in dance music of all kinds. In music notation, notes that require a specific accent are marked with an accent symbol (>) or a "wedge" (∧).

2. A feature of most drum machines, allowing beats to be emphasized by increasing the volume either of a particular instrument or of all instruments sounding on that beat.

Access Time

In a disk drive or other mass storage device, the time taken to find and retrieve a particular piece of information or block of data. For a disk drive, this is time taken up by the lateral motion of the head assembly (seek time) and waiting time for the disk to rotate sufficiently for the area of interest to be under the head (rotational latency). *See also* Fragmentation.

Accidental

1. Sharp or flat symbols placed in groups in a key signature to establish the basic key of a piece of music, or individually within the music to indicate a temporary alteration of a note.

2. A note which is not normally part of the current Key.

Ack

Abbreviation of Acknowledge. One of the characters transmitted for the purposes of Handshaking in a data transfer. The character is sent back to the transmitting device by the receiving device to confirm that the last block of data has been received. It also occurs as part of the Sample Dump Standard as a System Exclusive message of a Non-Real Time type with a Sub ID#1 value of 127.

Acoustics

1. The study of sound and the way it behaves.

2. The contribution a room makes to any sound which occurs in it, and by extension the "sound" of the room or studio itself. This is determined by its shape, dimensions and the construction materials used.

Active

Electronic circuits are commonly divided into two classes: active and passive. In rough terms any circuits which contain valves or semiconductors (transistors, diodes or integrated circuits) can be called active. Circuits which contain only resistors, capacitors or inductors (coils, transformers etc.) can be called passive. The definition is sometimes considered from the aspect of Gain. Generally, semiconductor circuits are able to increase the gain of the signal while non-semiconductor circuits are not. For this reason, active also implies the ability to increase gain while passive implies the lack of such an ability.

Active Input

See Transformerless Input.

Active Loudspeaker

A type of loudspeaker which has amplification circuitry built in. If there is only one amplifier driving all Transducers, the terms powered speaker or powered monitor are preferred.

Active Sensing

A System Real Time message with a status byte value of 254 transmitted, in the absence of other data, every 300 ms by some MIDI devices. If it then fails to appear, a receiving device equipped with active sensing will assume that the connection has been broken (the cable has fallen out) and will silence all voices currently playing. The message requires no data bytes.

Adagio

A slow or leisurely tempo: 66–76 beats per minute.

ADAM

Acronym from Akai Digital Audio Multitrack. A format developed by Akai for recording twelve tracks of digital audio data on a standard Video-8 cassette. The tape runs at four times the normal Video-8 speed and gives about 15 minutes recording time at the industry standard sampling rate of 44.1 kHz.

ADAT

Acronym from Alesis Digital Audio Tape. A format developed by Alesis for recording eight tracks of digital audio data on a standard S-VHS cassette at industry standard sampling rates.

ADC

See Analogue to Digital Converter.

Additional Information

See Set Up.

Additive Synthesis

See Synthesis.

ADSR

Abbreviation of Attack, Decay, Sustain, Release – these being the parameters which appear on certain types of Envelope Generator. Some envelope generators may feature additional parameters such as Delay [3] (before the attack) or a second decay, etc.

ADT

Abbreviation of Auto Double Tracking. *See* Double Tracking.

Aeolian

See Mode.

AES

Abbreviation of Audio Engineering Society. A body involved in the specification and development of technical standards in the audio industry.

AES/EBU

A professional digital audio connection standard or interface specified jointly by the Audio Engineering Society and the European Broadcast Union. The standard allows two audio channels to be encoded in a serial data stream and transmitted via a Balanced Line connection (using XLR connectors). The domestic variant is called SPDIF and uses Unbalanced Line on phono connectors.

AF

See Audio Frequency.

Aftertouch

A facility on some keyboards and other MIDI controllers which can be used to introduce modulation (vibrato etc.) to notes currently playing. On a keyboard it is activated by pressing the keys down further after the note has been turned on. Two types are defined by MIDI: Channel Key Pressure and Polyphonic Key Pressure.

AI

See Artificial Intelligence.

Algorithm

1. In a computer, a sequential group of rules which, taken as a whole, will solve a specific problem. Each rule is sufficiently unambiguous that it can be executed by a machine. The algorithm can be considered as a symbolic representation of the problem. Generation of the algorithm is one of the stages of writing a computer program. The more accurately the algorithm models the problem, the more effective will be the program which results from it. *See also* Software.

2. In Yamaha's implementation of John Chowning's system of FM synthesis, an algorithm is a particular configuration of a number of Operators. The algorithm determines how many operators will be Carriers, how many will be Modulators and what the signal connections will be between these. In some ways it is analogous to a Patch on a modular synthesizer.

Algorithmic Composition

The use of, or a facility within, software to help music composition. Essentially computer-generated music. Sometimes called computer-aided composition.

Aliasing

1. In audio, the effect which occurs in a digital audio device when a cycle of a sinewave present in an audio signal is subjected to less than two sampling events, thus ignoring the advice given by the Nyquist Sampling Theorem. The resultant signal will no longer be a sinewave and will be lower in frequency than the original. In practice this will normally only occur with the high audio Partials if the sampling rate is significantly less than about 40 kHz and no anti-aliasing filters are fitted to the encoder. The upper trace in the diagram is a 20 kHz sine wave, sampled at about 30 kHz (the vertical lines). The lower trace shows the output regenerated from the samples. As you can see, it is a distorted wave of a much lower frequency.

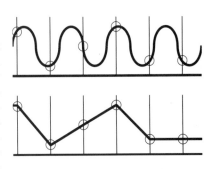

2. In digital video systems, an effect that occurs to a greater or lesser extent when a curve is displayed on a video screen. On close inspection, it is possible to see that the curve is approximated by jagged steps or "jaggies". A similar phenomen is noticeable on digitally printed images, especially with low resolution printers. This is an analogous effect to that described in Aliasing [1].

Alignment The precise adjustment of tape heads and associated equipment for optimum performance on a tape recorder. *See also* Line-Up.

Alla Breve A term historically related to medieval note lengths, in which the breve was one of the shortest notes. In modern usage, the term usually refers to $\frac{2}{2}$ time (often indicated by the alternative "Cut C" time signature of ($\mathbb{C}$) – this has the feel of two minim (half note) beats per bar, as opposed to the more common four crotchets (quarter notes) per bar of $\frac{4}{4}$ or $\mathbf{C}$ time. In commercial and popular music, it is frequently used to mean "half time" – i.e. play twice as fast.

Allegretto A slightly slower tempo than Allegro.

Allegro A lively to reasonably fast tempo: 116–150 beats per minute.

All Notes Off A Channel Voice message which instructs a MIDI device to silence any voices currently playing. A typical situation for its use might be where a sequencer is controlling a number of devices on several channels. Should you stop the sequencer playing, the software could either transmit a Note Off message for each note currently playing or it could simply send a single All Notes Off message for each channel, leaving the receiving device to do the work. The message is actually a type of Controller Change message with a data byte value of 123. *See also* All Sounds Off.

Alpha Test *See* Bug.

All Sounds Off A Channel Voice message which instructs a MIDI device to silence any voices currently playing and to mute the audio output, as if a MIDI volume message of zero had been received. Muting the output effectively stops even those sounds with a long decay that might continue after a Note Off message has been received. The message is actually a type of Controller Change message with a data byte of 120. *See also* All Notes Off, Reset All Controllers.

Alternating Current An electrical signal which, unlike Direct Current, changes state with time. Mains electrical supplies and audio signals (try not to confuse the two) are AC. Alternating Current is normally considered to vary positively and negatively around a zero reference point, i.e. one complete cycle of change might start at 0, rise to some higher positive value, fall back to 0 and then continue downwards to some negative value before rising again back to 0, thus completing the cycle.

Alto Italian for high. Used originally for a high male vocal part with a range roughly from the E below middle C upwards for two octaves. This was often sung by adult males with a falsetto voice, castrated males or boys. In modern usage, alto is also used for the female voice of similar range, more properly termed Contralto. By extension, instruments which operate in a similar range may also be prefixed by the term: e.g. alto sax. The alto clef, used principally by violas ("altos" in French), has middle C assigned to the centre line of the stave. *See also* Baritone, Bass, Clef, Soprano, Tenor, Treble.

AM Abbreviation of Amplitude Modulation. An encoding process whereby an audio signal is used to modulate the amplitude of a carrier signal so as to allow radio transmission.

Ambience The reverberant quality of a room.

Ambisonics A method of stereo recording which is claimed to give a better representation of the Field[1] in which the recording took place. Generally credited to Professor Felgett of Reading University, this system aims to give a three-dimensional impression of the ambience surrounding a musical performance and requires a decoder and extra pair(s) of loudspeakers.

Amp Abbreviation of amplifier or ampere.

Ampere The SI Unit of electrical current. *See* Electricity.

AMPLE Acronym from Advanced Music Programming Language and Environment. A system of hardware and software for BBC computers, developed by Hybrid Technology Ltd. for music production.

Amplification An increase in the amount of some quality such as signal level. The property exhibited by amplifiers. The opposite of attenuation.

Amplifier A device for altering (usually thought of in terms of increasing) the Amplitude of a signal. Each channel in a mixing desk is effectively an amplifier and, for the purposes of automation, the fader can be replaced with a VCA. The most commonly encountered amplifier is the one used to power loudspeakers in a monitoring system. Almost all stages through which a signal passes in the programme chain are specialized types of amplifiers which overall should ideally have Unity Gain.

Amplitude The relative value of a signal, its volume or magnitude. The height of its waveform.

Anacrusis *See* Beat[1].

Analogue Often used in a very vague manner, this word has a number of interpretations:

1. Anything opposite in meaning to Digital.

2. Any device made from discrete electronic components whose function is to process a sound directly without the involvement of any sort of computing.

3. A copy of something in another form. The magnetic coating on a recorded tape is an analogue of the changes in air pressure we perceive as sound.

Analogue Synthesizer
A synthesizer which uses analogue circuitry to generate its sound. To some extent superseded by digital technology in the early '80s but now enjoying a fashionable revival.

Analogue to Digital Converter
The encoding part of a digital audio device whose function is to Sample an analogue signal and derive a numeric (binary) value from it at regular intervals.

Andante
At a walking speed: 76–94 beats per minute.

Andantino
Confusingly this can mean either a little faster or a little slower than Andante, although generally taken to mean faster.

Anechoic
Without echo. Said of an acoustic which is "free field" (i.e. without boundary or reflecting surfaces) and specifically of a room which is designed to produce no reverb or other echo effects. This is achieved by giving the walls very irregular surfaces of considerable and varying depths so that (in theory) all sound waves which strike them are completely absorbed. Rooms of this type are used to test audio equipment such as loudspeakers and microphones and for other types of research.

Answer
See Fugue.

Anti-Aliasing Filter
A filter which is fitted to the front of an analogue to digital converter, whose cut-off frequency is set to somewhat less than half the sampling rate of the digital audio system. Its purpose is to remove any sinewave content which the system would be unable to sample twice (or more) in one cycle, and therefore to eliminate the Aliasing which might otherwise happen. *See also* Reconstruction Filter.

Antiphonal
A term used to describe music that is played or sung in alternating sections by two separate groups of performers – it originated in the practice of using two choirs to sing the Antiphon (part of the Roman Catholic liturgy). Antiphony became a particular feature of the Venetian style, as the architecture of (particularly) St Mark's, Venice allowed the two choirs or instrumental groups to be widely separated. The interesting spatial effects that could be achieved in this manner were extensively exploited by Venetian composers such as Gabrieli.

AOR
Abbreviation of, variously, Adult Oriented Rock or Album Oriented Rock; sometimes Album Oriented Radio. A tendency of some FM radio stations in the early '70s to play longer album tracks (to break up the monotony of singles) led to "album-only" radio stations. This in turn caused record companies to promote rock albums in addition to singles, thus solving a basic marketing problem experienced by them in connection with some forms of rock music (*see* Heavy Metal). The result was a monotony of ever-longer rock album tracks.

APRS
Abbreviation of Association of Professional Recording Studios. An industry body set up to ensure a uniform standard of service and practice in the area of sound recording.

Aria
Italian for air (song). Generally indicates a composition for solo voice with accompaniment – also, by extension, a lyrical instrumental piece. More particularly, from the late 17th century, it refers to a substantial vocal item which might appear in an opera or religious work. Such arias typically begin with an instrumental introduction followed by a first vocal section in the tonic key, a short instrumental episode, a second vocal section in a contrasting key, concluding with a repeat of the first section without the introduction. This repeat, which was often elaborately ornamented by the singer, was seldom written out: the indication *Da Capo* or *Dal Segno* being used instead and leading to the description of the entire structure as Da Capo aria.

Arco
Italian for "with the bow". An instruction to players of the string family of instruments (violins, violas, 'cellos etc.) that they should return to using the bow, in effect cancelling a *Pizzicato* instruction. This is the most common way to play a string instrument.

Arpeggiator
A facility offered on some synthesizers which will automatically spread or arpeggiate a chord. The order in which the notes of the chord will be played can usually be selected by the user. The timing of the notes will be derived from an internal clock, from a trigger output of a drum machine or sequencer, or from MIDI Clock. Some stand-alone MIDI processors provide this facility, a notable example being the Oberheim "Cyclone". Some sequencers offer an arpeggiation facility as an editing option. *See also* Auto Accompaniment.

Arpeggio
A chord with its notes spread so that they are played consecutively in ascending or descending pitch order. From the Italian *arpeggiare* – to play the harp.

Arrangement
1. A version of a piece of music for resources other than those originally intended. This may be an instrumental version of a vocal number, a piano reduction of a band piece, or may involve altering other parameters of the original, such as its harmony, rhythm or structure.

2. In sequencers, a term sometimes used for the general layout of tracks, channels and patches rather than the complete Song[2]. This template can often be saved as a separate file.

Articulation

The way of characterizing notes (usually in a melody) by the precise control of their individual lengths to produce or eliminate gaps between them. The terms Staccato and Legato reflect the two extremes of articulation. It is one of the most important ways by which music can be shaped into phrases.

Artificial Intelligence

The concept (almost an article of faith for some) that computers will be able to, or can now, behave in a manner that resembles human intelligence. For example, they will be able to learn to perform a task rather than require programming, be able to adapt to changing levels or types of input, to perform deductively, to reason and possibly even to imagine. More strictly, the branch of computer science which deals with such problems as pattern recognition and knowledge-based or expert systems. Many new technologies are contributing to developments in this area including neural networks and bioelectronics.

Art Music

A broad term to describe music which is not folk, jazz or other types of popular music. Historically it is music which would more likely have been available to an elite within a society (not necessarily a western one either), such as royalty, the church or other influential group. It is music which tends to have been written down or notated and to have had an identifiable author or composer. Designations of Musical Periods, such as baroque, generally refer to western art music. The term classical, which strictly relates to a specific period, is often loosely used to encompass all art music.

ASCII

Acronym from American Standard Code for Information Interchange. One of a number of standard systems which determine how a specific character is represented numerically in a computer. Thus the character A is represented by the number 65 (1000001 in binary). ASCII is a seven-bit code and thus allows 128 characters to be uniquely defined. The intention was to ensure that text data could be transmitted from one machine to another. There is a so-called "extended ASCII" which is an eight-bit version of ASCII used by IBM-compatible PCs. *See also* UKASCII, EBCDIC.

ASIC

Acronym from Application Specific Integrated Circuit. Essentially an IC (usually an LSI) made for a particular function, and which can replace an assembly of general purpose integrated circuits which do the same job: e.g. the sound generating and processing circuitry of a synthesizer.

Asynchronous

A form of data transfer between two devices which have separate, free running clocks, and where no attempt is made to synchronize them. In order to ensure that data is not missed, each byte is preceded by a Start Bit and succeeded by a Stop Bit. MIDI is asynchronous.

A Tempo

Italian for "in time". An instruction to return to a previous speed, usually encountered after some change in tempo. Not necessarily the same as Tempo Primo.

Atmosphere Microphone

A microphone used to pick up audience noise or other environmental sounds in a live broadcast or recording, in order to give some "atmosphere" to the production.

Atonal Music

Strictly speaking, music which tends not to have a sense of being in a particular key. Atonality seeks to avoid the hierarchical properties of Tonal Music. It began to appear during the early 20th century as composers sought new means of expression. The term is also used in a more restricted sense to refer to the pre-serial music of composers such as Schoenberg, Berg and Webern. *See also* Serialism.

ATRAC

Acronym from Adaptive TRansform Acoustic Coding. A method of data compression developed by Sony for their MD system. ATRAC exploits the way the human ear and brain work – particularly the phenomenon known as Auditory Masking, where tones which are quieter than others in the same or adjacent frequency bands are ignored. ATRAC divides the audio signal into 52 frequency bands. Unlike Philip's similar PASC system, the frequency bands defined by ATRAC are not of a constant width. Narrow bands are used for lower frequencies, with each higher band being 20% wider than the one below it. Below 500 Hz the bands are about 100 Hz wide, whereas above 13.5 kHz they are over 3.5 kHz wide. In sampling, ATRAC does not use all 16 bits for every sample, but distributes the bits so that only the most active bands are sampled. ATRAC samples sustained signals less often than variable signals, so constant sounds use less data than percussive ones. Periods of silence generally use no bits at all – unlike conventional sampling processes, where all 16 bits are used to describe silence. The data compression ratio achieved by ATRAC is approximately 5:1 when averaged out, and this easily enables Sony to obtain the same duration on Mini Disc as CD.

Attack Time

1. The time taken for a sound to reach maximum loudness or timbre from silence. The attack is, essentially, the start of a sound.

2. Of a Compressor or Limiter, etc: the time the device takes to respond to a transition in the signal level beyond the Threshold.

3. Of an Envelope Generator: the time taken for the envelope to reach its maximum level from its off or zero position. If the EG is being used to control an amplifier (VCA or DCA) the time taken to reach maximum loudness from silence. *See also* Envelope Generator.

Attack Velocity

See Velocity.

Attenuation

A reduction in the amount of some quality such as signal level. The property exhibited by attenuators. The opposite of amplification.

Attenuator	A device for reducing signal level, also known as a pad. Some microphone inputs on mixing desks have this facility, where the latter term is preferred.
Audio	Relating to sound or hearing.
Audio Frequency	The range of frequencies which can be experienced by an average human being. The range is defined as 20 Hz to 20 kHz for convenience but, for most people, the upper limit is closer to 17 kHz, and this continues to reduce with age. Dolphins are believed to hear up to 70 kHz.
Audio Mixer	*See* Mixing Desk. Strictly speaking, a more accurate term for a mixing desk which is specifically used for audio signals.
Audio Signal	Electromagnetic transmission of audio frequency information. The sound is encoded as variations in voltage (or other quality) for the purpose of conveying the sound information from one point to another.
Auditory Masking	A function of the mechanism of hearing, whereby a high level of sound in a given frequency band reduces the apparent level of another sound in the same or adjacent bands.

Augmentation

1. The increase of a major or perfect interval by one semitone to make an augmented interval.

2. The appearance of a musical idea in note durations which are longer than those used for its first appearance. This technique was often used in the polyphonic music of the middle ages and renaissance, as well as in contrapuntal music (e.g. Fugues) of the baroque and later musical periods.

Auto Accompaniment	A facility on some electric keyboards, organs and music software, to generate a musical backing derived from single notes played by the user. Usually used in conjunction with a pre-set drum pattern, which will determine the style of the accompaniment.
Autocorrect	*See* Quantization [1].
Autolocator	A device for controlling the transport system of a tape recorder. In addition to providing remote control of play, fast forward, rewind, pause, stop and record modes, the device will allow specific sections of the programme on tape to be located for the purposes of drop-in/drop-out recording etc., referenced to some type of timecode such as SMPTE. Usually a number of locate points can be stored in the device. Some sequencers also have an autolocate facility.
Automation	A system where manual (human) control of a process is replaced or enhanced by machine (usually computer) control. The most obvious musical application is Mixing Desk automation where faders, mutes and even equalisation can be controlled in part or in whole by a computer. The change in control settings can be continuous but is more likely to be in terms of "snapshots" of particular mixer settings. These are stored in order and the computer then fades from one to another. The duration of such fades is usually programmable. Many mixing desks are now equipped with MIDI allowing mutes, at least, to be set from a sequencer, often using Note On messages.
Autopanner	A device for processing a signal so that it can be made to appear at various positions in a stereo image.
Auxiliary	A Bus allowing a signal to be sent from a mixing desk prior to the main output, usually to provide an input to Effects.
Auxiliary Messages	In a MIDI Implementation chart, a classification of MIDI messages which includes Active Sensing, All Notes Off, Local On/Off and Reset, and which describes whether this particular MIDI device responds to any of these messages.
Azimuth	The angular relationship between the tape head gap and a line at 90° to the edge of the tape. Even a slight variation in this relationship will reduce the high frequency content of the reproduced signal.

B	The right-hand part of a stereo signal.
Backbeat	A popular music term referring to the second and fourth beats in a four-beat bar, often emphasized by the drummer. *See also* Beat [1].
Backing Track	Pre-recorded music used by a singer or other musician during performance and which augments or entirely replaces other performers. This has become increasingly popular as musicians attempt to recreate the sound of their studio recordings live on stage. *See also* PA Version.

Backing Vocals

In popular music, extra vocal parts which fill gaps in, or harmonize with, the lead vocal line. Usually sung by specialist session singers. Sometimes abbreviated to bvox.

Backup

1. A copy of data which has been taken from a computer system and is stored separately from it. The intention is that the data can be restored to the computer in case of accidental loss of the original. The backup may be made on floppy disk, magnetic tape, RAM card, etc.

2. A source of power, such as a battery, used when the main source of power has been removed. Normally encountered in devices such as synthesizers etc. whose memory contents are preserved by an internal battery when the device is switched off. *See also* Uninterruptible Power Supply.

Baffle

1. In a recording studio, a structure designed to absorb or scatter sound waves in order to control the acoustics of the room. They are usually placed on the walls or ceiling, and may range in construction from expanded foam tiles less than a metre square, to substantial wood, plaster and Rockwool wedges several metres long.

2. One or more sheets of wood (or other material) inside a loudspeaker cabinet, serving both as a fixing for the Transducer(s) and as a means of directing the sound waves, particularly to avoid Cancellation of waves from the front of the loudspeaker by those emanating from the rear.

Balance

1. A control (usually on domestic hi-fi) which adjusts the relative volumes of the left and right channels.

2. A control on a synthesizer which adjusts the relative volumes of two different sounds which it can voice simultaneously. It should not be confused with Pan.

3. One of the defined MIDI Controller Change messages with a status byte value in the range 176–191 and a first data byte value of 8, which has the same function as Balance [2].

Balanced Line

A method of conveying an audio signal from one point to another using a cable with two wires, which gives high immunity from EMI [2]. A conductive Screen [2] forms an earth or current return path, while the two wires carry versions of the signal, one of which is 180° out of phase relative to the other. These are called the "hot" and "cold" lines. At the destination the lines are summed by an amplifier with two inputs, one of which is 180° out of phase. As a result of this process there is no net Cancellation of the audio signal; however, any noise which appears in both lines will be cancelled out (by inversion) at the summing end.

Ballad

A form of song which narrates a story, particularly in folk music traditions. Also used to refer to any sentimental song.

Band

1. A synonym for track on a record or tape.

2. A range of frequencies.

3. A group of musicians.

Band Part

A notated form of a piece of music, derived from a Full Score, usually containing only the music for a single instrument or pair of similar instruments.

Band Pass

1. *See* Filter.

2. A security pass which allows personnel backstage before, during or after a performance.

Bandwidth

1. The range of frequencies a signal possesses, or that a piece of equipment will pass, between specified upper and lower limits. It should not be confused with frequency response, which concerns itself not only with the upper and lower limits but also how frequencies are amplified or attenuated between these two points.

2. One parameter on a Parametric Equalizer.

Bank

In synthesizers, an array of different sounds. For example, 64 different sounds may be arranged in two banks of 32 each or eight banks of 8 each (a Roland favourite). Bank is also a term used for the groups of audio outputs in hard disk multi-track recording systems.

Bank Select

One of the defined MIDI Controller Change messages with a status byte value in the range 176–191 and a first data byte of 0 for MSB, followed by a repeat of the status byte and a data byte of 32 for LSB. The two acting together define one value from a 14-bit range and select which bank any subsequent Program Change message will affect. This method gets round the problem of Program Change messages having only 128 possible values. As Bank Select messages have two data bytes, and the program change is a further byte, the total number of programs or sounds which can be selected is 2,097,152 (128 x 128 x 128).

Bantam

A type of jack connector preferred for professional use in recording studios, particularly on Patchbays. The connectors are about half the size of common jacks but are more robust and reliable. They are also about 10 times more expensive.

Bar

In written music, a grouping of pulses into a convenient unit which falls between two barlines. A barline is the vertical line which crosses the stave at regular intervals. The bar begins with the downbeat and ends immediately before the next downbeat, and will contain a constant number of beats of the type determined by the Time Signature. A bar of $\frac{4}{4}$ will have four quarter-note (crotchet) beats.

Baritone

From the Greek, meaning "deep sounding". A male voice, pitched between bass and tenor, with a range extending from F or G above Middle C downwards for about two octaves. By extension, instruments which operate in a similar range may also use the term. e.g. baritone (a brass band instrument) or baritone sax. *See also* Alto, Bass, Soprano, Tenor, Treble.

Baroque

See Musical Periods.

BASIC

Acronym from Beginner's All-purpose Symbolic Instruction Code. *See* High Level Language.

Basic Channel

In a MIDI device, the Channel [2] on which that device receives fundamental messages which govern its operation, e.g. Reception Mode changes. In Mono mode (Mode 4) the basic channel is the lowest numbered channel.

Bass

1. Audio frequencies below about 200 Hz.

2. The lowest voice or musical part. A bass voice has a range from about E above middle C downwards for around two octaves. By extension, instruments which operate in a similar range may also be prefixed by the term: e.g. bass clarinet, bass guitar. In orchestral terms, bass by itself usually refers to the double bass. *See also* Alto, Baritone, Clef, Soprano, Tenor, Treble.

Bass Tip Up

See Proximity Effect.

Baud Rate

The rate at which binary data is transmitted, expressed as the number of bits per second. MIDI data is transmitted at 31.25 kbaud (31,250 bits per second).

Beat

1. In Measured Music, the sensation of a basic pulse from which all rhythm in the piece is derived. Beats are of three types: downbeat is a strongly accented pulse, such as the first in the bar; offbeat is any pulse other than the downbeat; upbeat (or anacrusis) is a special case of offbeat, which immediately precedes the first beat of the bar and hence the bar line.

2. The unit of time determined by 24 MIDI clock pulses, normally representing a quarter-note (crotchet).

Beating

An effect which occurs when two or more oscillators are not at exactly the same frequency, or when two strings in an instrument are not at exactly the same pitch. This results in cyclic cancellation, in effect a type of tremolo. The rate of the effect increases proportionally to the distance in frequency between the two oscillators or strings. Musicians listen for an absence of beating to indicate that two notes are perfectly in tune.

Bebop

A species of jazz arising in the '40s and characterized by an increased complexity or diversity of techniques, including extreme tempi, alteration of accents within bars, odd phrase lengths, richer harmonic language (such as use of flattened fifths), the use of chords in a soloistic manner and very rapid solo passages. Miles Davies, Dizzy Gillespie, Thelonius Monk and Charlie Parker are the best known exponents of this style.

Bel

See Decibel.

Bern Copyright Convention

See Copyright.

Betamax

A domestic standard cassette system for making analogue video recordings. The commercially less successful of two such systems which first appeared in the early 1980s. The other, which has persisted, being VHS. Both formats have been pressed into service as a medium for recording digital audio data. Betamax was used in Sony's F1 system, while VHS's improved successor, S-VHS, is used in the Alesis ADAT digital audio multitrack system.

Beta Test

See Bug.

Bhangra

A diverse range of popular music emerging among indigenous and expatriot Punjabi communities. Modern forms are the result of a meeting of traditional Punjabi festival music with western rock and pop music forms. As it develops it increasingly draws on parallel developments in dance music such as Hip Hop, and has come to include some of the cultural aspects (breakdancing, clothing, fashion etc.) of those forms. Bhangra had religious origins and was performed, along with Giddha (women's solo songs), at the festival of Vaisakhi. However, its modern forms are enjoyed by Asians of Christian, Jain, Hindu, Muslim and Sikh persuasion throughout the world, as well as by an increasing white audience exposed to it via acid and House Music at "raves". It is denigrated by some Punjabis, who regard it as a further corruption and dilution of their culture, and by "world music" enthusiasts, who regard it as too commercial. Bands such as Alaap, Heera and Holle Holle, are typical of early '80s British bhangra bands, while DCS, Golden Star and Culture Shock reflect later trends.

Bias

See Tape Bias.

Bidirectional

A form of data transfer which allows a device to receive and transmit data simultaneously. MIDI has provision for an In socket and Out socket and to this extent may be considered bidirectional.

Bidirectional Mike

See Figure-of-Eight Microphone.

Big Band

A form of Jazz dance music which evolved during the Swing era of '30s and '40s, and the jazz bands that play in that style to this day. As the name suggests, it was typified by a move away from small ensembles to full instrumental sections playing en masse in a soloistic manner. Most big bands will have a rhythm section (drums, acoustic and/or electric bass, guitar and piano), a horn section of trumpets and trombones, plus a reed section of clarinets and saxes. Count Basie, Duke Ellington, Benny Goodman and Glen Miller are perhaps the most famous exponents. More modern developers of this style include Loose Tubes and Courtney Pine.

Binary

A way of representing any number using only two symbols, "0" and "1". Binary is a base 2 numbering system and follows the same rules as the more familiar base 10, or decimal, system. In decimal, each column is 10 times bigger than the one to its right (1000, 100, 10, 1) while in binary each column is 2 times bigger (1000, 0100, 0010, 0001 or 8, 4, 2, 1 in decimal). Any decimal number can be represented in binary although it may require more columns. In binary, the columns are called binary digits, or bits for short. Binary is used in computers since the presence or absence of a voltage can represent the two digits "1" (on) or "0" (off). Many MIDI publications print numbers in binary as they are often written by computer engineers who work in binary every day. Because of the relatively large number of columns or bits used to represent numbers, binary numbers are sometimes compressed into Hexadecimal (base 16) form, where one hexadecimal digit (a hit?) represents four binary digits. *See also* the conversion table on page 109.

Binary Form

A musical structure which consists of one musical idea (often repeated), followed by another (also often repeated). The first section may end in the "home" key, or in that of the second part. The latter will almost invariably begin in a different key (often the dominant) or at a different pitch level from the first, but will not generally contrast greatly with it. Binary form is sometimes represented by the letters AB. The form was commonly employed in dance movements (minuets, gigues etc.) during the 17th and early 18th centuries, but appeared less frequently later due to its inability to sustain a listener's interest during the larger scale works which were beginning to appear. Gradually the scheme was enlarged into the so-called rounded binary form (ABA) by repeating the first idea to end the piece. This in turn led to the development of Sonata Form.

Binaural

A method of recording in stereo, using microphones positioned equivalently to human ears, e.g. on a dummy head or separated by a disc of wood or plastic. The process gives a strong sense of space, but only on headphones, and is less convincing on loudspeaker systems.

Bit

Acronym from Binary digIT.

1. The positional column in a binary number system indicating the magnitude of that column or its power of 2. *See also* Binary.

2. In digital systems, an individual pulse in a pulse train which carries binary information. e.g. a sample value from an analogue to digital converter. Bits are usually grouped in eights (a byte), or fours (a nibble). The number of bits a system uses to describe numbers (the Word size) sets the limit to the maximum count or resolution of the system. In general, the greater the number of bits a digital audio system uses to encode the signal, the greater the dynamic range. As a rough guide, dynamic range improves by 6 dB for each bit added to the word size. Thus 8 bits gives a dynamic range of 48 dB, 12 bits gives 72 dB and 16 bits, 96 dB.

Bitmap Graphics

One of the two principal ways of generating graphics on a computer, using individual dots to form the image. So called because, when dealing with black and white pictures, each dot (usually corresponding with a Pixel on the monitor) can only be on or off, and may thus be represented by a single Bit in the computer's memory. Bitmap graphics produce larger files and poorer quality images, especially when scaled up in size, than the alternative Vector Graphics method.

Block

In a mass storage device such as a disk drive, the smallest amount of data that can be accessed is called a block, it being quicker to locate a fixed minimum amount. A block is typically 512 or 1024 bytes. Also used in a general way to describe an amount of data which is being transmitted or processed.

Bluegrass

A form of American country or folk music originating in the Appalachian mountains, using bowed or plucked string instruments such as violin or "fiddle", banjo, guitar, mandolin and Dobro, and typified by very fast and virtuoso performance. Bluegrass was popularized in the '40s by Bill Monroe and his Blue Grass Boys. The film "Deliverance" featured an example of the style in the soundtrack episode "Duelling Banjos" which was released as a single in 1973. Its modern form is sometimes called "Newgrass".

Blues

A form of folk music which originated in the southern states of USA among Afro-Americans at the end of the 19th century. It evolved from plantation and other work songs, and from existing forms of African music. Its early development is closely linked to that of Jazz, although the latter shows a greater European influence and diversity of type while the blues is somewhat more conservative. It is typically played on the guitar or piano, often to accompany lyrics of a melancholy nature. A prominent feature is the ambiguous tonality due to use of both major and minor forms of the third and seventh in the same melody, as well as occasional use of the augmented fourth. Taken together, these notes in the melody are known as the "blue notes" and contribute to the "bitter-sweet" sound of the blues. Its most common form is a slow, quadruple time elaboration over a repeated 12 bar bass. In time, forms of popular music such as Rhythm & Blues and Rock & Roll were derived from it.

Blumlein, Alan
The inventor (almost father) of stereo. While working for EMI[1] in the '30s, he filed (among others) British Patent 394 325, which described a number of techniques for making stereo recordings and cutting a two channel, single groove record by varying the lateral and vertical position of a disc cutting tool with axes at 45° to the surface of the record. Many of the techniques described in what must be the most important audio patent ever filed were not actually implemented until the late '50s, some time after his patents had expired. Blumlein was killed in a wartime aviation accident while he was working on the principles of Radar – ironically enough the accident was caused as a result of a safety check adjustment of an engine.

Blumlein Pair
Crossed pair microphone technique described by Alan Blumlein in the '30s, where two relatively directional microphones cross one another at an angle of 90° so that each microphone is at an angle of 45° to the centre of the sound source.

BNC
A type of connector favoured for video and digital audio work. It is a coaxial connector superficially similar to a television aerial connector. It is fitted with a bayonet-type locking mechanism to prevent inadvertent disconnection.

Boogie Woogie
A variant form of blues played on the piano. The 12-bar harmonic pattern of the blues is stated by an Ostinato bass, often in quavers in the left hand, accompanying improvised material in the right. It originated in American bars and brothels during the early 20th century. Boogie Woogie reached a peak in popularity around 1935-45 with performers such as Meade "Lux" Lewis.

Boom
1. An extendible pole to which a microphone can be fitted, and which allows an operator to tilt and point the microphone at a target. Used in outside broadcast and in television studios for audience discussions, etc.

2. In general recording, any sort of microphone stand with extending sections that allows a microphone to be positioned above a performer or some section of an orchestra, etc.

Bootleg
An illicit copy of something, most commonly an audio recording or computer software. Also specifically used to refer to an audio recording made by a member of the audience at a live performance. Bootlegging, like many forms of rip-off, has become something of an underground cult. Bootleg recordings of a deceased artist's last performance are much sought after by collectors and can change hands for spectacularly large amounts of money despite their often poor quality. Bootleggers are sometimes seen by some (i.e. those who have never had their creative output stolen from them) as working-class heroes striking a blow against commercialism.

Bouncing
See Track Bouncing.

Boundary Effect
See PZM.

BPM
Abbreviation of Beats Per Minute. The number of beats which occur during one minute – an indication of tempo. The term is used in MIDI as an equivalent to the MM seen in art music. In popular music, the beats are almost always assumed to be crotchets (quarter notes). *See* Metronome.

BPS
Abbreviation of Bits Per Second. *See* Data Rate.

Break
A solo or section of reduced instrumentation in a piece of music – or even a complete silence. In Afro-American music it is derived from songs of the early 1900s which were interrupted by a dance solo of tap or shuffle steps, this interruption being known as the break. In modern usage the term usually implies an opportunity for an instrumental solo. As "breakdown" it refers to the reduction to percussion towards the centre of a song which is a common feature of much dance music, and which has replaced the more traditional Middle Eight.

Breakjack
A type of jack socket fitted with switching terminals, so that insertion of a plug breaks an existing connection.

Breakpoint
On synthesizers and samplers, the specific value at which the tracking of scalable parameters, such as velocity, starts to take effect, or at which the nature of the scaling changes. For example, it might be possible to scale the volume of a sound so that it decreases from the bottom of the keyboard towards middle C and increases from that note to the top of the keyboard. In this case, middle C would be the breakpoint. *See also* Scaling.

Breath Controller
1. A device which a performer blows into, bites or presses with their lips, allowing them to articulate a sound generated by a synthesizer or sampler. First seen as an adjunct to Yamaha's DX synthesizer, and later developed into an elaborate MIDI Controller[1].

2. One of the defined MIDI Controller Change messages with a status byte value in the range 176–191 and a data byte value of 2, which implements the function described in (1) above. It is usually assignable to some parameter in a synthesizer, such as filter cut-off or volume, etc.

Bridge

1. Meter bridge. A structure mounted at the rear of a mixing desk, or on other equipment such as a tape recorder, which contains a number of VU or PPM meters. This allows the user to ascertain and compare the signal levels at various points in the programme chain.

2. Bridge mode. A method of driving a single load, such as a loudspeaker, from two similar (ideally identical) amplifiers in order to double the power presented to the load. Thus a stereo amplifier operating at 200 WPC could provide approximately 400 Watts into a single load in bridge mode. Many stereo amplifiers designed for PA work offer this facility.

3. See Middle Eight.

Bridge Passage

A section of music which links two musical ideas. This is normally necessary because the ideas are in different keys and the bridge passage effects a modulation from the key of the first idea to that of the second. *See also* Middle Eight, Sonata Form.

Bright

Term used to describe a sound which has a preponderance of upper-mid or high frequencies, or to describe the sound of an acoustic area which is comparatively rich in reflecting surfaces, such as a stone room of the type currently fashionable for drum recordings.

Brio

Italian for vigour, e.g. *con brio* – with energy.

BSI

Abbreviation of British Standards Institute. A body responsible for the establishment of standards (particularly of safety) for products and services in Britain. The standards are numbered and products conforming to one or more standards may display the BSI "Kitemark" which includes the number of the relevant standard.

Buffer

An area of memory used for temporary storage of data, particularly as an intermediate stage between two devices which operate at different speeds. The presence of the buffer allows the data to be held until the slower device is ready to accept it.

Bug

A defect or error in computer hardware or, more usually, software, which results in incorrect operation. To some extent bugs are inevitable. Indeed, there is a body of mathematical thought which suggests that it is impossible to prove that a program is without error. This is an important issue for software-controlled systems which are required to be "intrinsically safe", such as flight automation or nuclear and chemical process control. Most software houses rely on two-tier testing of their products. In-house or Alpha Tests are designed to check that the program functions according to the design specification. Beta Tests are carried out externally by computer magazines and specialist users and are intended to check that the program doesn't do anything beyond the design specification, like re-formatting the user's hard disk or transferring the contents of his or her bank balance to an account in the Cayman Islands. A computer system which exhibits bugs is sometimes described as "flaky".

Bulk Dump

The act of transferring a large amount of data between two or more devices in a network. More specifically, it refers to transfers of System Exclusive data in MIDI, e.g. the Sample Dump Standard.

Bulk Eraser

A device for erasing spools of tape whereby the whole spool is placed in a strong magnetic Field[3] generated by an electromagnet. This erases all areas of the tape simultaneously without having to run it through a tape machine.

Bulk Tuning Message

A System Exclusive message of the Non-Real Time type with a Sub ID#1 of 8, that allows the exchange of tuning data between MIDI devices as well as other devices such as computers. This allows microtonal scaling or different temperaments by defining a specific pitch value (in a frequency range from 8.1758 Hz to 13,289.73 Hz in steps of .0061 of a cent), for each of the 128 notes in the MIDI range. Two messages are involved: a bulk tuning dump request message which is transmitted by a device in order to signify that it is ready to receive, and a bulk tuning dump message which contains the data for 128 tuning programs, each containing 128 pitch values.

Bulletin Board

A computer equipped with a Modem, intended to provide a data resource for access by users with similarly equipped computers, usually via the public telephone network. The process of making the initial contact is sometimes called "logging on". Bulletin Boards often have the electronic equivalent of a club atmosphere, with sections aimed at those with various particular interests. Charges often depend on the usefulness of the data offered. Many, including those run by universities, are a good source of cheap software, both Public Domain and Shareware.

Bus

Also spelled Buss. In a Mixing Desk, a path via which the user can route a signal from one or more inputs to a specified destination. Typical destinations include: Groups, Mix, Auxiliary send, Foldback, Monitor, etc. Therefore one might speak of "routing inputs 1–8 to the mix bus" meaning that inputs 1–8 will appear at the mix output.

Busking
Term for the ad hoc performance of music in the street or other public place, usually for money. Also describes the rough, or partially improvised, performance that might result from an incompletely notated score or inadequate rehearsal.

Bvox
See Backing Vocals.

Bypass
A facility on an Effects Unit, such as a Flanger, which allows the user to switch the incoming signal directly through to the unit's output, thus cancelling the effect so that a comparison may be made quickly between the effected and un-effected signal.

Byte
In digital systems, a group of 8 bits. The largest decimal number a byte can represent is 255. *See also* Word.

Cable
An assembly of several wires, contained in an insulating sheath, to convey an electrical signal or signals between two points. Audio cables may have a conductive layer (the Screen [2]) wrapped around and common to all of the wires in the cable. The purpose of the screen is to protect the signal in the wires from EMI [2] by providing a low impedance path to earth. In principle, a cable always contains more than one wire; however, in some screened cables with apparently only one wire, the other "wire" is in fact the screen. For audio work a single signal connection requires a cable with at least two wires. In some cable the screen is arranged as a coaxial sheath around the central wire. Because the distance to the screen is constant and comparatively small at all parts of the central wire, the immunity to EMI is quite high. When large numbers of wires are involved (say, more than four) it is common to refer to the cable as multicore.

CAD
Acronym from Computer-Aided Design. The D is also variously taken to stand for Drawing, Drafting and stock market Dealing. Other computer-assisted tasks include CAEngineering, CAManufacture, CALearning, CAComposition and (increasingly nowadays) CABankruptcy.

Cadence
From Latin *cadere* = fall. A type of musical punctuation, indicating the end of an idea or preparing the ground for a transition to a new idea. Essentially a juxtaposition of two chords. In tonal music four types of cadence are recognised. Two of these fall to the tonic chord: the Perfect cadence moves from dominant to tonic; the Plagal cadence moves from subdominant to tonic. Imperfect cadences move from any chord to the dominant, and Interrupted cadences from the dominant to any chord other than the tonic. It can be seen that all of these cadences involve either the tonic or the dominant chords, and the most common (the perfect) involves both. For this reason, cadences are an effective way of establishing or identifying the key of a musical passage.

Cajun
A form of folk music of the French speaking settlers of Louisiana, USA. These settlers were deported from the newly British colony of Nova Scotia, which the French knew as Acadia, and called themselves Cadiens or Cajuns. Afro-American communities in the area developed their own version of this music, called Zydeco. Essentially dance music, Cajun is characterized by syncopation, two-step rhythms and the alternation of sung and played verses. Instruments used include the diatonic accordion, fiddle (usually played with a drone string), guitar, harmonica and metallic percussion such as triangle and even wheel rims. Modern versions, of course, supplement this with amplification and drums. Rockin Dopsie is probably the best known modern exponent.

Calypso
A type of song, indigenous to Trinidad, which often takes the form of satirical social commentary. Usually sung by a solo performer, occasionally with chorus. Closely linked with the Mardi Gras festival and appearing in the late 19th century, at about the time this event made the transition from a rather aristocratic colonial ball to the African street festival which we recognize today. The music is very rhythmic and incorporates many influences including African, European and Latin American from nearby Venezuela. Witty lyrics, often improvised, are matched to one of a limited number of traditional melodies in a speech-song style. Calypso continues to develop, with a line of descent through to Soca. Well known exponents include Mighty Sparrow, Lord Kitchener and, more recently, David Rudder.

Cancel
One of the characters transmitted for the purposes of Handshaking in a data transfer. The character is sent back to the transmitting device by the receiving device to indicate that it wants transmission to cease. It also occurs as part of the Sample Dump Standard as a System Exclusive message of the Non-Real Time type, with a Sub ID#1 value of 125.

Cancellation
The situation which occurs where a signal is mixed with a completely out-of-phase copy of itself. The simultaneous mixture of waveforms of exactly opposite polarity results in no net signal level. Although

complete cancellation is rare, the effect can occur to a lesser degree (as a drop in volume) in some microphone set ups, although it will probably only be noticeable at certain frequencies. In the diagram, trace (a) is a sine wave, while (b) is the same signal inverted, 180° out of phase. Trace (c) is the result of mixing the upper two signals together: i.e. zilch, diddly-squat, nada compadre.

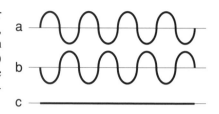

Cans

See Headphones.

Cantabile

Italian for in a "singing" style.

Capacitor

An electronic device with the ability to store an electrical charge. Capacitance is measured in Farads: in practice a Farad is too large to be useful, so the unit is prefixed by micro, nano, etc. Physically, two conductive plates separated by a dielectric material that will hold an electrical charge. This assembly may then be rolled up and sealed in a tube. Widely used in electronic circuits. Theoretically a capacitor presents an infinite impedance to DC (it will not allow it to pass); with increasing frequency this impedance decreases (i.e. a capacitor will pass AC to a greater or lesser degree depending on frequency). It has the opposite characteristic to an inductor. Any conductor has some capacitance. Also called condenser.

Capacitor Microphone

See Electrostatic Microphone.

Capo

1. Italian for "head": the beginning of a piece of music. *Da Capo* – from the beginning. *See also* Aria.

2. Capo Tasto: a device which is clamped to the fingerboard of guitars and other fretted instruments to alter the pitch of all the strings, providing instant transposition.

Capstan

In a tape machine the tape is moved by the effect of friction between a rotating motor-driven pillar (the capstan) and a freewheeling rubber roller (the pinchwheel).

Card

An alternative term for a printed circuit board.

Cardioid Microphone

A microphone with a heart-shaped polar diagram (Greek: *Kardia*, heart). Occasionally called unidirectional microphone.

Carrier

1. A radio frequency signal which is modulated by an audio frequency signal, allowing the audio signal to be broadcast by a radio transmitter.

2. In FM Synthesis, the Operator at the bottom of a stack in an Algorithm, through which the composite effect of other modulating operators connected to it is heard.

Cartridge

1. In broadcasting, an enclosed loop of ¼" tape, used mostly for short recordings of five seconds to one minute, e.g. jingles, etc.

2. On record decks, the Transducer mounted at the end of the pick-up arm.

CAV

Abbreviation of Constant Angular Velocity. In a mass storage device, such as a disk drive, it refers to the fact that the disk rotates at a constant speed. This means that the data rate will increase for a track at the edge of a disk and decrease for a track in the centre of the disk, in much the same way as the outside pair of skaters in a line spinning around a central skater will be going much faster than the pair on either side of the central skater, although the speed of rotation of the line of skaters is constant (try and imagine it). *See also* CLV.

CCIR

Abbreviation of Comité Consultatif International des Radio Communications. European body which formerly determined broadcasting standards. Now a representative on the IEC.

CD

Abbreviation of Compact Disc. A digital audio storage medium consisting of a 5-inch disc on which digital audio data is recorded in a manner which allows it to be read by an optical laser for replay. They cost about £1 to make, box and label, yet get sold in the UK for up to twelve times that amount; i.e. 1200% mark up. Someone's making loadsadosh. *See also* Glass Master.

CD-I

Abbreviation of Compact Disc–Interactive. A standard whereby image (maps, pictures, etc.), text and sound data are placed on a CD, along with a program which enables a computer to present all this information to a user in an Interactive manner. A typical example might combine maps with pictures of geographic locations, descriptive text and even sounds which are heard in the locality. In principle, anybody can access the information at will. In practice, there are often limitations on what is possible. But imagine a perfect system. You plan a holiday to Madagascar. You go to your local library and insert the *Madagascar* disc in a computer CD drive. You ask about hotels in Antananarivo. The screen shows *Avenue de L'Independence*. You tell the computer to look north. The screen shows the view in this direction. A voice tells you that the *Hotel Anjary* is to your left. You tell the computer to turn left. The hotel appears on the screen. You tell the computer to go inside and look at a bedroom and the kitchens, meanwhile a voice tells you about the rooms and what sort of food is on offer. You decide to stay at this hotel. The library computer accesses the hotel's computer and makes a reservation. Alternatively, you could stay home and learn to write fugues from a CD-I on J. S. Bach.

CD+MIDI   A type of CD which includes both digital audio data and MIDI data. This means that a recording of the sound of a musical performance, and the MIDI data used to generate it, are simultaneously available to the user, although in some cases the MIDI data might be for additional musical parts which do not appear in the sound recording. In any case this allows the user to "play with" the performance by choosing different Patches, etc, on their MIDI network. Obviously, the CD player will have to be fitted with a MIDI Out socket. So the guy who asks the sales assistant which channel his Hi-Fi midi system should be set to, may not be asking such a daft question after all.

CDP   Abbreviation of Composer's Desktop Project. *See* University Music Systems.

Cent   A unit of pitch equal to 1% of a semitone. 50 cents is a quartertone.

Changes   A term employed by jazz musicians to refer to the chord patterns of Standard songs used as the basis for improvisation: e.g. "let's use the changes of Cherokee".

Channel   **1.** A section of equipment which deals with a signal in isolation from others, allowing it to be treated separately, e.g. in a Mixing Desk.

2. A feature of the MIDI Specification which allows a receiving device to have messages sent specifically to it, and for these messages to be ignored by other devices on the MIDI network. An analogy with television is sometimes made. Transmitters send out signals for a number of different stations simultaneously. When you set your television to receive a particular channel, all others are ignored. A neighbour with a TV tuned to a different channel would receive a totally different programme at the same time. In MIDI, a device will receive instructions for channels other than its own but will not respond to them. The MIDI specification makes provision for sixteen channels in any one MIDI network. In MIDI messages, the channel number is encoded by the last four bits of the Status Byte.

Channel Key Pressure   A Channel Voice message with a status byte value in the range 208-223, used to implement a type of Aftertouch whereby only one note of a chord needs to be pressed down for all the notes of the chord to be affected (i.e. all the keys on that channel). The message requires one data byte.

Channel Message   A classification of MIDI messages which only affect devices on a MIDI network set to a particular Channel[2] (i.e. all non-System messages). They are further subdivided into two groups: Channel Mode and Channel Voice. *See also* MIDI Message.

Channel Mode   *See* Reception Mode.

Channel Voice   A classification of MIDI messages relating specifically to a musical performance, where features of the performance (notes, articulation, etc.) are individually described by a unique message. They have status bytes with values in the range 128–239 and include Note On, Note Off, Polyphonic Key Pressure, Channel Key Pressure, Program Change, Pitch Bend, Controller Change. These messages all include a specific channel number, allowing similar messages to address different devices on the same MIDI network. The message will only be implemented by a receiving device whose Channel[2] matches that of the message.

Channelize   The process of redirecting MIDI Channel messages from one channel to another. This is often carried out by sequencers so that the user does not have to keep adjusting the transmit channel of the master keyboard in order to hear the sounds of MIDI devices on different channels.

Chaos   A broad area of scientific study concerning systems which involve change or motion where there is feedback, so that small alterations to the initial conditions of a system can produce radically different results. The area is more properly known as "non-linear dynamics". A good example of such a system is the weather, and the work of meteorologist Ed Lorenz is one of the earliest examples of what is now known as "chaos science". The recognition of the importance of small differences, so often discounted in traditional science, is a key aspect of this new approach. Another is the insight gained by mathematicians from studying non-linear equations, and particularly those attractive objects called Fractals (a term invented by Benoit Mandelbrot), one of which, the so-called Mandelbrot beetle, is shown in the entry on Fractal Music. He had noticed that Noise, in the form of errors on computer data lines, was self-similar: i.e. the large-scale pattern of errors tended to repeat at ever smaller scales and thus could not be eradicated. He therefore suggested the strategy of protecting the data against inevitable noise by using Error Correction. It now appears that self-similarity is a universal organizing phenomenon in areas as diverse as music, heart failure, population growth, economic trends and even the structure of the universe. It is the multi-disciplinary relevance of chaos that makes it such a powerful tool for problem solving. It also tends to produce beautiful pictures and "interesting" music.

Chart Music   *See* Popular Music.

Chase Lock   In a system where two or more devices (such as a VTR and tape recorder) are synchronized together, the process by which the slave follows or "chases" the master to ensure it is at the right place in time.

Checksum   A simple means of error detection employed in data transfer between devices in a network. The checksum is a numeric value which is the result of some calculation performed on the data being transmitted. It might simply be the sum total of all the data but other, more elegant methods tend to be used. The resulting value is then transmitted along with the block of data. The receiving device performs the same calculation on the data and compares the result with the checksum it has received. If there has been no error in the transmission (i.e. no data lost or changed) the checksum values will be identical. If the receiving device produces a different result, it will normally request that the data be sent again. In general the checksum can only tell a receiving device that a transmission error has occurred – it does not carry sufficient information to allow the error to be corrected. This limits the usefulness of checksums to data transfers which are non-real time, e.g. System Exclusive transfers where it doesn't matter how long it takes for the data to be transmitted. In situations where data has to meet a deadline (e.g. CD playback) it is desirable to be able to detect and correct the error. *See also* Error Correction.

Chip

See Integrated Circuit.

Chord

Two or more notes sounded simultaneously.

Chorus

1. A process which, by applying a constantly changing short delay of about 40 milliseconds to a sound such as a guitar, and altering the pitch very slightly above and below that of the original sound, gives the effect of a number of guitars playing the same music.

2. Originally one of the defined MIDI Controller Change messages with a status byte value in the range 176–191 and a first data byte of 93. It is assigned to the parameter in a synthesizer which alters the depth of the effect described in Chorus [1]. More recently this message has been reassigned as one of five generalized Effects Depth messages. *See* Effects Control.

3. The group of singers who perform as a unit in opera, oratorio, musicals, etc. (the term choir is always preferred when the singers are taking part in a church service). By extension, the sections of a work written for such a group are also called choruses: e.g. the Hallelujah chorus from *Messiah*.

4. *See* Song [1].

Chromatic

Pertaining to the full semitone scale, as opposed to Diatonic.

Chromium Dioxide

A magnetic material (CrO_2) used as the primary coating on audio and video recording tape. It has superior characteristics to Ferric Oxide but is inferior to "metal" tapes.

CIRC

Acronym from Cross Interleaved Reed-Solomon Code. *See* Error Correction.

Circle of Fifths

Also known as Cycle of Fifths. A convenient way of thinking of the 12 major or minor keys as a circle, arranged in steps of a fifth, which can be read in either direction. Starting from C major and proceeding clockwise, the key signature of each new key gains one sharp until F# major is reached. Theoretically, more sharps could be added *ad infinitum*. However, as F#-major can also be written as Gb, it is more convenient to continue round the circle in flat keys, removing a flat at each step until C is reached once more. In an anticlockwise direction, the circle could be viewed as a series of perfect Cadences, with each new tonic key becoming the dominant of the next. For this reason it is widely used for Modulation [2], especially to (or back from) a remote key (i.e. one on the far side of the circle).

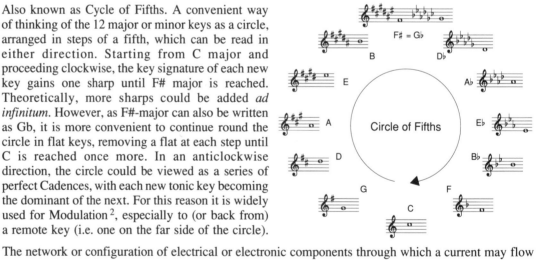

Circuit

The network or configuration of electrical or electronic components through which a current may flow in a device. The term can refer to the theoretical notion, the diagram, or the physical form of the device. It is sometimes used to refer to a piece of electronic equipment. *See also* Printed Circuit Board.

CISC

Acronym from Complex Instruction Set Computer (pronounced "sisk"). Essentially a microprocessor which has an elaborate and powerful instruction set which is ideal for implementing a general purpose microcomputer such as a PC. *See* RISC.

Classical

See Musical Periods.

Clean

Said of a signal that is free of distortion.

Clef

In written music, a symbol placed at the beginning of the stave which assigns a pitch to a specific line on the stave and, by inference, to all of the other lines and spaces. Three clef symbols are commonly used, each derived from the medieval forms of the letters G, F and C. The third of these (unlike the other two) can appear on different lines of the stave.

Click Track

A track on a multi-track tape recorder which has a pre-recorded metronomic click to help musicians play in time. The click track would be routed via Foldback to the musician's headphones. This is very important when a band is playing (or, heaven forbid, miming) to a backing track during a "live" performance. If the drummer is wearing headphones at the next gig you go to, you will know what is going on. In some cases, devices such as drum machines are able to accept this as a synchronizing signal.

Clipboard

In a computer, a temporary memory area which can be used to store sections of text or pictures so that they can be moved within the current program, or transferred from one program to another. The clipboard generally holds only one thing at a time and this will usually not be preserved if the computer is switched off. Many programs use the clipboard to store (automatically) the last item deleted by the user: it can then usefully be retrieved if the deletion is subsequently regretted. *See* Copy, Cut, Paste.

Clipping

A form of distortion which occurs when a system attempts to pass or produce a signal which is greater than its dynamic range will allow. Typically, the system will adequately track the input signal up to a certain point in the waveform beyond which it cannot go. It will remain at this level until the input signal drops back below this point. This effectively clips the tops off peaks in the input signal, making them appear slightly square. Most commonly encountered in the mix bus of mixing desks, where the combined signal level from many channels exceeds the bus's dynamic range, and in power amplifiers, where the input signal exceeds the ability of the power supply to provide current at the required level. Sometimes called table-top distortion.

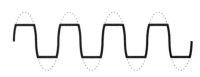

Clock

In a computer, a high frequency oscillator (typically 5 MHz or more) which generates a pulse wave. This is used as a timing reference to ensure that each of the separate sections of the computer (memory, CPU etc.) operate in a synchronized manner.

Clone

A term used to describe a device which offers the same facilities and compatibility as an established product made by a different manufacturer. Most commonly encountered to describe IBM-PC type computers made by companies other than IBM.

Closed Circuit

A system of audio or video transmission for use within a building or other linked sites.

CLV

Abbreviation of Constant Linear Velocity. In contrast to CAV, a mass storage system that has a disk whose speed varies to keep the data rate at the head constant, irrespective of the head's position on the disk. CD is an example of this method.

CMRR

Abbreviation of Common Mode Rejection Ratio. In a Balanced Line connection, the common mode is the noise whose phase is common to both lines. The degree of Attenuation of common mode by the inverting amplifier is called the rejection ratio and, like other gain reduction processes, is quantified by a negative number of decibels.

Coaxial Cable

See Cable.

Cocktail Party Effect

The phenomenon of human discrimination between items of equal volume in an audio signal, e.g. the ability to hear one conversation out of many at a party. Related to Auditory Masking.

Coda

Italian for "tail". A musical passage which gives a sense of completion to a movement or work. This may be as little as an extended Cadence or can be a quite substantial musical episode in its own right.

Codetta

An Italian diminutive derived from coda meaning "a little tail". A short musical passage which links subject and answer in the exposition of a Fugue, or appears at the end of a Sonata Form exposition.

Coding

The process of altering the form of a signal. This may allow a transformation of the signal which was not possible in its original form, e.g. in noise reduction processes like Dolby. Alternatively, it may simply be used to take advantage of side effects of the new coding. For example, in PCM (used in digital audio) coding allows recording and replay with low noise levels, and low interchannel Crosstalk. There are normally two complementary stages: encoding is the process which converts from the original to the new form, decoding is the process which converts back from the new to the original form.

Coherent

See Phase Coherent.

Coil

See Inductor, Moving Coil.

Coincident Pair

A microphone technique used for stereo recording in which two microphones are placed at an angle of 90° (or thereabouts) and quite close together.

Col

Italian prefix meaning "with the". For example, *col legno* – with the wood – is an instruction to string players to use the wooden side of the bow.

Cold

The conductor which carries the out-of-phase component of the signal in a Balanced Line transmission system. According to English tradition, this is pin 3 of an XLR (pin 2 is hot and pin 1, earth).

Coloration

The unintentional overemphasis or enhancement of a range of frequencies in a signal by a piece of equipment through which it passes, e.g. a loudspeaker.

Combo

1. A combination of loudspeaker(s) and amplifier in one, usually portable, box. Used by guitarists, keyboard players, etc, for stage amplification. *See also* Guitar Amp, Keyboard Amp.

2. A small ensemble of musicians, particularly in jazz.

Commercial Music

Music, of whatever type, that is primarily intended to make money for people, hopefully including the composer. This may be music to support a film, advert or corporate promotion video, or it may simply refer to chart music.

Common Time

See Time Signature.

Compander

A device which combines the functions of both a Compressor and Expander[2].

Companding Converters

An analogue to digital converter and digital to analogue converter pair, which uses a non-linear scale: i.e. one that has larger steps towards peak amplitude and smaller steps towards minimum amplitude. This scale increases the ability of the converter to resolve small changes in low amplitude signals, thus reducing distortion, but with the penalty of increased noise. The overall effect is as if the signal had been compressed before the conversion and expanded after.

Compatibility

1. The degree to which different pieces of equipment can be used or connected together or are interchangeable: e.g. whether you can successfully replay a tape recorded with one type of noise reduction on a player equipped with another.

2. The degree to which stereo recordings can be mixed to mono and not lose quality.

Compound Time

See Time Signature.

Compression

A gain control process which ensures that a signal falls within a required dynamic range. *See also* Compressor.

Compression Ratio

1. The ratio of the number of decibels change in input level to the number of decibels change in output level of a compressor, once the Threshold has been exceeded. Normally in the range 2:1 to 20:1 or more.

2. In data compression, the ratio of uncompressed to compressed data. An indication of the saving in space otherwise required to store the data.

Compressor

A device for reducing the dynamic range of a signal. Essentially it is a non-linear amplifier: the output level is not directly proportional to the input level. A linear amplifier ideally has a 1:1 relationship between the input and the output at Unity Gain – in other words, it will produce an output swing of 1 dB for an input swing of 1 dB. A compressor need not exhibit such a linear relationship, and the degree of non-linearity is indicated by the compression ratio. Thus, with a compression ratio of 2:1, a compressor will produce an output swing of 1 dB for an input swing of 2 dB. The reduction in maximum output that this represents is then compensated for by an output level control to restore the gain to unity. The effect is to increase the average loudness of the signal without increasing its gain. In practice the effect is triggered by, and operative above, a Threshold. In some cases, a very high ratio (20:1 or more) is used to ensure the output does not exceed a certain value that might otherwise Over Modulate a tape track for example. *See* also Expander[2], Limiter.

Computer

A device, usually electronic (the hardware), which processes input data according to a set of instructions (the program or software) in order to produce output data. Most computers conform to "von Neumann" architecture, which means, in essence, that they perform instructions one after the other and cannot do more than one thing at a time, although they may do serial operations so quickly that they appear parallel to our sluggish minds. Computers can be broadly classed according to speed or power in decreasing order: supercomputers, mainframes, minicomputers and microcomputers or personal computers (PCs). However, the distinctions are not always clear cut and many microcomputers are now as powerful or fast as the mainframes of a few years ago. Computers are encountered in audio work, where they are used to manipulate MIDI or digital audio data: the most common are the Atari ST range (in the UK), the Apple Macintosh and the IBM-Compatible PC. Almost all pieces of music technology available today are also effectively computers.

Computer Generations

Computers can be categorized according to power and type of technology into "generations" in the sense that each new generation is different from the last by virtue of some improvement in technology or design. First generation computers (c. 1951) used valve technology and magnetic or paper tape storage. The second generation (c. 1961) used transistor technology and had separate systems to handle input and output, thus freeing the CPU, and were programmable via a High Level Language. The third generation (c. 1965) used SSI and MSI Integrated Circuits with hard disk storage, thus reducing physical size and improving reliability. The fourth generation (c. 1984) used LSI and VLSI technology and allowed Networking and Multi-tasking. The fifth generation of the 1990s uses VLSI technology with parallel processing, using RISCs or transputers, particularly in Artificial Intelligence and expert systems applications.

Con

Italian prefix meaning "with", as in *con amore* – "with love".

Concert Pitch Established by the International Organization for Standardization in 1955, the agreed reference frequency of 440 Hz. for the note A above middle C. Notated: A = 440. *See also* Pitch.

Condenser *See* Capacitor. (Condenser is American for capacitor).

Condenser Microphone *See* Electrostatic Microphone.

Conductor **1.** A material which allows electricity to pass through it. All common metals have this property. A cable can be considered to be a conductor encased in an insulator.

2. The person who instructs an orchestra or other musical group on how a piece of music should be played (tempo, dynamics, balance, etc) thus ensuring a consistent interpretation. He or she will frequently carry out this task at the actual performance of the piece.

Connector A two-part device which joins wires, cables or pieces of equipment to allow a signal to pass from one to another. A connector consists of a plug and a socket. Usually (but not always) a plug has pins or poles and is therefore referred to as "male"; a socket usually (but not always) has holes into which the plug poles or pins fit and is therefore referred to as "female". The process of joining of a connector is sometimes called "mating". In audio, three connector types are commonly used: XLR, Jack and Phono. Although a connection may be established permanently, the nature of a connector is to be temporary and more convenient than, say, soldering the wires or cables together. Most problems (crackles, drop outs, signal loss) in studios can be attributed to connectors. We can send men to the moon, but we can't fit two bits of metal together so that they make a reliable electrical contact.

Console **1.** Alternative term for a computer terminal.

2. Alternative term for a mixing desk or vision mixer.

Contiguous Literally meaning "alongside" from Latin *contigere,* to touch. In a mass storage device such as a hard disk, it refers to the practice of allocating blocks of data so that they are physically next to one another on the disk. This is advantageous as it means that, once a track on the hard disk has been accessed, the head need not move again until that track has been completely read.

Continue A System Real Time message, with a status byte value of 251, which will cause a MIDI device to resume playing the current Song[2] from the point at which it was last stopped. Usually only implemented by drum machines and sequencers. *See* also Active Sensing, MIDI Clock, Reset, Start, Stop.

Continuity In an electrical circuit with a number of connection points, the degree to which all the connection points function correctly. A continuity tester is used to determine whether a signal which starts at point A satisfactorily reaches point E, via B, C, D.

Continuity Announcer A broadcaster whose main job is to introduce the next programme, occasionally provide station information and generally fill in time. The intention is to give a sense of continuity between one programme and the next. Exponents of this art become expert at the "slinky-link" – a masterful turn of phrase which can establish a connection between programmes as diverse as Patagonian Nose-Flute Technique and the World Series.

Continuo An instrumental part, commonly found in baroque music, which carries the bass line and indications of essential harmony. In addition to being played by bass instruments, the part was usually improvised upon (or "realized") by chordal instruments, such as harpsichord, organ, lute or guitar. The latter supplied or reinforced the harmony using a system known as Figured Bass, in which chords are indicated by numbers and other symbols which describe the intervals to be played above the given bass.

Continuous Controller A Controller Change message with a status byte value in the range 176–191, and a first data byte value in the range 0–63, which is used to introduce some kind of continuous change in the sound, for example gradually increasing vibrato. Values 0–31 take one additional data byte, while values 32–63 can be paired with these to provide an additional data byte if greater resolution is required. Compare with a Switched Controller which allows a change between only two conditions, for example the Sustain pedal.

Contralto *See* Alto.

Controller *See* MIDI Controllers.

Controller Change A Channel Voice message with status byte values in the range 176-191, which allow for various musically useful effects such as vibrato or sustain to be added to currently active voices. The first data byte values determine the type of controller and these are divided as follows: values 0–63 are used for Continuous Controllers, values 64–90 for Switched Controllers, values 91–95 for Effects Depth, 96–101 for Data Controllers, 102–121 are currently undefined and 122–127 are used for the All Notes Off, Reception Mode and Local Control messages. The message usually takes one additional data byte.

Control Room In audio, the soundproofed room which houses the recording equipment such as mixing desk, effects units and tape recorders. It is usually adjacent to the studio, to which it is connected by a soundproof window and cable ducts. In television, the equivalent area is called a sound control room. *See also* Machine Room.

Control Voltage	*See* CV & Gate.
Conversion	Many processes which occur in audio involve conversion of one form of something into a related form of something else, e.g. from pressure waves to electrical waves (in a microphone), to numeric data (in digital equipment) or to magnetic fluctuation (in tape and hard disk). Conversion always involves loss, as you will know if you have ever bought or sold foreign currency. Even in its original form of pressure waves, a sound is not immune from conversion in its journey from source to listener. All matter in the universe represents an amount of energy with relatively high organization Energy does not like to be organized and will do anything in its power to become less organized. As a result, all matter will eventually become heat. This energy-to-heat conversion is called entropy, and it is the process which will ultimately lead to the "heat death" or end of the universe. Sound pressure waves are actually a way for energy (kinetic energy) to convert itself into heat. They "prefer" to be heat and they achieve this aim by involving themselves with objects they meet via friction. The objects in the path of the pressure waves will absorb some of the energy and in the process warm up slightly. This includes the listener! So next time you feel hot, turn the music down.
Copy	In a computer, a command which enables a previously selected section of text or picture to be repeated elsewhere, either within the current program or another. *See also* Backup, Cut, Paste.
Copy Protection	The prevention of the copying of computer software, generally through the use of Dongles, keys or registered-user passwords. Also used for devices which prevent inadvertent overwriting of data, such as the knock-out tabs on audio and video cassettes, or the write-protect shutters on floppy disks and RDAT cassettes. *See also* Encryption, Hacking, Password Protection, SCMS.
Copyright	The rights of an individual automatically (without taking specific action): (a) to prevent unauthorized copying of anything original he or she creates; (b) to control the distribution of any copies; and (c) to benefit exclusively from their exploitation. Such rights are formalized in the statute law of many countries, and in international agreements such as the Bern Copyright Convention. The USA revised its copyright law in 1978. In the UK, the 1988 Copyright, Designs and Patents Act replaced the 1956 Act and its amendments. Such laws generally define copyright as a property right (sometimes "Intellectual Property") which exists in any original artistic, dramatic, literary or musical works, broadcast or cable programmes, film or video, sound recordings, typographic layout or computer software which exists in a tangible material form. Ideas or concepts unexpressed in any form are not generally included. The 1988 British Act defined for the first time in that country an individual's "Moral Rights": (a) to be identified as the author of a work and to ensure that the work is not falsely attributed to another (Paternity); and (b) to object to derogatory treatment of the work (Integrity). Generally, copyright lasts throughout the author's life and for 50 years thereafter and/or 50 years from the date of first publication. It is important to note that it is not only the composer's work that is protected in music: separate copyrights may well apply to the lyrics, the typesetting of the printed page, any editorial additions and to the work of performers involved in any recordings of it. The merit or quality of the work is irrelevant. It is up to the holder of copyright in a work to enforce his rights, if necessary through court action, although an external agency can collect fees on the holder's behalf. In Britain such administration is most commonly carried out by the Mechanical Copyright Protection Society (MCPS) or the Performing Rights Society (PRS).
Counterpoint	From Latin *contrapunctum* = against the note. The practice of combining two or more melodic lines simultaneously in a composition. These may be different musical ideas (free counterpoint), or the same idea appearing at staggered time intervals (and perhaps slightly modified) so as to overlap with itself. This latter is called imitative counterpoint, as each new entry seems to imitate the preceding one.
Countersubject	A musical line which fits with the main theme (subject) in a Fugue or in counterpoint generally.
Counter Tenor	English derivative of "contra tenor". *See* Tenor.
Country Music	A form of American popular music derived from the folk music traditions of the white settlers, particularly those from the British Isles. Country and Western is typified by cloyingly sentimental ballads, but other country music includes Hillbilly and Bluegrass which often call for spectacular instrumental virtuosity. The oldest traditions are found in the east of the USA, particularly in the area around the Appalachian mountains. Other areas have local specialities, such as the cowboy songs of the mid-west, and may also reflect the ethnic influences of a region, such as the Creole aspects of Cajun and Zydeco, or the Hispanic flavour of Tejano or Tex-Mex.
Cover Version	In popular music, a version of a piece made by a band or artist other than the one originally associated with the work. This may be a result of the cynical exploitation of an already proven and successful formula, a want of originality, or a feeling that the original could be re-interpreted in a new way. This last often occurs in Crossover, where a song from one market is "covered" for another. A notable example of this was Eric Clapton's USA No.1 hit, "I Shot The Sheriff", a cover of a reggae track, little known to white audiences, by Bob Marley. The success of the cover was largely responsible for Marley's elevation to international stardom.

CPS Abbreviation of Cycles per Second. *See* Hertz.

CPU Abbreviation of Central Processor Unit. In a computer, the device or integrated circuit that actually carries out the computing processes.

Crescendo Italian for becoming gradually louder, often abbreviated to *cresc*. The effect is notated by the symbol ◁———, colloquially known as a "hairpin". *See also* Diminuendo.

Crippleware An ironic term which describes versions of computer software with some crucial features disabled (they might not load or save data, or they might quit after a short period of running). Often issued free to demonstrate the software to potential users.

Crossfade A gradual transition from one signal to another, such that the first signal is reduced in volume as the second is increased in volume.

Crossover **1.** A device for diverting certain portions of the spectrum of an audio signal to loudspeakers of various sizes so that each speaker receives frequencies that it can handle with optimal performance. Essentially a series of filters: high pass for the tweeter, band pass for the mid range, and low pass for the woofer. The crossover may be Passive and therefore post-amplifier, or may be Active and pre-amplifier. In the latter case an amplifier is generally required for each speaker present.

2. A music business term that describes a record released for consumption by one market but which finds wider popularity, particularly in the mainstream pop and chart music markets. The increase in popularity of Reggae during the early '70s, and its influence on modern popular music is an example.

Crosstalk The superimposition of an audio signal from one Channel [1] onto another, one tape track onto another, or one cable onto another. It is usually considered undesirable.

Crotchet Note (♩) or rest (𝄽) whose duration is one quarter of a semibreve. Also known as quarter-note.

CRT Abbreviation of Cathode Ray Tube. A large valve used in televisions and computer monitors.

Cue **1.** An indication to start a performance or recording. The indication may be audible (usually over headphones) such as a verbal command, or a sound already recorded on another track, or it may be visible such as a light or arm gesture e.g. the "thumbs up".

2. The appearance in a Band Part of music played by another instrument, which serves as a reminder to the player of an imminent entry. Often printed in small notes.

Current *See* Electricity.

Cursor The solid or flashing mark on a computer monitor, which indicates a point in text or graphics where additions or alterations can be made. On some systems, it can be moved with a Mouse [1].

Cut **1.** In a computer, a command which removes a selected section of text or picture, etc. The portion removed may be temporarily stored in memory (perhaps in a Clipboard) so that it can be retrieved or moved elsewhere, either within the current program or into another. *See also* Copy, Paste.

2. In film, the instruction issued to terminate filming of a particular scene. Also, a particular edited version of the film.

3. In audio, used to indicate a reduction of a particular frequency or band of frequencies. Also used to refer to the production of a master for CD or vinyl disc production and, by extension, an archaic way of referring to an LP record.

Cut C Time *See* Time Signature.

Cut Off The frequency at which a Filter takes effect. For example, in a low pass filter with a cut off of 200 Hz, frequencies above this point will tend to be removed.

CV and Gate Prior to MIDI, a limited system of interconnection between synthesizers. The system comprised a control voltage (CV) which determined what pitch to play, and a gate signal which turned the sound on when present and off when absent. The system was inherently monophonic and a CV and Gate was needed for each note to operate. There were a number of difficulties with this system as each manufacturer used different standards. Although a relationship of 1 volt per octave was common, there was no agreement about which octave to begin in. Also, some manufacturers had their gate signal upside down, or used a trigger pulse instead of a gate; the basic rule was "If it was made by A, it won't talk to B". Now you know why MIDI was invented.

Cycle of Fifths *See* Circle of Fifths.

Da

Italian for "from". For example, *Da Capo* means "from the beginning".

DAC

See Digital to Analogue Converter.

Daisy Chain

A type of MIDI network in which devices are connected one behind the other. In a network of four devices, a message generated by device 1 for device 4 is passed through (and ignored by) devices 2 and 3. The connection is made between the MIDI In socket of one device and the MIDI Thru of the previous device. *See also* MIDI Socket, Star Network.

Damper

1. A piece of cloth or other material which is used to absorb sound energy.

2. A specific example of Damper [1] fitted to pianos, harps and other percussive or plucked instruments, which is used to reduce the time taken for a note or notes to decay. *See also* Sustain [2].

DASH

Acronym from Digital Audio Stationary Head. A family of formats for recording digital audio data onto open reel tape. Developed by Sony but also used by other manufacturers. *See also* Pro-Digi.

DAT

See RDAT.

Data

The information operated on by a computer as it executes a program. In general, computer data is intended to represent some aspect of the "real" world, i.e. it is symbolic. In digital audio, data represents sound. In digital video it represents an image. The word is derived from the Latin *dare* meaning things given and the word is therefore strictly plural, the singular being datum. However, this book avoids using the form "the data are ..." on the basis that it will irritate more people than it will please.

Database

A category of computer software which allows a user to collect information or data about a number of different types of things, and keep it in a standard format. The user can then search through the information to find specific items of interest. The term is also used to refer to the collection of data itself. An address book is a database, and database software is often used by companies to keep the address information of customers. This is more useful than a paper address book, as the program will normally be able to find and print a list of names and telephone numbers for, say, all customers from Richmond, so that a salesman can then hassle them on the 'phone. Properly speaking, the total collection of information is called a datafile. It is divided into records, where each record is a unique set of information e.g. an entry in the address book for a specific person. Each record, in turn, is divided into fields, each one containing a particular unit of information e.g. a telephone number, a county, or a post code. Databases are useful for purposes other than address lists: stock control and statistical research are common uses. This glossary was stored in a database, rather than a word processor, so that entries could be made at random and then sorted into alphabetical order prior to printing.

Data Byte

The part of a MIDI message which describes the amount of change of some parameter identified by the Status Byte. Data bytes always have a value of 127 or less.

Data Cartridge

Essentially a RAM or ROM in a plastic box, which plugs into a synthesizer or other device. It allows alternative versions of the device's internal memory to be stored, or new sounds, etc, to be added.

Data Compression

A process whereby a quantity of data is reduced in order to occupy less space in a mass storage device or take less time to transfer between devices. A simple example of computer data compression is the reduction of large areas of solid colour to a few instructions and co-ordinates in a compressed graphics file. In audio, data compression is used most notably in Philips' DCC format (PASC system) and Sony's MD format (ATRAC system). Although some reduction in quality might be expected, the results of some early subjective tests seem to suggest that people actually prefer PASC or ATRAC processed audio to that of uncompressed CDs.

Data Controller

A Controller Change message with a status byte value in the range 176–191 and a first data byte value in the range 96–101, which is used to set some parameter in the receiving device, for example the data increment and decrement switches on a synthesizer.

Data Entry

See Data Slider.

Datafiler

A portable device for the replay of previously recorded MIDI data: useful in live performance.

Data Rate

The rate at which data is transferred from one place (e.g. a hard disk) to another (e.g. a computer). It is usually measured in bits or kilobits per second (kb/s), but occasionally (and confusingly) in bytes per second. Sometimes called transfer rate. *See also* Baud Rate, Shannon's Channel Capacity Theorem.

Data Slider

A Potentiometer fitted to a device such as a synthesizer which allows parameters within the device to be adjusted for programming, etc.

Data Thinning

A facility which allows a user to reduce the amount of MIDI data produced by Continuous Controllers such as pitch bend, aftertouch, etc. Often found as an editing facility on sequencers. In practice, the full output of the controller is recorded and then the user can, by various means, "shave" some of the data off while auditioning its effect. Usually it is possible to maintain the effect of the pitch bend or whatever with far less data than was originally recorded.

dB

See Decibel.

dB(A)

A decibel-based unit intended to represent a human perception of loudness. A measuring device with a scale in dB(A) will have an equalisation which gives the device a similar response to that of the ear. Such a device might be used to assess a noisy environment, such as an airport or late night party, in order to determine the level of auditory risk for humans.

dB(m)

See dB(u).

dB SPL

A decibel-based unit intended to give an absolute measurement of sound pressure (intensity), where 0 dB = 20 µPa (micro Pascals). The human range of hearing is related to this scale, with 0 dB SPL being the threshold of hearing and 120–140 dB SPL (depending on which reference book you use) being the threshold of pain. The scale below shows the relationship between µPa and dB SPL, as well as giving some rough indications of the sound levels of various phenomena:

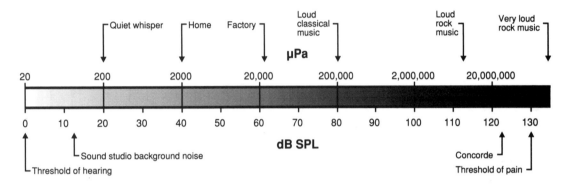

dB(u)

A decibel-based unit intended to allow signal voltages to be directly compared, and which takes 0.775V = 0 dB(u) as the reference point: also known as dB(m).

dB(v)

A decibel-based unit intended to allow signal voltages to be directly compared, and which takes 1V = 0 dB(v) as the reference point.

DBX

A commercial noise reduction system for analogue tape recording. It is based on the principle of pre-Emphasis to boost high frequencies by about 12 dB per octave, followed by 2:1 Compression of the signal during recording. On replay, the signal is expanded and then de-emphasized. Tape noise is reduced when the high frequencies are cut back to their original levels, effectively improving the Signal-to-Noise Ratio by up to 30 dB. The order of pre-Emphasis, Compression, Expansion and De-Emphasis is important to minimize the fluctuations in background noise which would otherwise be apparent with the hard compression used. Although effective in its primary purpose, the system can cause a "pumping" effect on low frequency transients. It also does not handle stereo material well, sometimes allowing the stereo image to wander. This is not a problem on multi-track Portastudios, where DBX is commonly found. For other proprietary noise reduction systems *see* Dolby.

DC

See Direct Current.

DCA

Abbreviation of Digitally Controlled Amplifier. A type of amplifier where the amount of gain is controlled remotely by a digital control signal, or where the amplification is implemented digitally. Sometimes found on synthesizers and samplers. *See also* Digital Signal Processing.

DCC

Abbreviation of Digital Compact Cassette. A system, devised by Philips, for recording a digital audio signal on a cassette which is similar to the standard audio cassette. The system also has the dubious advantage of allowing pre-recorded analogue tapes to be played. As the DCC tape speed has to be the same as the original compact cassette standard (1⅞ ips) the data rate is reduced to below that ordinarily required to achieve CD-quality performance. To compensate for this, a data compression system known as PASC is employed which means that CD-like performance can be achieved at a quarter of the normal data rate. Surprisingly, the results of some early subjective tests seem to suggest that people prefer PASC processed audio to that of the CD standard (a similar effect is noted with regard to Sony's ATRAC data compression system developed for their rival format MD). At the time of writing, some doubts are being expressed over the future of DCC in the light of competition from the existing RDAT format and Sony's MD format.

DCF

Abbreviation of Digitally Controlled Filter. A type of Filter where the cut off frequency is controlled remotely by a digital control signal, or where the filter is implemented digitally. Sometimes found on synthesizers and samplers. *See also* Digital Signal Processing.

DCO

Abbreviation of Digitally Controlled Oscillator. A type of Oscillator, where the frequency is controlled remotely by a digital control signal, or where the waveform is generated digitally. Sometimes found on synthesizers. *See also* Digital Signal Processing.

DC Offset

An AC signal is considered to rise and fall about a continuous central zero point of 0V DC. When the signal rises and falls about a point at some other DC voltage level, the signal is then said to have a DC offset. This condition is generally undesirable in equipment intended to be connected together and can result in clicks in the signal. If a signal with a considerable DC offset is presented to a loudspeaker, the loudspeaker will move in and out around some position other than its natural rest point; this limits the excursion of the coil in one direction and, in the long term, may burn out the coil altogether. However the DC

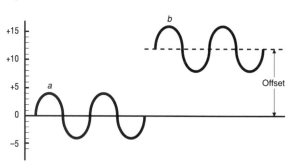

Trace a is centred around 0 and has no DC offset. Trace b is centred around 13 on the scale and therefore has a positive DC offset.

offset can be removed by passing the signal through a capacitor which will allow the AC component to pass, but which will present a high impedance to the DC component and thus effectively filter it out. This state of affairs is deliberately exploited in Phantom Powering, where the microphone signal has a DC offset of 48V which is removed by capacitors in-line with the signal.

Dead

1. Said of an acoustic with a short reverberation time (also called a dry acoustic).

2. The termination of life in an organism. The condition of those who do not distinguish between different types of AC signals, such as audio and mains, or who interfere with safety earth schemes.

Dead Side

The part of a microphone's response pattern that causes a low or zero output from the microphone.

Decay

1. The time taken for a sound to reach minimum loudness. The end of a sound.

2. In acoustics, the time taken for reverberation to die away. *See* Reverberation Time.

3. Decay Time. In an Envelope Generator, the time taken to move from the point of maximum level to another level, usually the sustain level. If the EG is being used to control an amplifier (VCA or DCA) the time taken to reach a constant level following an initial rise to maximum loudness. Synthesizer users are apt to use the term "release" for the end of a sound. *See also* Envelope Generator.

Decibel

A ratio-based measure of some quality, usually sound level, power or voltage, compared to a reference amount. One-tenth of a Bel, but used in preference to Bels, which are too large for practical purposes. It is often qualified to indicate which property is being compared, such as dB(A), dB(v), etc. One might talk about a Signal-to-Noise Ratio of –80 dB(v): this would be a comparison between the amplitude of the signal (which we want to hear) and the noise (which we don't). In this case, the signal voltage is the reference point and would be called 0 dB(v), whatever the actual value was. The noise voltage would thus be 80 dB(v) smaller, again irrespective of its actual value. The logarithmic nature of the decibel scale allows us to compare two values of enormously different magnitudes with conveniently small numbers. For example, in terms of absolute pressure level, human hearing covers a range of 20 µPa to 200,000,000 µPa: any arithmetic on this basis is quite tedious. The same range expressed in dB SPL is 0 -140 dB SPL: much more convenient.

Decoding

See Coding.

Decrement

Terse word for decrease by one, although sometimes incorrectly used with larger values, as in "decrement by ten". *See also* Increment.

Decrescendo

Italian for "becoming gradually quieter". The term *diminuendo* is more commonly used.

De-emphasis

The principle of cutting high frequencies in a pre-recorded signal during replay. It is usually complemented by a (Pre-)Emphasis process which performs the reverse function at the time of recording. Used to compensate for the difficulties in recording high frequencies on some media.

De-esser

A device for removing excessive sibilance from recorded speech or singing.

Default

The condition adopted by a device when it is first powered up and has not yet received instructions which would cause any change to that condition. Most machines will simply be in whatever condition they were in prior to being powered down. Others will be completely blank, or in some more or less useful predetermined condition set by the manufacturer.

Degaussing

The process of demagnetizing a metal component in an electronic device such as a tape recorder or computer monitor, where the residual magnetic field might distort the sound or image.

Delay

1. A period of time by which two events are offset, or by which an expected event is late. In audio, a sound might arrive at a microphone at two (or more) different times due to having taken paths of different lengths, e.g. directly and via reflection from walls, etc.

2. A process whereby an audio signal is temporarily stored (recently in a digital device, but originally in a tape machine). Delay units are used to simulate echo by mixing the delayed signal with the direct or, in the case of radio broadcasts involving live telephone conversations, they are used to allow a period of grace before transmission, during which any rude bits can be censored: this is known as "profanity delay". Delay is also used for various purposes in electronic circuitry: e.g. in a CD player having only one DAC, a sample which represents the left audio channel needs to be delayed until the equivalent right channel sample becomes available.

3. In an Envelope Generator, a variable period of time which can elapse between a key press or other trigger and the start of the Attack Time [3].

4. A facility offered on some sequencers: see MIDI Delay [1].

Delta Times	See Standard MIDI File.
Demisemiquaver	Note (♪) or rest (𝄾) whose duration is 1/32 of a semibreve. Also known as a thirty-second note.
Demo Tape	A tape made by an unknown artist to demonstrate their talent to a prospective agent or record company, or made by an established artist to give an outline of a proposed album. Amateur demos were traditionally of a rather dubious technical quality, even though the recorded performances sometimes displayed a certain raw energy. With the advent of cheap technology, however, it is now quite common for demo tapes to be of such high quality that they can be released as they stand without the need for re-recording. This is particularly true of dance music (Hip-Hop, House Music, etc.) – much of the material released in this market has been produced by untrained engineers working in bedroom studios and is no less successful for that.
Desktop	A generic term for a type of personal computer system that is reassuringly large enough to occupy most of your desk, thus providing you with an excuse not to do any paperwork. Originally coined to distinguish such devices from larger, stand-alone mainframes and minicomputers, and now useful also to distinguish desktop computers from their smaller laptop and notebook counterparts.
Desktop Publishing	Also called DTP. A category of computer software which allows a user to layout and generate complex documents such as magazines, books, display adverts, brochures, etc. Programs will allow text to do such fancy things as "flow" around a picture so that it follows the boundary of the image, as well as respond to more mundane aspects of layout and style. Although superficially similar to a Word Processor, DTP is optimized for the creation and altering of layouts – the positioning, rather than the initial keying-in, of the text. Various text files will usually have been generated using a word processor, which has facilities such as a spelling checker, before being imported into the DTP program.
Detune	**1.** In a synthesizer with two or more oscillators per voice, a facility for altering the frequency of one oscillator relative to the other(s). This can give a richer sound quality due to Beating between the oscillators or, with extreme settings, can produce discernible intervals in pitch.
	2. Originally one of the defined MIDI Controller Change messages with a status byte value in the range 176-191 and a first data byte of 94. It is assigned to the parameter in a synthesizer which alters the depth of the effect described in Detune [1]. More recently this message has been reassigned as one of five generalized Effects Depth messages. *See* Effects Control
Development	The transformation or exploration of a musical idea or group of ideas. *See* Sonata Form.
Diatonic	Pertaining to the division of the octave into a scale of five tones and two semitones. There are two types in common usage in western music. The diatonic Major scale has the interval series tone, tone, semitone, tone, tone, tone, semitone. The diatonic Minor scale has the interval series tone, semitone, tone, tone, semitone, tone, tone. Music which includes notes outside of the diatonic scale currently in force is said to be Chromatic. The layout of a piano keyboard clearly shows the relative positions of tones (T) and semitones (S) in the diatonic major scale of C and the diatonic (or "natural") minor scale of A, since no black notes are needed. Shifting these scales to start on any of the eleven other available pitches will produce more complex patterns (as the scale on the right indicates), providing the stock-in-trade for many a piano teacher:

Diatonic Major Scale of C   Diatonic Minor Scale of A   Diatonic Minor Scale of C

DI Box	*See* Direct Injection.

Digital Said of any electronic device in which some quality, such as an audio or video signal, is encoded in numeric form, according to a coding scheme such as PCM. Digital Signal Processing (DSP) or "done in the digital domain" are phrases used to indicate processes carried out on an encoded signal by manipulating the numbers which represent it.

Digital Domain The concept of expressing real events numerically. Thus, when a signal is converted into digital form and then modified arithmetically so that the signal is altered in some way, this is said to take place in the digital domain. If the digital data which represents a sound is transferred from one piece of equipment to another without conversion, the transfer is said to be entirely in the digital domain.

Digital Signal Processing The arithmetic manipulation of a signal which has first been converted into digital data. For example, if a sound has been converted into digital form, making all the numbers 45% bigger will increase the amplitude of the sound, thus implementing a digital amplifier. In principle, any process (equalisation, gain control, echo, reverb etc.) can be applied to a sound in this way. DSP can be also used to generate sounds from scratch instead of relying on an existing set of data. This is the principle behind most digital synthesizers.

Digital Synthesizer A synthesizer which uses digital techniques to generate its sound. To some extent this superseded analogue technology in the early '80s.

Digital to Analogue Converter The decoding part of a digital audio device whose function is to sample binary values at regular intervals and derive an analogue signal from them.

Diminuendo Italian for becoming gradually softer, often abbreviated to *dim*. The effect is notated by the symbol ▷, colloquially known as a "hairpin". *See also* Crescendo.

Diminution **1.** The reduction of a major or perfect interval by one semitone to make a diminished interval.

2. The appearance of a musical idea in note durations which are shorter those used for its first appearance. A technique sometimes used in polyphonic music of the middle ages and renaissance, and contrapuntal music (particularly fugues) of the baroque. The opposite of Augmentation.

3. A method of ornamentation whereby notes of long duration are broken into a number of shorter notes, often of different pitches. A trill is the most basic example. In its most elaborate English form it was known as "division" and was the principle means of demonstrating virtuosity and improvisational skill in the 17th century.

DIN Acronym from Deutsche Industrie Normale – the German industrial standard, like a technical version of the BSI. The body responsible has promoted technical standardization in many areas. In audio, most commonly encountered with reference to tape equalisation and connector types.

DIN Sync A method of synchronization between devices such as drum machines (but not tape recorders), initially implemented by Roland (later adapted by Korg and others), which was common before MIDI became standard. Its name comes from the use of the same type of five-pin DIN connector which was later to be used for MIDI. In its original form, it comprised a gate signal used for stop/start and a pulsed clock signal at 24 PPQ. Korg later increased the pulse rate to 48 PPQ. Each device would normally have been equipped with a switch to determine whether it was a Master or a Slave.

Diode A type of valve or semiconductor device, generally having two terminals called anode and cathode, with the property of allowing current to flow in one direction only. If presented with an AC signal, it will inhibit one of the phases of the signal (positive or negative) while passing the other. Which phase is affected will depend on the position of the diode relative to the signal. This feature is often exploited to convert AC to DC, the practice being called Rectification (Americans sometimes call diodes rectifiers). A Light Emitting Diode (LED) will emit light while passing current; these are almost universally used for front panel indicators on modern equipment.

DIP An acronym of Dual In-line Package: a standard method of packaging fragile integrated circuits inside an oblong plastic or ceramic case with two rows of metal legs or pins, one on each of the long sides of the rectangle. The package has increasingly been used for components other than integrated circuits, such as resistor arrays and switch arrays.

DIP Switch An array of miniature (and fiddly to operate) switches, usually in groups of eight, which are sometimes fitted to electronic equipment to allow the user to change the default settings of that device. The switches might select frame rate on a synchronizer or channel number on a MIDI device, etc.

Direct Current An electrical signal which, unlike Alternating Current, does not change polarity with time (i.e. it has a frequency of 0 Hz). Batteries and power supplies inside equipment produce DC.

Direct Injection The practice of connecting a non-microphonic signal, such as an electric guitar, to the microphone input of a mixing desk. This almost invariably entails the use of a device called a DI box which matches the usually high impedance of the guitar to the low impedance of the microphone input. The guitar signal is connected to the DI box and the output of the DI box is plugged into the microphone input.

Directivity Pattern *See* Response Pattern.

Directory

In computer systems, a term used to describe a collection of files in a mass storage device, such as a Hard Disk. Typically, there will be a "root" directory from which will branch various sub-directories which the user may set up to contain related files, such as those needed for a database.

Direct to Disk Recording

1. The practice of recording digital audio data onto a hard disk for later replay or editing. This is currently quite expensive, as approximately 10 Megabytes of storage are required for one minute of stereo. However, it has many advantages, particularly in speed of access for editing and for the integration of digital audio tracks with sequenced MIDI data. The phrase was first coined by New England Digital in connection with their Synclavier system.

2. (archaic) The practice of recording directly (without tape) to a master disc, which was then used to press subsequent vinyl discs.

Dirty

Said of a signal that contains significant distortion.

Disc

1. Compact Disc (CD), a plastic disc with digital audio or other data encoded optically on its surface.

2. (archaic) Gramophone record.

3. Computer Disc: *see* Disk.

Disco

A form of popular music and associated club/dance culture which emerged during the early '70s in Europe and America. It started in clubs which found it cheaper to play records than to have live musicians, and was also associated in the early days with the burgeoning sex industry in major cities. For whatever reason, these areas also tended to contain clubs popular with gay men who quickly adopted disco as their own musical identity. When the music finally reached the mainstream market it was stripped of its gay associations and many consumers were unaware of the connection until a band called Village People rather forcibly reminded them with a string of hits including the controversial and occasionally banned "YMCA" and "In the Navy" (nothing promotes a record better than a banning order). The playing of records in clubs led to the creation of club DJs whose role became more and more creative and distinct from that of radio DJs. Record companies began printing BPM figures on record sleeves to assist DJs who wanted to make a smooth transition from one record to another on an adjacent turntable. Creative use of double turntables led to Scratching, Hip Hop, etc. I am glad I have been able to define disco without once mentioning Saturday Night Fever. Oh Damn.

Disk

A magnetic disc for storing computer data. *See also* Floppy Disk, Hard Disk. The spelling "disk" is more common in computer parlance, while "disc" is usually used for audio and visual media.

Distortion

Any deformation of the information content of a signal. In audio this would cause a change in sound quality, due to alterations in the relative levels of existing partials or to the introduction of new partials. This is sometimes called harmonic distortion.

Dither

1. In digital audio, the principle of adding a small amount of random White Noise to the signal with the intention of reducing the distortion which occurs when the signal level falls between resolution steps close to zero, i.e. those encoded by the LSB. The added noise increases the average amplitude slightly, so that the signal can be resolved by the LSB. This reduces the distortion at low levels but increases the noise. It is considered that noise is more acceptable than distortion. The amount of dither signal added is one-third of the LSB. Thus, for a 16-bit converter encoding a range of 2 volts, the LSB is equivalent to a difference of 30.5 μV ($2 \div 65,536$ V) which gives us a dither amount of 10.166 μV. *See also* Quantization Error.

2. In digital video, a method of interpolating colour information between adjacent Pixels so that, for example, an 8-bit imaging system with only 256 discrete colours can appear to represent a wider range of colours.

Dixieland

A type of jazz associated with white musicians performing in New Orleans in the early part of the 20th century, and a subsequent revival of this style in the late '30s. Prominent use of clarinet, trumpet or cornet, and trombone is typical. Although Afro-American musicians had been playing jazz for some time, it was little known outside the southern states before being promoted by white groups such as The Original Dixieland Jazz Band. The origin of the word "Dixie" may, according to one explanation, come from the French word Dix, printed on $10 bills by a New Orleans bank, Louisiana having been a French colony until 1803.

DJ

Abbreviation of Disc Jockey. A person who operates turntables upon which discs are played, either for radio broadcast or in clubs. With the gradual demise of vinyl records in favour of other audio media, the term now describes a person who replays recorded music irrespective of the medium upon which it is stored. In the opinion of some, club DJs are more creative than their radio counterparts and are often musicians in their own right. *See also* Scratching.

DMA

Abbreviation of Direct Memory Access. Many computers require their CPUs to spend precious time looking after the movement of data in and out of memory. If a computer uses DMA, the memory is controlled by a dedicated processor (MMU) which frees the processor from this tedious task. This has the effect of speeding up the main task that the CPU is trying to carry out.

Dobro	Acronym from DOpyera BROthers. An acoustic guitar fitted with a metal resonator to give it a louder and more strident tone than usual. Invented by John Dopyera in the early 20th century.
Dolby	Commercial noise reduction systems used in analogue tape recording. Types B, C and HX are commonly found on domestic equipment such as cassette decks, while types A and SR are found in recording studios. Manufacturers pay a licence fee to the Dolby Corporation for the use of the system in their equipment. Essentially, the Dolby circuitry selectively boosts quiet (low-level) signals (just in the higher frequency range in Dolby B) to take them above the level of tape noise. On replay, an inverse process cuts these boosted levels, and with them much of the inherent tape noise, improving the Signal-to-Noise Ratio by about 10 dB (Dolby B), 10 or 15 dB depending on frequency (Dolby A), or up to 20 dB (Dolby C). Dolby HX Pro (Headroom eXtension) adds control of recording bias and equalisation by the high frequency component of the signal. This improves the high frequency saturation of the tape during recording, without introducing distortion. Although described as Pro, it was developed by Bang & Olufson and is marketed under license by Dolby for use primarily in domestic equipment. Dolby SR (Spectral Recording) is a noise reduction system developed for use on professional analogue tape recorders. Instead of dealing with just low-level signals in various frequency bands, its circuitry processes the changing spectral properties of the entire signal over time and frequency, claiming to offer a level of performance audibly equivalent to 16-bit digital recording with a dynamic range of around 80 dB. *See also* DBX.
Dolby Stereo	A system developed by Dolby which allows a stereo optical track on 35 mm ciné film to carry four analogue audio channels, using a proprietary matrix encoding scheme. On 70 mm film, six audio channels are recorded on separate magnetic tracks laid onto the film. Not to be confused with Dolby's noise reduction systems. *See also* SR.D.
Dolce	Italian for sweetly.
Dominant	*See* Scale.
Dongle	A type of Copy Protection for computer programs, consisting of a cartridge containing a ROM or custom IC which plugs into a socket on the computer. Its presence is required, and verified, by a piece of software before the program will run. If the dongle uses a ROM, it will probably contain a serial number which matches that of the software. If it contains a custom IC, this will usually perform a mathematical function on a value generated by the software, the result of which is already known to the software. Given the wrong answer, which includes no response, the software may not load or it may start up in a "demo mode" where it runs with key features, such as the ability to load or save files, inhibited. *See also* Hacking.
Doppler Effect	An acoustic effect encountered when the source of a pitched sound is moving relative to the listener. Especially conspicuous if the source moves towards the listener, passes and then moves away, as with a car horn or fire engine bell. As the source approaches, the sound has its normal velocity plus the velocity of the vehicle. This effectively shortens the wavelength of the sound, causing it to rise in pitch. The reverse happens as the vehicle moves away. The effect is exploited in the Leslie Cabinet, in which loudspeakers are effectively rotated relative to the user, resulting in slight pitch changes and a corresponding Chorus effect. The Doppler Effect occurs with any wave phenomena: the light from stars, for example, is shifted in colour (the Red Shift) as they move away from the earth.
Dorian	*See* Mode.
DOS	Acronym from Disk Operating System. Used as a generic term for a variety of Operating Systems on IBM-compatible PCs: e.g. MSDOS, DRDOS.
Dot Matrix	*See* Printer.
Dot Pitch	An indication of the Resolution of an imaging device, such as a Printer, Monitor[3] or Scanner, given in dots per inch: *see also* DPI.
Double Flat	*See* Flat.
Double Sharp	*See* Sharp.
Double Tracking	In multi-track recording, the re-recording of a performance onto a new track for playback simultaneously with the original, giving the effect of more than one musician playing or singing the part. Possible the earliest example was Les Paul's "guitar orchestra" of the late '40s and early '50s, in which he played all the parts himself and which featured a double-tracked melodic line. A similar effect can be achieved from only a single take by copying the material onto another track, first delaying it by a few milliseconds, and then mixing it with the original. This is known as Auto Double Tracking, or ADT.
Downbeat	*See* Beat[1].
DPI	Abbreviation of Dots Per Inch. An indication of the resolution of graphic imagers, such as computer monitors and printing systems. The higher the number, the greater the ability to show fine detail. Laser printers commonly operate at 300 DPI and this is quite adequate for most purposes; typesetting-quality printers operate at 1200 or more DPI.

Drawbar

On a Hammond organ with tonewheels, a slider that shortens the distance between the axle bearing the wheels and the transducer which converts their spinning patterns into an audio signal. This has the effect of introducing a particular pitch component (Harmonic) into the sound to alter its timbre. While similar in purpose to a stop on a pipe organ, it has the advantage of being variable in intensity as opposed to a stop's simple on/off action. Drawbars have been retained on more recent electronic organs of the Hammond type, but their function is now to act as simple faders that adjust the gain of different oscillators.

Drop Frame

A standard Timecode frame rate developed for the American television system. Black and white images use 30 FPS while colour images use 29.97 FPS. As it does not make sense to have .97 of a frame this odd value is derived from 30 FPS by dropping two frames in every minute which is not a multiple of ten. Thus 108 frames will be dropped per hour. (30 FPS x 3600 seconds is 108,000 frames; this, minus 108 is 107,892 frames, and divided by 3600 gives 29.97).

Drop In

A method of recording new material into a track which has already been recorded. This might be done to correct some mistake which occurred on the first take. It will usually be followed by a Drop Out [3] at the end of the insert, leaving the rest of the original take intact. Obviously the choice of drop in and drop out points is critical: for precision work it is sometimes preferable to use an Autolocator to carry out these procedures. Sometimes called "punch in". Most sequencers offer a similar function for MIDI data recordings.

Drop Out

1. Reduction of signal level caused by a recording or editing error, or by a defective coating on the tape.

2. A similar failing in a digital recording due to an irrecoverable data error.

3. Switching out of record mode on a recording system, perhaps at the end of a section which is being corrected, so as to leave previously recorded material intact. Sometimes called "punch out". *See also* Drop In.

Drum Machine

A specialized type of synthesizer which produces percussion and related sounds, and incorporates a sequencer that allows the sounds to be arranged in rhythm tracks.

Drum Pads

A set of pads which ideally have a similar response to the heads of acoustic drums when struck with sticks. They are made for two purposes: quiet drum practice and, when fitted with suitable transducers, to play electronic (usually sampled) drum sounds. If equipped with MIDI, drum pads can also act as a controller, allowing drummers to trigger any type of synthesized sound across a MIDI network.

Dry

Said of an acoustic with a short reverberation time (also called a dead acoustic).

DSP

See Digital Signal Processing.

Dub

See Dubbing, Reggae.

Dubbing

The copying of audio and/or video material from one recording or medium (disc, tape, etc.) to another. In particular, the addition of music, sound effects, dialogue, etc. to a film or TV soundtrack.

Ducking

The use of a gain control device, such as a Compressor or VCA, to reduce automatically the level of one signal when another appears. Most commonly used by DJs to lower the music signal whenever they talk into the microphone. So called because the music signal "ducks" to avoid the microphone signal, as if the latter was a low-flying aircraft.

Dummy Head

An artificial head which is the same mass, volume and shape as an average human head. Also known as a *Kunstkopf*. Its purpose is to facilitate a stereo microphone system which uses a pair of microphones mounted in the position of ears. This is gives a very strong binaural, or enhanced stereo, effect – but only on headphones; the effect is not so noticeable on speakers, and in fact may lead to poor reproduction.

Duplet

A pair of notes (or rests) executed in the time normally taken by three of the same value, most commonly occurring in compound-time music. The inverse of a Triplet.

Dynamic

1. A type of microphone. *See* Moving Coil.

2. Dynamic(s), a vague term which in some way conveys the sense of motion or variety in a procedure or activity, such as the "group dynamics" of the members of an ensemble as they prepare for a performance.

3. Dynamics. In music, a general term referring to degrees of loudness.

Dynamic Range

The difference between the loudest and quietest parts of a performance. Also the difference between the highest and lowest signal levels of a programme, expressed in decibels.

Early Reflections

In Reverberation, the first pattern of reflected sounds which appears after the Pre-Delay. To some extent, the intensity of the early reflections indicates the reflective properties of the material from which the room is constructed. If they are very clear and pronounced the room is probably made of a very reflective surface such as stone. Conversely, if they are somewhat less clear then a listener will imagine that the room is less "church like" and more domestic.

Earphones

See Headphones.

Earth

1. AC mains supplies are based on the principle that the current can "return" to the power station via the ground or earth. As this path presents the lowest impedance, the electricity supply "prefers" to travel down it. For this reason, it is desirable to connect the metal chassis of most equipment which operates at mains voltage levels directly to earth, giving a preferred path for "loose" electricity (e.g. if a wire bearing a live level should work free). This is a safety feature and should not be interfered with. Unfortunately, the side effect is that some earthing schemes can result in earth loops which in turn give rise to hum. The simple and tempting solution is to unearth the equipment, which sometimes will get rid of hum and possibly get rid of the person who does this. *See also* Dead [2], Earth Lift, ELCB.

2. The planet, third from the sun, on which we live. Variously personified in philosophy and religion. One personification which has reached a current vogue is that of "Gaia". Many people fear (with some justification) that our greed will kill Gaia, or she will wreak revenge on mankind for its negligence of her. Either way we loose unless we change our attitude.

Earth Lift

A facility on some equipment to assist in eliminating earth loops and the hum they can cause. Generally, and certainly on well-designed equipment, this does not break the connection between Screen [2] and chassis earth, or worse still, between the chassis and the earth pin of a mains plug. Instead, it introduces a small but significant impedance (usually a resistance of between 10 and 100Ω), thus reducing the tendency of the current to flow along the loop and the level of any hum being caused in the process.

Earth Loop

The situation which arises when two pieces of equipment, each having an established chassis earth internally connected to signal earth, are then connected via a screened cable. This forms a relatively large loop from chassis earth to signal earth (screen), signal earth to signal earth and chassis earth back to chassis earth. Because the electrical pathway formed in this manner has a finite impedance, a difference in potential may occur from one end of the loop to the other, allowing an AC signal (probably at mains frequency) to form in the pathway. This signal will then manifest itself as an irritating hum, which in some cases may be louder than the intended signal. The solution is to break the screen connection between the two pieces of equipment, ideally at the end of the cable that is plugged into a receiver such as a mixer or amplifier.

EBCDIC

Acronym from Extended Binary Coded Decimal Interchange Code (pronounced "ebsdick"). One of a number of standard systems which determine how a specific character is represented by a numeric value in a computer. Thus, the character A is represented by the number 193 (11000001 in Binary). EBCDIC is an eight-bit code, allowing 256 characters to be uniquely defined. The intention was to ensure that text data could be transmitted from one machine to another. EBCDIC was originated by IBM. It should not be confused with so-called "extended ASCII" which is an eight-bit version of ASCII used in IBM-compatible PCs. *See also* ASCII, UKASCII.

EBU

1. Abbreviation of European Broadcast Union. A body involved in the specification and development of technical standards in the audio/video industry.

2. A Timecode standard developed by the EBU [1] (from SMPTE) to integrate video devices with audio. It was subsequently adopted by the audio industry, initially for audio to video synchronization and subsequently for synchronization of tape machines, drum machines, sequencers and other time-reliant devices. The timing and other information is carried in 80-bit messages generated 25 times a second (one message for each frame of video). A similar code has been implemented in America by the SMPTE, but the rate is 30 messages per second as the American television system has this frame rate. It is common for people to refer to all timecodes as SMPTE, in much the same way as all vacuum cleaners are called Hoovers.

Echo

The audible repetition of a sound in its entirety, usually some time after the original has ended. Also used incorrectly to refer to Reverberation.

Echo Chamber

A room used to produce echo effects or, more correctly, Reverberation. Sound is replayed by a loudspeaker in a reverberant room. One or two (for stereo) microphones placed some distance away in the room pick up the modified sound and this signal is then mixed back into the programme. Most normally dimensioned rooms are only big enough to provide reverb effects rather than true echo. As sound travels at about 334 m/s you will need a room dimension of about 160 metres to generate a one second delay so, unless you are using an aircraft hangar, it probably isn't strictly an "echo" chamber

Echo Mix
The relative amount of "dry" (original) signal to "wet" (effected) signal in echo and reverb units, etc.

Echo Unit
A device for producing echo effects. These used to be based on modified tape machines (tape echo), but are now usually digital devices.

Editing
The practice of altering a recording (or data in a computer) by removing or repeating sections, or by changing the order in which sections occur. Tape editing on open-reel recorders is achieved by cutting the tape into pieces and then sticking it back together to give the desired effect. This is less practical with digital recording, where more precise editing can be done using a computer or purpose-built equipment to manipulate data. The main reasons for editing a recording are: to join together the best takes from a number of different recordings of the same piece to give the finest possible performance, or the conversion of a long piece into a shorter one and vice versa (typically to generate a 12" version of a 7" single).

Editor
A category of software which allows a computer user to adjust synthesizer parameters remotely via MIDI, using System Exclusive messages, etc. The larger screen of the computer often makes this an easier operation than the synthesizer's own user interface. *See also* Librarian.

EDL
Abbreviation of Edit Decision List. *See* Playlist[2].

Effects
1. A range of processes applied to an audio signal for creative purposes, such as echo, reverb, flanging, etc.

2. Effects Unit: a device for implementing Effects[1].

3. Sound effects or FX. Pre-recorded or live sounds which are used to promote realism in a studio broadcast, e.g. recordings of traffic noise or the sea.

Effects Control
Two classes of Controller Change message with a status byte value in the range 176–191, and a first data byte value in the range 91–95 (Effects Depth), or 12–13 (Effects Controls 1 and 2) which are used to introduce and adjust some kind of effect such as reverb.

Effects Controls 1 & 2
Controller Change messages with status byte values in the range 176–191, and a first data byte value of 12 or 13. These are intended to be assignable to parameters (other than depth) which appear in a synthesizer or effects unit and which control some aspect of an effect such as reverb time or pitch shift. They operate in conjunction with Effects Depth messages; the two message types taken together are called Effects Control.

Effects Depth
1. A parameter on a synthesizer, effects unit, etc, which can be adjusted by the user to alter the amount of a particular effect, such as reverb, delay or chorus.

2. Effects Depth Controllers. Controller Change messages with status byte values in the range 176–191, and a first data byte value in the range 91–95, which are used to implement the function described in Effects Depth[1]. These were formerly (pre-1991) assigned to specific effects, but are now generalized and operate in conjunction with Effects Controls 1 and 2 messages; the two message types taken together are called Effects Control.

Effects Send / Return
A facility on a Mixing Desk or other audio device which allows a signal to be sent to an effects unit and for the processed signal to be returned. It may consist of just a stereo jack configured as an Insert Point, or it may have additional level and EQ controls, etc. *See also* Auxiliary.

Efficiency
A measure of the effectiveness of a system which converts energy from one form to another, usually expressed in terms of the useful output as a percentage of the input. For example, loudspeakers are not particularly efficient since much of the electrical input supplied from the amplifier is converted into heat rather than the desired sound. The term is also used with regard to computer Algorithms, such as those used for data compression, to describe their effectiveness.

ELCB
Abbreviation of Earth Leakage Circuit Breaker. A device fitted to the mains electrical supply which monitors any current flowing to earth. The device will disconnect the supply if this current exceeds about 30 mA, as this probably indicates some form of connection (including the possibility of human contact) between the live parts of the circuit and the earth. Although similar in effect to a fuse, ELCBs are more sensitive and are designed primarily with human safety in mind.

Electret Microphone
See Electrostatic Microphone.

Electrical
To do with electricity, though more commonly used to refer to devices which make use of wires, switches or transformers, and which typically work with mains level voltages or currents. This usage makes a vague distinction between such devices and those which use resistors, capacitors, inductors, valves or semiconductors, which typically work with low voltages or currents, and which are described as electronic. *See also* Electricity.

Electric Guitar

The first electric guitar was probably the Rickenbacker Electro Spanish guitar, played in public by a jazz guitarist, Jack Miller, in Los Angeles in 1932. However, there had been many, essentially amateur, experiments in amplifying guitars in the '20s. The earliest production model was an electric Hawaiian guitar, first advertised by Leo Fender in 1936-7. Les Paul is credited with the invention of the solid-bodied guitar in 1946 and its subsequent rapid adoption in pop music. *See also* Dobro, Guitar Amp, Pick Up [1].

Electricity

A form of energy involved in stationary or moving charged particles such as ions, and the potentially dangerous force imparted by this energy. Principally associated with electrons and specifically of electrons in a metal conductor such as a wire. It is one manifestation of the Electromagnetic force. Electricity is normally described in terms of two interrelated qualities: potential difference (measured in volts and commonly called voltage) and current (measured in amperes or amps). This relationship can be likened to the height of a head of water in a tank or reservoir (voltage) and the flow of that water in pipes (current). Current and voltage can be considered separately, but they are only aspects of one phenomenon and cannot exist independently. Like most forms of energy, electricity is used by humans to do work, and most people will be aware of the mains voltage supplied to their homes. The amount of work that can be done by electricity is expressed in VA (voltage multiplied by current). Electric supplies are divided into two classes depending on whether the voltage is steady state (DC) or varies with time (AC). Electricity is also used to convey information such as an audio signal, but in these cases the voltages and currents involved are very small, typically millivolts and milliamps.

Electric Keyboard

A term for basic electronic musical instruments, from nasty organ / piano simulators up to devices that approach the sophisticated editing facilities offered by synthesizers. Features such as Auto Accompaniment and preset drum patterns are often included, while MIDI may be offered on more expensive models. Usually used for recreational, rather than professional, purposes. *See also* Keyboard Lab.

Electro-Acoustic Music

A form of art music which may involve electronically generated sound, tape loops, samples, etc., as well as conventional instruments, voices, and possibly electronic treatments of these. It may be performed live, or simply played to an audience via a replay device like tape or CD. In the context of electro-acoustic music, operation of a PA is sometimes called "diffusion", as the operator may place sounds in the stereo (or quadraphonic) field, or apply effects according to directions in the score. To this extent, the PA operator is as much a performer as anyone else. Leading exponents have included Babbitt, Stockhausen and Varèse. *See also* Musique Concrète.

Electromagnetic

There are four known forces operating in the universe. Two of them (the Weak and Strong nuclear forces) are harnessed by man to generate electricity and to degenerate entire populations. The effects of the other two, gravity and electromagnetism, are more mundane experiences. Electricity is one manifestation of the electromagnetic force, magnetism is another. These two manifestations are mutually affective. That is, a Magnetic Field [3] can influence an electric field and vice versa. This is because an electromagnetic wave consists of both an electric field and a related perpendicular magnetic field. The electromagnetic spectrum consists of (in order of increasing frequency) radio waves, microwaves, infrared light (heat), visible light, ultra violet light, X-rays and gamma rays. All electromagnetic waves propagate at the same speed which (for convenience and because it was the first form of electromagnetism to have its velocity measured) is called the velocity of light: 299,792.458 kilometres per second.

Electronic

To do with electrons, though more commonly used to refer to devices which make use of resistors, capacitors, inductors, valves or semiconductors and which typically work with low voltages or currents. This usage makes a vague distinction between such devices and those which simply switch, divert or carry voltages (generally mains supply voltages) and which are described as electrical. *See also* Electricity.

Electrostatic Microphone

Class of microphone, of which condenser and electret are types, in which air pressure changes cause changes in the capacitance of a condenser (Capacitor). The capacitor is normally biased by a voltage which is supplied from batteries or via Phantom Powering down the signal cable from a mixing desk. The Electret is an exception, as this requires such a small biasing voltage that it is possible to charge it up permanently at the time of manufacture: Sennheiser use a proprietary biasing scheme which utilizes RF instead of a DC voltage.

Electrostatic Loudspeaker

A loudspeaker with a transducer that uses the audio signal to vary the strength of an electric field which, in turn, induces vibration in a metallic or metalized membrane. In principle, it is the reverse of an Electrostatic Microphone and quite different from the more common electro-magnetic Voice Coil arrangement. Made popular by the manufacturer Quad and used mainly for domestic hi-fi, as its power output is fairly low. *See also* Loudspeaker.

E-Mail

Acronym from Electronic MAIL. The sending of text, graphics or other data such as MIDI files or software, from one computer to another. Particularly used with reference to computer communication over telephone lines using Modems. *See also* Bulletin Board.

EMI

1. A famous record company (abbreviation of Electrical Musical Industries).

2. Abbreviation of Electro-Magnetic Interference. All systems where an electrical signal is used to represent some quality, such as sound in an audio signal, are prone to interference from electromagnetic fields in the vicinity of the cable carrying the signal. This can induce an erroneous voltage which appears at the receiving end of the signal flow as a spurious noise. Hum is the most common example of this. Other examples include the clicks and pops generated by thermostats and light switches.

Emphasis

Also called pre-emphasis. The principle of boosting high frequencies in a signal prior to recording. It is usually complemented by a de-emphasis process which performs the reverse function on replay. It is used to compensate for the difficulties in recording high frequencies on some media.

Emulator

A system which allows a computer to run applications written for a different type of computer. Emulators usually cause software to run at a slower speed and, since they occupy memory space, may not leave sufficient room for larger programs to load at all.

Encoding

See Coding.

Encryption

The encoding of data to make it secure from unauthorized users or to allow recovery from errors which may occur in data transmission. *See also* Error Correction, Hacking, Password Protection.

End in / End out

Of a spool of magnetic recording tape. Describes whether the end of the music or speech recorded on the tape is on the outside of the spool – i.e. it has been played on to the right hand reel (end out) – or whether the beginning is on the outside of the spool, i.e. it has been rewound on to the left hand reel (end in). For tape storage purposes, end out is preferred as this causes any Print Through to occur behind the real event rather than in front of it.

Engineer

Also known as sound engineer. The person responsible for technical aspects of a recording or broadcast. Such a person will have the responsibility of ensuring the best possible recording or broadcasting quality, and will also ensure that equipment is lined-up with this aim in mind. In some cases this person may also repair defective equipment.

Enharmonic

1. A partial or sinewave component of a sound which bears no simple arithmetic relationship to any other partial in the sound. *See also* Harmonic, Sound.

2. A term to indicate alternative ways of notating the same musical pitch, such as B-sharp and C-flat.

Envelope Generator

A device which produces a control signal which varies in level with time. The simplest of these (sometimes called ADSR) has four parameters: Attack Time, Decay Time, Sustain Level and Release Time. Thus it has three time constants and one level constant. Such a device is often found on synthesizers, where it is usually used to control the volume of an amplifier, the cut off frequency of a filter or the frequency of an oscillator. More complex arrangements involving a series of time and level constants are available, particularly on digital synthesizers. These are called multistage envelopes and may involve six or more paired time and level parameters:

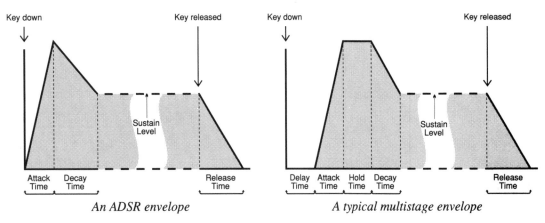

An ADSR envelope   *A typical multistage envelope*

EOX

Acronym from End Of eXclusive. A MIDI message in the form of a status byte with a value of 247, used to indicate the end of each System Exclusive message.

EP

Abbreviation of Extended Play. A seven-inch record with a longer playing time than a normal single, recorded at 33⅓ or 45 rpm.

Episode

A section of secondary importance in a musical structure. Specifically, a contrasting passage in a Rondo form, a linking passage in a Sonata form movement or an idea which links the middle entries of a subject following the exposition of a Fugue.

EPROM

Acronym from Erasable Programmable Read-Only Memory. A type of memory IC which can be written to, read many times, subsequently erased (by exposure to ultraviolet light for about an hour) and then written to again. The fact that the chip can be re-programmed in this way distinguishes it from ROM and other types of WORM. There is also EEPROM where the first E stands for electronic and specifies an electronic method of erasure.

EPS

Abbreviation of Encapsulated PostScript. An agreed standard format for embedding a PostScript file within a longer file, such as the text of a book. Typically the EPS file will represent a graphic image (perhaps of music notation from a scorewriting program) and will consist of the PostScript commands necessary to print the image. Bitmapped data to provide a version of the image for screen display may optionally be included.

EQ

See Equalisation.

Equalization

In the early days of recording it was necessary to compensate for frequency losses caused by the equipment through which a signal passed. This compensation (broadly speaking a sort of tone control to boost high frequencies) was called equalization, as the net effect of the loss plus the compensation was intended to make the signal "equal" to its original form. Occasionally this meaning is still used but, as recording technology improves, the need for compensation is less and equalisation tends now to be used as a creative effect. Equalization or EQ is now fitted as a standard section (in a much more elaborate form than that described above) on many mixing desks and effects units. It may also be provided by a stand alone unit in the form of a Graphic or Parametric Equalizer.

Equal Temperament

A convenient system for dividing an octave into 12 pitch steps, each of 100 cents. This has the effect of making all semitones equal in size, compromising to various degrees the uneven spacing created by pitches derived from the natural harmonic series. Tuning to equal temperament became necessary once composers wanted to write in any key for instruments of fixed pitch, such as the harpsichord. It should be understood that, say, the note A which appears in F# minor is naturally slightly flatter in pitch than the note A which appears in C major. This would normally be dealt with intuitively by a proficient player on an instrument with continuous pitching, such as a violin. A keyboard instrument would, in theory, need to be retuned for each new key to take such differences into account. This is clearly impractical, so various compromises in tuning were attempted, the most successful of which – equal temperament – distributed the errors in pitch equally between all notes. In celebration of this, J. S. Bach wrote 48 Preludes and Fugues, two sets in each of the 12 major and 12 minor keys.

Erase

1. To remove, deliberately or accidentally, a pre-recorded signal on a tape. Most tape recorders have a special magnetic head set aside for this function, which operates when the machine is put into record mode. If a complete tape is being erased for re-use, it is often more convenient to use a "bulk eraser", where the whole spool of tape is placed in a strong magnetic field generated by an electromagnet. This erases all of the tape simultaneously without having to spool it through a tape machine.

2. To remove data from a data storage device, such as a floppy or hard disk. In practice the actual data is not erased, but the directory area of the storage device, which keeps a record of the location of data, is altered. As it is no longer possible to find the data, it might just as well not be there. Systems that allow an "un-erase" are able to reconstruct the directory, and therefore find the data, as long as no new information has been recorded since the erasure was carried out. Also, the removal of data from a memory device such as an EPROM. Generally this cannot be undone.

Error Correction

A process whereby data which is being transferred from one place (e.g. a compact disc) to another (e.g. the D/A converters of the CD player) can be protected against minor errors. The data has extra pieces of information, called "keywords", interleaved or combined with the original data. Then, if there is a problem in the data path (e.g. a scratch on the CD surface) which leads to the keyword becoming corrupted, the error can (in most cases, but not always) be corrected. This is possible because the combination of interleaving method and known keyword enables the nature of the error to be calculated and therefore reversed. There are many methods, but the most frequently encountered is Cross Interleaved Reed-Solomon Code (CIRC). *See also* Checksum.

Errors

An inescapable fact of life: errors can occur. This is because of a fundamental property of the universe called entropy. Tidying a room requires effort, letting it get untidy requires no effort at all. It is easier to break things than make them, etc. Organization requires energy, and as physical systems (such as the universe) tend towards the lowest energy level possible, this is the same as saying they like to be as disorganized as possible. A system of data transfer between devices is a highly organized thing. Any piece of data is required to have a specific value at a specific time. Unfortunately, there is an infinite range of other values, any of which the data can assume. Even if the data is stationary (stored on a hard disk for example) it can become corrupted and the chances of corruption become greater if you start shifting it around between devices, or from one part of a device to another. Broken wires, EMI[2], who knows – perhaps the phase of the moon – all conspire against the integrity of our little piece of data. There are two things one can do: detect the error and have the data retransmitted in the hope that the error doesn't recur (*See* Checksum) or detect the error and correct it (*See* Error Correction). Both of these increase the organization or energy of the system. *See also* Chaos.

Espressivo

Italian for expressively.

Exciter

A device for artificially enhancing a signal by adding new Partials to it. These devices are said to compensate for loss of high frequencies in analogue tape recording systems, impress A&R men and generally right the wrongs of the world. Used subtly they can indeed clarify a complex and dense mix. In practice they tend to get overused and you can generally spot an "excited" mix a mile off.

Executive Producer
A non-functional person with peripheral involvement in a recording or broadcast, whose feelings would be hurt if their name did not appear on the record sleeve, cassette or CD inlay, etc. Usually such a person will appear in the control room from time to time and make comments such as "I think that ambient mic wants to be a bit further away", or (particularly when his advice is followed) "It's beginning to sound quite good now!". Essentially he is there to ensure that the people who actually do the work have a guaranteed source of irritation in case the recording process is trouble free.

Expander
1. A synthesizer, without a keyboard or other master controller, often packaged in a standard 19" rack mounting box. Also called a Tone Module.

2. A device opposite in function to a Compressor, i.e. it is linear above the Threshold, while its gain drops non-linearly below this. Thus, with a expansion ratio of 1:2, an expander will produce an output swing of 2 dB for an input swing of 1 dB. The effect is to increase the dynamic range of a signal, particularly when the lower limit of the dynamic range has been determined by the presence of background noise such as tape hiss.

3. A printed circuit board which can be added to equipment after manufacture or purchase, to improve it or increase its capacity: e.g. a memory upgrade board for a computer.

Expansion Ratio
In an Expander [2] that is working below its Threshold, the ratio given by the number of decibels change in input over the number of dBs change in output. Typical ratios are in the range 1:2 to perhaps 1:20. Expansion Ratio is the opposite and complement of Compression Ratio.

Expansion Slot
A socket provided on a piece of equipment, usually a computer, which allows additional hardware components to be added.

Export
In a computer, the act of placing data generated by the current program into a format which can be accessed and understood by a different program. This leads to a number of standardized file formats, of which the Sample Dump Standard and Standard MIDI File formats are examples.

Exposition
The initial appearance of a musical idea or group of ideas. *See* Fugue, Sonata Form.

Expression
One of the defined MIDI Controller Change messages with a status byte value in the range 176–191 and a data byte value of 11. It is usually assignable to some parameter in a synthesizer, such as Volume or Filter Cut Off.

Extemporization
See Improvisation.

f
See Forte.

Fade
1. Slow alteration of the level of a signal, usually using a potentiometer. Fade-in starts with no signal and gradually increases the level. Fade-out starts with a signal present and gradually decreases the level, normally to silence. *See also* Crossfade.

2. Of a piece of music, usually commercial music, the repeated section at the end of the song which is subjected to a gradual fade-out. *See also* Outro, Song [1].

Fader
A control on one channel of a mixing desk for adjusting the level of that channel relative to others. This is generally a slider, although strictly the term could be applied to a rotary control. *See also* Potentiometer.

Fairlight CMI
The trade name of one of the first commercially available Computer Musical Instruments (hence CMI). Originally designed in the late 1970s by Australian Kim Ryrie, it was named after a ferry which crosses Sydney Harbour. Although it was intended primarily as a digital synthesizer, it is better known as a sampling / sequencing workstation. Despite its comparatively limited specification by modern standards (and perhaps more because of its considerable cost) it is now considered something of a classic. Often compared to the Synclavier, it somehow never quite managed to keep up with the developments offered by that instrument.

False Entry
See Fugue.

Falsetto
A singing method that allows adult male singers to produce a high (alto or above) voice. It developed in church music at a time when it was not considered acceptable to admit women into choirs. The distinctive timbre of the falsetto voice has more recently been exploited by pop musicians such as the Bee Gees and Jimmy Somerville.

Farad
The SI Unit of capacitance.

Feedback

1. A loop connection from the output of a device or system to its own input. This is usually run through a level control, as unrestricted feedback can lead to oscillation in the device or system. An oscillator is, in fact, an amplifier with a high degree of feedback. Feedback occurs as a parameter in an echo unit and essentially determines the number of distinct repeats which are audible. Sometimes called regeneration.

2. A situation which can arise in PA systems where a microphone picks up its own amplified signal via the loudspeakers, causing a vicious circle of unintended over-amplification. *See also* Howlround.

3. A specific application of Feedback[1] in FM synthesis, where at least one operator in each algorithm is equipped with a feedback loop.

Feel

The emotional response, usually disciplined by stylistic awareness, created by a musician through the music being performed. This is generally communicated to others by the detailed, although often intuitive, control of the timing and articulation of the musical events – particularly to music which "swings", although it is a condition of all well-performed music. *See also* Interpretation.

Fermata

Italian for pause: an instruction to linger on a note or rest. It is notated with the symbol ⌒ colloquially known as an "eyebrow".

Ferric Oxide

Gamma Ferric Oxide (Fe_2O_3) is a magnetic material used as a primary coating on recording tape. It has inferior characteristics to both Chromium Dioxide and "metal" tapes.

ff

See Fortissimo.

FFT

Abbreviation of Fast Fourier Transform. *See* Fourier.

Fibre Optic

A method of data transmission in which a light beam (usually generated by a laser) is shone along a thin glass "cable". The light beam is turned on and off very rapidly in order to represent the bits of the digital Word. The system can carry a much greater rate, and therefore amount, of data than most conventional electronic means and is virtually immune to EMI[2].

Field

1. The subjective environment which a listener perceives while listening to sound. Stereo is an attempt to model such a field.

2. The area around one or more microphones, within which it is intended to record sound.

3. The spatial area of influence of the electromagnetic force. There are two fields manifested by this: electric field and magnetic field.

Fifth

The interval between a note and the one seven semitones above or below it. *See also* Interval.

Figured Bass

A method of indicating harmonies to be played in an improvisational manner above a bass line. Particularly encountered in the Continuo parts of works from the Baroque era, where the figures attached to the bass are "realized" by chordal instruments such as harpsichord, organ or lute. The figures define the intervals above the bass note which form the chord required: they may be supplemented by additional symbols, such as accidentals to indicate that a note is to be sharp, flat or natural, a line to show that the chord is to be held or repeated over subsequent bass notes, or the words *tasto solo,* meaning that no chords are required. Several shortcuts are employed in figured bass, particularly omitting the figures 3 and 5 when the context makes it clear that these intervals are required. Thus, an absence of figures on a particular bass note normally implies adding a 3rd and a 5th to make a root position triad, the most common chord of all.

Figure of Eight Microphone

A microphone which is sensitive to sound arriving at the front and rear of the capsule, but has virtually no sensitivity to sound arriving at the sides. So called because its polar diagram is shaped like a figure eight, although a three dimensional picture would show it to be like two tear drops with their sharp ends touching and their blunt ends furthest away from one another. *See also* Cardioid, Hypercardioid, Omnidirectional, Response Pattern.

File

In a computer, a quantity of data which has been previously stored in such a way that it can be retrieved. The storage medium will probably be a floppy disk or hard disk. In general, the file is identified by a name which must be unique, unless it is the intention of the user to overwrite (and therefore destroy) the existing data with a new set. The act of creating such a file is called "saving" or "closing", while the act of retrieving the data is called "loading" or "opening".

File Dump Standard

A part of the MIDI specification which allows the interchange of Standard MIDI File type data between MIDI-equipped devices via a MIDI cable, as opposed to a disk transfer. It is a Universal System Exclusive message of the Non-Real Time type, with a Sub-ID #1 of 7. One point of interest is caused by the restriction of the MIDI data byte format to 7 bits, where the MSB is always set to zero. Information stored in the device in 8-bit form has to be repackaged in blocks of eight MIDI data bytes (each of which has only seven useful bits) representing only 7 bytes from the transmitting device. The extra byte is composed of the seven MSB(it) chunks that are effectively suppressed by MIDI.

Fill

An instruction found in popular music, particularly in drum parts, for the performer to improvise a florid embellishment in the bar or bars so marked. Often used to signal a transition between sections (e.g. between verse and chorus) or to mark the end of a song, where the colloquialism "monster fill" invariably gives the green light to a drummer.

Film Soundtrack

The audio component (dialogue, music, effects, etc.) of a film presentation. There is usually a requirement for sound to be synchronized to images. This has been achieved by a variety of means including the recording of sound on optical tracks etched into the film emulsion alongside the frames, fixing magnetic tracks on the film surface, synchronizing the film with a separate tape machine by means of mechanical sprockets, and electronic sync using systems such as SMPTE. *See also* Dolby Stereo, LC Concept, Optical Track, SR.D.

Filter

An arrangement of electronic components (normally capacitors and inductors) which allows some frequencies to pass, while attenuating others, relative to a specific frequency called the Cut Off. Passive filters only attenuate frequencies or bands of frequencies while active filters can also boost them. To some extent any component, even a piece of wire, will function as a passive filter. The process can also be done in the digital domain. Filters come in a variety of forms, the most basic being high pass, band pass and low pass. HP removes frequencies below the cut off, BP removes frequencies either side of a band centred around the cut off, and LP removes frequencies above the cut off. Additional types exist, such as a comb filter which is usually achieved using a delay unit. *See also* Flanger, Resonance.

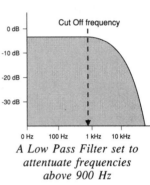
A Low Pass Filter set to attentuate frequencies above 900 Hz

Fine

Italian for finish (pronounced *fee-nay*). An indication in music to show that the performance should finish at that point – used when the printed end of the music directs the performer to repeat an earlier section. For example, *Da capo al fine* means "return to the beginning and play up to the word *fine*".

Firmware

In a computer system, the physical medium in which the software is contained. e.g. a floppy disk, ROM or magnetic tape, as distinct from either the abstract form of the software itself, or the hardware which is controlled by it. As an analogy, a human is a system of hardware, firmware and software. The hardware is the biomechanical aspects of the body (skeleton, skin, heart and other organs), the firmware is the spongy tissues of the brain which, it is believed, contain the software or the abstract thinking processes which, ultimately, control the hardware.

First Movement Form

See Sonata Form.

Fish

Any member of a family of vertebrates bearing scales and living predominantly under water, breathing through gills. In a planet which is three-fifths water, it stands to reason the Earth has quite a lot of them. Many species are particularly beautiful and can be kept in small (or preferably large) tanks in your living room, with the exception perhaps of the Vietnamese catfish *(pangasianodon gigas)* found in the Mekong river which, at up to 2 metres and weighing up to 300 kg, is the world's largest freshwater fish. That is bigger than many American footballers. For some reason fish are strongly associated with the surrealist movement in art and literature, for example, the surreal competition in the film "The Meaning of Life", where they play spot the fish, or the well known light bulb joke: Q. "How many surrealists does it take to change a light bulb?" A. "Fish!"

Fishing Rod

1. An extension pole for a hand-held microphone. Similar in function to a Boom, but lighter and more suitable for close-up work. Also called "fishpole".

2. A light, hand-held pole on the end of which is mounted a line and hook. Used to catch fish, for recreation or necessity.

Flaky

See Bug.

Flanger

An electronic effects unit. It functions by delaying part of the signal for a few milliseconds, causing phase shifts (technically, a comb filter response) when the delayed signal is subsequently mixed with the original. The delay time is rarely constant, but is varied in the manner of an LFO, to give a distinctive sweeping sound. Originally flanging was a tape effect resulting from slowing one machine relative to another by pressing on the flange of a tape spool. Popular in late '60s: Itchycoo Park, etc.

Flat

The condition of a note which is, either deliberately or accidentally, lowered in pitch. This might be by only a few cents or as much as a tone (double flat). In music notation a flat is indicated by the symbol ♭ (i.e. lower the note by a semitone) and a double flat is shown by the symbol ♭♭.

Flat Response

A frequency response which, when plotted graphically, produces an essentially flat line throughout the frequency band of interest (usually 20Hz – 20 kHz). This is an ideal response as it shows that the input signal will not be unduly amplified or attenuated at any frequency in the given range. For analogue equipment, deviation from flat of less than about 2dBs can be considered flat enough. Digital equipment is usually flat within 0.5dB across the human audio range.

Floppy Disk

A device for long-term storage of computer data. The device is so called because of the floppy plastic disk surfaces which it uses rather than the hard metal surfaces of hard disks. These plastic surfaces have a lower density of storage and slower speed of operation than hard disks. Floppies have a capacity ranging from about 300 Kilobytes to (currently) about 1.44 Megabytes or more. Floppy disk drives are often fitted to samplers, where they can store up to about 20 seconds of mono sound, depending on the Sampling Rate.

FLOPS

Acronym from FLoating-point OPerations per Second. An indication of the numeric processing or "number crunching" speed of a computer. *See also* MIPS.

Flutter

Unintentional changes in pitch caused by rapid speed variations in tape recorders or record players. Such variations may be due to a worn or defective pinchwheel or capstan, faulty motors or unreliable varispeed control electronics. *See also* Wow.

Flux Density

Of a magnetic system such as magnetic tape, a measure of the amount of magnetism in a given area. In magnetic tape, an area with greater flux density will replay louder than one with lesser density. Measured in Webers (Wb), though for audio purposes the nanoWeber (nWb) is preferred.

Flying

1. The practice of suspending equipment such as microphones, loudspeakers etc., above the heads of the performers or audience. It constitutes a major insurance overhead.

2. The temporary effect of letting go of a structure upon which one is climbing. The duration of the effect will depend on the height of the structure at the point you let go.

FM

Abbreviation of Frequency Modulation. An encoding process whereby an audio signal is used to modulate a radio frequency carrier signal so as to allow radio transmission. This system can give better quality than AM, and allows stereo operation.

FM Synthesis

Frequency Modulation synthesis. A method developed by Dr. John Chowning and marketed by Yamaha. The principle is that one oscillator (the Modulator) alters the frequency of another (the Carrier). As both oscillators generally operate in the audio frequency range, this results in a change in timbre, rather than pitch. In practice it is more useful to combine the oscillators with an amplifier and envelope generator in a package called an Operator and this is the basic unit of sound generation. The waveforms were originally sinewaves but later versions of the system allow different waveforms or even digital recordings (samples) of acoustic sounds to be used. There are a number of operators in a Voice, and the relationship between the operators (how they are connected) is described by an Algorithm.

Foldback

An audio signal which is diverted from the control room into the studio area for replay through headphones or (occasionally) a loudspeaker. This allows the musician to hear a mix of live and pre-recorded material while performing. The signal is normally obtained from a pre-fade Auxiliary send on a mixing desk.

Foldback Mix

The relative mixture of sources in a Foldback signal which a vocalist or instrumentalist prefers to hear while their performance is recorded.

Folk Music

A broad term for a particular type of Popular or non-Art Music. It is associated with, and often describes, the everyday activities of those who are not the élite in a society, most often those now called the "working class". In the past, folk music was not normally written down by the people who performed it and is rarely attributable to any particular author or composer. Surviving examples have mostly been preserved by the rather unreliable method of oral tradition, i.e. by one person performing the music which another then learns by imitation. In more recent times, formally trained musicians have notated it for the purposes of study and to prevent pieces being lost. Most folk music was either song or instrumental dance music. Folk music continues to be a living tradition in many cultures: in the west it has become increasingly linked with pop music and has lost something of its oral tradition, although its origins as an expression of the experiences of the community are still evident.

Font

A set of letters, numbers and symbols of a given design. Traditionally, the term was used for each particular size of type of this design: e.g. 10-point Times was one font in the Times family of typefaces. However, the ability of computers to scale a single outline font to any dimension has led to the term now being used for a complete typeface (e.g. "Times Italic") encompassing all sizes. Most often encountered in DTP and Scorewriter programs. *See also* Point.

Foot Controller

One of the defined MIDI Controller Change messages with a status byte value in the range 176-191 and a data byte value of 4. It is usually assignable to some parameter in a synthesizer, such as Volume, Program Change or Filter Cut Off.

Form

The structure or "organization" of a work of art. Static works, like paintings, have forms that can often be grasped in a single visual experience. Longer structures found in literature and theatre have forms shaped by their narrative content. The more abstract nature of music requires clear and simple signposts if its structure is to be memorable, especially since it occurs over a period of time. Thus, most musical forms are based on proportions of repetition and contrast, particularly of themes or melodies, together with an underlying tonal plan which determines the pattern of keys used. A number of forms are well established: *see* Binary, Fugue, Rondo, Sonata, Ternary and Variation forms.

Formant

A group of Partials which are quite closely spaced. Typically, formants occur in clusters throughout the spectrum of many sounds, being especially prominent in the vowel sounds of speech, as well as in reed instruments and bells. Formants are very useful in synthesis for giving a natural quality to the sound: the comparative difficulty of producing them in Subtractive Synthesis might help explain the oft-perceived "electronic" nature of this type of sound generation.

Forte

Italian for loud (usually abbreviated to f). The number of such marks indicate the degree of loudness. Indications in the range *fff* to *fffff* all mean about as loud as possible.

Fortissimo

Louder than Forte: usually abbreviated to *ff*.

Forzando

A strong accent: usually abbreviated to *fz*.

Fourier

Fourier analysis is the reduction of a periodic function (e.g. an audio waveform) into its sinusoidal or Partial components. In other words, the waveform of even a complex tone can be mathematically reduced to its simple sine wave components – a series of partials whose frequencies are multiples of the fundamental frequency. An application is found in a form of Additative Synthesis (called resynthesis) where a live sound might be sampled and subjected to Fourier analysis in order to program a series of oscillators to rebuild the timbre from its sine wave components. The Fourier Series takes the form:

$$\frac{1}{2}a_0 + \sum_{n=1}^{\infty}(a_n \cos nx + b_n \sin nx), \text{ where } a_n = \frac{1}{\pi}\int_{-\pi}^{+\pi} f(x) \cos nx \, dx \text{ and } b_n = \frac{1}{\pi}\int_{-\pi}^{+\pi} f(x) \sin nx \, dx.$$

Baron Jean Baptiste Joseph Fourier (1768-1830) is the man responsible for all this mathematical gobbledygook (he was also an Egyptologist). A further application is the Fast Fourier Transform (FFT), a method of displaying information about a sound event based on a Fourier Analysis of the spectrum of the sound. The FFT is often encountered in systems which process digital audio in some way or other, e.g. the "sound mountain" display on the Fairlight, where the display shows how the frequency spectrum changed with time. The illustration, right, is a simplified version of a Fourier Fast Transform diagram, showing how the component frequencies of a complex single sound can be represented.

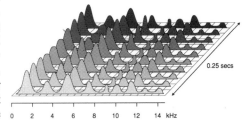

Fourth

The interval between a note and the one five semitones above or below it. *See also* Interval.

FPS

Abbreviation of Frames Per Second. *See* Frame Rate.

Fractal Music

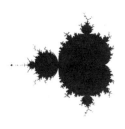

Any music which is generated according to the principles found in the discipline of fractal geometry, a branch of mathematics "invented" by Benoit Mandelbrot (he certainly invented the term "fractal"). This geometry concerns itself with objects generated by equations which describe non-linear dynamic systems (such as convection, turbulence or those little "crazy pendulums" with three or more magnets in the base) and particularly those involving complex numbers. Such systems are often called "chaotic" and the study of them, chaos science. There is currently a small number of computer programs available which iterate fractal equations and output MIDI messages and/or standard MIDI files. The diagram of the Mandelbrot set, left, shows an xy graph of values in the plane of "Real" and "Imaginary" numbers. By assigning musical parameters such as pitch and volume to the x and y axes it is possible to produce "music" as the set is calculated. Fractal images are frequently attractive, especially when seen in colour, even if the calculations needed to generate them seem obscure. Fractal music has not been so immediately successful. Whether this is because we are not used to it, or because of some inadequacy in the way the visual processes are implemented musically by the programmers, is hard to tell. However, it may be that this form of music will develop in useful ways in the future. Chris Samson, Robert Sherlaw Johnson and the author are among those producing fractal compositions. *See also* Chaos.

Fragmentation

A situation which may occur on computer disks containing files which have been repeatedly increased in length. The presence of other files will inevitably limit the amount of room for expansion. When this is exceeded, any extra data is automatically written to a new area of the disk, thus fragmenting what should be contiguous blocks of data. This causes data retrieval to take longer. In addition, some applications (such as Direct to Disk Recording) require files to be written contiguously, and thus fragmentation of the disk will limit the available space for data. Disk optimizing software will tidy up the disk and overcome this problem. *See also* Access Time.

Frame Rate

The number of video or film frames which appear in a unit of time. Normally given in Frames Per Second (FPS). 30 FPS is standard in America and 25 FPS is standard in Europe. *See also* Drop Frame, Timecode.

Frequency	In audio, the number of repeating cycles of change in air pressure, or oscillations in voltage, that occur in one unit of time, usually a second. Complex sounds are made up of many pure tones of different frequencies. Frequency is measured in units originally called cycles per second (CPS) and now called Hertz (Hz). For convenience, the human frequency range is divided into three bands: low frequencies (between about 20 Hz and 200 Hz), mid frequencies (between about 200 Hz and 5 kHz) and high frequencies (between about 5 kHz and 20 kHz).
Frequency Correction	*See* Equalisation.
Frequency Response	The response characteristics of a system or piece of equipment to different frequencies, often shown as a graph. Ideally, for audio work, such a graph should plot a flat line from below 20 Hz to above 20 kHz. In practice this is often not achieved, and the line will fluctuate up and down between these points, indicating that the equipment makes some frequencies louder or quieter than others. Humans have a well documented "non-flat" response – this is used to specify the dB(A) scale for determining loudness. The term should not be confused with Bandwidth, which concerns itself only with the attenuation above an upper limit frequency and below a lower limit frequency, and does not concern itself with the range between them. *See also* Flat Response.
FSK	Abbreviation of Frequency Shift Keying. A method of recording computer data (including MIDI information) onto audio tape, using two distinct frequencies to represent the binary states "on" and "off" of digital signals. It is most often found as a low-cost means of synchronizing MIDI devices such as sequencers to tape, and is sometimes implemented as a form of timecode.
Fugue	Strictly speaking, a formal musical structure which uses imitative counterpoint to develop or extend a musical idea or group of ideas. The terms "fugal" and "fugato" are sometimes loosely applied to any imitative music that starts like a fugue. A proper fugue has an "exposition", during which a musical idea (the "subject") appears in the tonic key, usually unaccompanied. This is repeated (the "answer") at a different pitch by a second part or "voice" while the first continues with the "countersubject". The answer is usually on or in the dominant, but sometimes the subdominant is preferred. Depending on the number of voices used, this pattern of entries is continued in different octaves until all voices have appeared, thus completing the exposition. While the exposition is fairly strictly formalized, and essential for a fugue to be worthy of its name, what happens thereafter is somewhat freer. Usually there will be further entries of the subject ("redundant entries") interspersed with "episodes"which may contain new material but are usually derived from the subject. These middle entries may be in keys other than the tonic or dominant and the episodes often effect the necessary modulation. The subject can appear in Augmentation, Inversion, Retrograde Motion, incomplete form ("false entry"), or with two or more entries occurring in close proximity ("stretto"), etc. The fugue will often conclude with a final entry of the subject in the tonic key.
Full Message	*See* MIDI Time Code Full Message.
Full Score	A notated form of a piece of music which contains the complete music for all instrumental or vocal parts, aligned vertically. It is generally the form in which the composer produces the original, and from which the conductor will direct. *See also* Band Parts.
Fundamental	The lowest frequency partial present in a (normally) musical sound. *See also* Harmonic, Sound.
Funk	This American slang word meant "a strong, unpleasant odour". It appears as early as the 17th century, describing the smell of tobacco smoke, and is probably derived from old French *funkier* (to smoke). In later usage it appears to have been applied specifically to sexual odours. It was then used to describe some forms of jazz which were considered degenerate by old hands, such as Rhythm and Blues. The word was taken up and used positively (i.e. in the titles of songs) by artists such as James Brown and became an important descriptive term for some types of disco music. In this sense it describes rhythmic attributes of the music, typically rapid and syncopated patterns usually in the guitar or bass.
Fuse	A safety feature on mains supply and other electrical systems. It comprises a metal wire mounted in an insulating carrier, connected at a point in the circuit close to the source of current. The strand of wire is a deliberately weak point in the circuit, and will rapidly destruct should the current exceed a predetermined value, thus isolating and protecting the rest of the circuit. It will not necessarily be fast or sensitive enough to protect a human from electrocution: *see* ELCB.
Fusion	A term to describe combinations of jazz with other musical forms, such as rock, and particularly the music of groups as diverse as Weather Report, Spiragyra and Loose Tubes. Sometimes applied to the combinations of ethnic music styles found in world music.
Fuzz	A term normally applied to the creative use of Distortion. The effect is often achieved by over- driving the input of an amplifier, or by using a specially designed Fuzz Pedal to simulate the same result. Mainly used by guitarists, but also found on electric organs and other keyboards.
FX	Specifically a script reference to pre-recorded sound effects for use in radio, TV or film production, but often used more generally as a short form of Effects.
fz	*See* Forzando.

Gain

The amount of amplification given to a signal by a piece of equipment, normally measured in decibels.

Gain Control

The process of altering the amplitude or gain of a signal. Amplifiers, Compressors and Noise Gates all implement gain control.

Gallows Arm

Type of microphone stand consisting of a vertical section, to the top of which is fitted a rod which carries the microphone. The angle this rod makes with the vertical section is adjustable.

Gamelan

A term describing both a type of music found throughout the Indonesian archipelago and the orchestra of instruments upon which it is played. The orchestra consists mostly of percussion instruments, both tuned (gongs, bells, xylophones etc.) and untuned (drums, wood blocks etc.). It often includes the *suling* (a type of bamboo flute), singers and occasionally bowed and plucked string instruments. The music is functional and is used to accompany religious ceremonies and rituals, dance and traditional puppet shows. Gamelans are tuned to one of two basic systems – "slendro" with five divisions of the octave, and "pelog" with seven – requiring a complete gamelan to have two sets of instruments. Pitch is not standardized and therefore the sound of each gamelan is unique. The main characteristic of the music is that no one performer predominates, ensured by the fact that each individual plays no more than a fragment of a melodic line. The music can only be perceived when all performers play their fragments in concert. While the traditional gamelan repertoire was complete before the 17th century, when European travellers first experienced it, there have been new compositions written both by Asian and western composers. It has also been a great influence on composers such as Debussy and, in particular, Minimalists such as Glass and Reich.

Gamut

An archaic musical term which, during the 11th century, was a name for the low G which is now notated on the bottom line of the bass clef. This was the lowest note described in the then current theoretical system of hexachords. This note was given the Greek letter gamma as its name and it was also known as "Ut", as it was the first note of the six-note group of the hexachord on G (the modern equivalent of "ut" is "doh"). Thus Gamut is a portmanteau of the words gamma and ut, in keeping with the practice of the time of describing note names in their most elaborate form. In later usage it came to mean a scale in the sense described in this glossary, and subsequently the entire range of possible musical notes or sounds. The word gamut is now more commonly used to refer to a complete range of anything, and is encountered with particular reference to colour imaging.

Ganged

A method of joining two controls so that a single action will adjust both by an equal amount. The stereo master gain control on a mixing desk is sometimes ganged, making it possible to fade left and right channels simultaneously in one movement.

Gate

1. *See* Noise Gate.

2. Gate signal. A pulsed voltage of variable duration which is used to instigate an event or process in an electronic device – the duration of the event is related to the duration of the pulse. It might be produced by a keyboard during the time that any key is pressed, or by a noise gate during the time determined by a signal which exceeds the threshold and the setting of the release time control. *See also* CV and Gate, Trigger.

Gated Reverb

The use of a Noise Gate to cause a sudden termination of a reverberation effect without allowing the normal decay phase to occur. This gives the sound a very unnatural "industrial" timbre and was much favoured for drums during the '80s. Its invention is frequently attributed to Phil Collins and his engineers.

GEM

See Operating System.

General MIDI

An agreed MIDI implementation, developed for consumer use, which specifies a recommended common set-up for MIDI devices. GM defines such things as the Keymap for 47 drum sounds and a list of 128 program numbers with associated standard sounds. There is also a table of various parameters for each of these Patches, including velocity response, output levels, keyboard and pitch bend range, envelope times and functions for other controllers, etc. The intention is to allow pre-recorded MIDI files, when replayed on any GM-compatible equipment, to use similar sounds and other parameters to the original arrangement. This is also very useful for the CD+MIDI standard. GS is a proprietory variation of GM, developed by Roland.

Gig

A term used in popular music in preference to the word concert and, by musicians working in any style, to the job of playing in a concert. It may possibly derive from the same root as jig (*gigue* in French), once a slang term for many kinds of popular music and dance.

Giga	Prefix meaning 1,000 million. Multiple of SI Units.
Gigabyte	1024 MBytes or 1,073,741,824 bytes. Not 1,000 million as you might expect, but the nearest power of 2 which is close to a billion: this is a result of the influence of binary numbers on computing.
Giocoso	Italian for merrily or joyously.
GIPS	Acronym from Giga Instructions Per Second. *See* MIPS.
Glass Master	A glass disc with a light-sensitive coating, whose surface can be "etched" with pits, representing binary data, by a laser beam modulated by an audio signal. This surface is then sealed with a coating of silver. Used as a master for the dies from which CDs are eventually pressed.
Glide	*See* Portamento.
Glissando	A continuous, but stepped, movement in pitch from one note to another. Harps and pianos give perhaps the best examples, although the effect is possible on most instruments. On instruments without fixed pitches (such as the violin, trombone or the human voice) it is easier to slide continuously without steps: this entirely different effect is known as *Portamento*. Strictly speaking, the two terms should not be confused.
Glitch	A term for an unexpected event, often with some annoying consequence. Particularly, a transient in the mains supply to a device such as a computer that causes it to "crash", the presence of an audible click in a recording, or a noticeable step effect on pitch shifters, harmonizers and looped samples.
GM	*See* General MIDI
GND	Abbreviation of Ground: *see* Earth.
Gospel	A form of popular music which originated in rural areas of America during the 19th century to accompany Protestant worship, often outdoors. The music was commercialized by Thomas A. Dorsey who first used the phrase "gospel songs" to refer to the single sheet publications of songs he had written or collected. The music, which was widely associated with Afro-American Christians from the southern states, was noted for its joyous, uninhibited (not to say egregious) celebration of religion. In the late '50s and early '60s artists in the fledgling rock and roll genre, such as Elvis Presley, Jerry Lee Lewis and Little Richard, brought this enthusiasm and passion into their own music and in so doing provided a vehicle for commercial exploitation of gospel music. While gospel has continued to develop in its own right through the next decades, it has also exerted a profound influence on mainstream popular music and, in particular, Soul.
Graphic Equalizer	A type of equalization device, where the user has control over the gain (cut or boost) of a number of narrow frequency bands (usually one half or one third of an octave). The controls are usually sliders mounted vertically in order of ascending frequency band from left to right. The relative positions of the faders give a graphic representation of the approximate frequency response of the equalizer The device may have two separate channels for stereo operation.
Graphics	The use of pictures (as opposed to text), particularly in computing, very often giving the advantage of making the computer more understandable or intuitive to use. Also, the manipulation of digitally stored pictures or video images by a computer. *See also* Bitmap Graphics, Vector Graphics.
Graphic User Interface	A means of representing objects or concepts in graphics, as opposed to text, on a computer screen. These icons can be manipulated using a Keyboard [2], Mouse [1] or other pointing device. A GUI is considered more intuitive and easier to use (especially by computer novices) than the text-based interfaces of older systems such as MS-DOS, used on IBM-compatible PCs. "Windows" and GEM are two popular implementations of a GUI.
Grave	Italian for very slowly. Pronounced "graah-vay".
Grazioso	Italian for gracefully.
Groove	**1.** The jagged track in the surface of a record within which the audio signals are encoded. **2.** An emotional feeling, generally pleasant, generated by a number of musicians interacting. A description of such a feeling. **3.** In popular music, the distinctive rhythmic "feel" of the music.
Group	**1.** On a mixing desk, a destination for one or more inputs which can be routed at will. In recording, the group is then sent to a track on the multi-track recorder. So the function of the group is to sum several inputs on the desk for sending to tape. The number of groups on a desk generally equals the number of tracks on the multi-track. **2.** A band of musicians.
Group Fader	A control which sums and adjusts the output of several other faders which have been routed to that group.
GS	*See* General MIDI.

Guard Band

A thin strip of metal, placed between the individual recording and replay transducers in a tape head, which has the effect of isolating the magnetic patterns of adjacent transducers. It results in a narrow unrecorded band between each of the tracks on the tape, helping to avoid Crosstalk.

GUI

See Graphic User Interface.

Guide Vocal

In multi-track recording, a preparatory vocal track to serve as a template for the later recording of instrumental tracks. It will eventually be replaced by a more polished final version.

Guitar Amp

Generally an amplifier and loudspeaker combo, optimized for use with electric guitars and other high impedance instruments. It is used primarily for live performance and also for recording when Direct Injection is not preferred.

Gun Microphone

A highly directional type of microphone used for long distance recording, e.g. for wildlife or surveillance. Also called "rifle" microphone.

Haas Effect

A psychoacoustic effect which allows humans to deduce the apparent location of sounds in an audio field, due to the relative delay between the arrival times at each ear. In the diagram, the sound of the bell arrives at the right ear shortly before it arrives at the left ear. This delay varies with the angle between the source of the sound and the head, allowing the person to locate the bell.

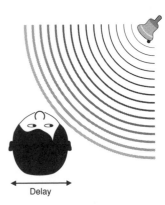

Delay

Most systems that implement Panning do so by controlling relative amplitude only, ignoring the Haas Effect. This reduces the effectiveness of stereo positioning on such devices. In principle, it would be possible to implement "pan-by-delay" on, say, a mixing desk (especially in the digital domain), but this approach has not generally been exploited by manufacturers despite the potential increase in realism – an exception being the Roland RSS.

Hacking

Originally a term to describe the emergency or temporary modifying of a computer system to fix a Bug. More recently used in the specific context of modifying a computer system without permission and, by extension, any unauthorized access to such a system. Hacking became a cult underground activity in the late '70s and early '80s when determined computer users found they could hack into systems which controlled billing of telephone and other utility services to their own financial advantage, as well as cause general mayhem. A war of attrition has developed between hackers and those that control the security of information on data networks. Hacking is also used to describe the practice of removing or bypassing Copy Protection systems, such as Dongles, to facilitate piracy of computer software. *See also* Virus.

Half Track

A tape machine which records on half of the tape width only. This allows the tape to be inverted at the end of its play time. The other half of the tape is now available for recording, thus doubling the recording time for a given length of tape.

Hammond

A type of electric organ and the name of the company (formerly the Hammond Clock Co.) that made it. It was first developed in 1933 by Laurens Hammond and was based on the tone wheel principle invented some forty years earlier by Dr. T. Cahill for his Telharmonium. In the Hammond organ, some 95 ridged metal wheels revolved past electro-magnets to generate an oscillating current which was then amplified to produce the sound. These wheels were contoured to offer a range of harmonics from which different tone colours could be produced. Integrated Circuits eventually replaced this mechanical system in the mid '60s. Probably the most popular electric organ ever, with over 2,000,000 built. *See also* Drawbar, Leslie Cabinet.

Handshaking

In data transmission, the process of checking that a receiving device is ready to receive, or that a transmitting device is ready to transmit. Also, the method whereby such checking takes place. In MIDI it occurs in System Exclusive, where messages are sent between two devices to ensure that both are present and that both have received or transmitted blocks of data. For this to happen there must be a direct unfiltered connection between the MIDI In and MIDI Out on both machines. If your System Exclusive transmission won't work, check that there is a two-way connection between the devices involved. *See also* Ack, Cancel, Nak, Wait.

Hard Copy

A copy of data (words or images) printed on paper, as opposed to appearing only on screen, or existing only in computer memory or on computer disk.

Hard Disk

A device for long term storage of computer data. The term refers to the stack of metal platters it contains, as opposed to the single flexible plastic disk used in "floppies". Metal surfaces allow much greater density of storage and much higher speed of operation. Hard disks start at about 10 Megabytes and currently go up to about 1.2 Gigabytes (equivalent to more than 1000 floppies). Very large hard disks (above, say, 150 Megabytes) are usually encountered in specific applications where large amounts of data need to be stored, such as digital audio in "direct-to-disk" recording.

Hardware

The electro-mechanical parts of a system, especially a computer system where the term is used to draw a distinction between the physical machine, the Firmware and the abstract Software that instructs it. As an analogy, a human is a system of hardware, firmware and software. The hardware is the biomechanical aspect of the body (skeleton, skin, heart and other organs), the firmware is the spongy tissue of the brain, and this, it is believed, contains the software or abstract thinking processes which, ultimately, control the hardware.

Harmonic

1. A special case of a Partial, normally occurring in "musical" sounds, whose frequency has a simple mathematical relationship to other partials. Generally they are all integer multiples of a particular fundamental frequency. *See also* Enharmonic, Sound.

2. A special effect used by musicians, particularly string players, of isolating a Harmonic [1] in order to produce a pure, often silvery tone.

Harmonic Distortion

See Distortion.

Harmonizer

See Pitch Shifter.

Harmony

In music, the perceived effect of the combination of notes of different pitch to form or imply a pattern of chords. Also, the analysis and theory of hierarchical relationships between chords, which can result in statements such as "this chord is the dominant of that chord".

Head

1. *See* Tape Head.

2. In jazz, the opening tune, often played by all the musicians in unison. If the whole piece is closely based on this melody and its associated chords, it is termed a "head arrangement".

Header

Additional information which prefixes a block of data, either on disk or for the purposes of data transfer between devices. Headers usually represent a description of the block of data which follows. Commonly encountered in MIDI System Exclusive transfers. For example, in Yamaha System Exclusive transfers, the first six bytes are header information: SOX, Yamaha's ID number (67), status and channel, format type, and two bytes whose combined value states how many bytes the following data block contains.

Headphones

Essentially a pair of loudspeakers small enough to fit over the ears.

Headroom

The capacity of a recording or broadcasting system to pass a signal above the normal working level (0 dB) before the onset of distortion. This is typically the area on a VU meter or PPM which is numbered positively and sometimes coloured red.

Heavy Metal

A term first used in the song "Born to be Wild" and taken from "Naked Lunch", a book by William Burroughs, then applied to a form of popular music which appeared during the late '60s on both sides of the Atlantic. Arguably descended from blues, via R & B, it is essentially a type of rock guitar music with excessive amplification. The Jimi Hendrix Experience were, perhaps, the prototype for Heavy Metal, which then reached peak development with bands like Black Sabbath (arguably the first HM band), Deep Purple and Led Zeppelin. Commercially the form presented a problem to record companies, being very much "album" music with long tracks not easily converted into singles. It tends to be a live phenomenon, as performance tours of prodigious length are required to market the more expensive record format. Aficionados of this type of music are likely to have long hair, enjoy the company of motorbikes and indulge in "headbanging" – a form of aerobic exercise involving rapid rotary motion of the head in time to the music. The playing of an imaginary or "Air Guitar" is also commonplace. Because of imagined and real interests in witchcraft and the occult on the part of some artists, heavy metal is experiencing a certain notoriety, and has become a target of fundamentalist Christian groups in the USA.

Hemidemisemiquaver

Note (♬) or rest (𝄿) whose duration is a sixty-fourth of a semibreve. Also known as sixty-fourth note.

Hertz

The SI Unit of frequency, in particular the number of times something occurs in one second, abbreviated Hz. Named after Heinrich Rudolph Hertz (1857-94). The unit is sometimes alternatively expressed as CPS (Cycles per Second).

Hexadecimal

A numbering system using base 16. It is often used as a compact way of representing binary values since one hexadecimal digit is equivalent to four binary digits. The system requires 16 different symbols: the normal 0-9, supplemented by the letters A-F. The binary number 0000 0101 0001 1110 (or 1310 in plain ol' decimal) is represented by 051E in hex. *See also* the conversion table on page 109.

HF Damping

The reduction of high frequency components in a signal due to propagation (movement through a material). This may be propagation through a wire or other electronic broadcast medium, in which case the effect is caused by line impedance or other electronic effect. Alternatively, it may be acoustic propagation through air (or, less likely, some other medium such as water) in which case damping is more noticeably caused by absorption of the high frequencies by materials other than the main propagation medium, such as curtains, furniture, etc. The high frequencies have shorter wavelengths: this makes it easier for materials to "trap" them (because the material thickness is considerable when compared to the wavelength) and convert some of their energy into heat.

Hi-Fi

Acronym from High Fidelity. A term used since the late '40s to describe domestic audio equipment. It originally implied a superlative standard of performance at a time when such a standard was difficult to achieve, thus the term was of some consequence. More recent advances have ensured that virtually every product on the market is able to perform to a High Fidelity standard, and the term now simply describes domestic, as opposed to professional, equipment.

High Level Language

A computer programming language that is reasonably close to ordinary human language. Its significance is best understood by comparing it to low level language. This is the language the CPU responds to, with each part of a program instruction being expressed as a numeric machine code which has to be executed in a single machine cycle. In a high level language, the command PRINT "so and so" would have to be compiled or interpreted by an interim process into a number (possibly hundreds) of machine code instructions, which are then executed. While it is possible, if laborious, to program in a low level language, most people prefer to work with a high level language as it more closely resembles the language used in everyday thinking. Basic, C, Forth, Pascal and PostScript are just a few of the many high level languages.

High Pass

See Filter.

Hip Hop

A strand in the development of Rap music. Essentially the New York form of Rap. Hip hop is not simply a musical phenomenon, and cannot be viewed apart from other aspects of Afro-American (and particularly New York) culture. Particular clothes, language and elaborate graffiti are attributes of Hip Hop as much as the music. Technology is a major aspect of the music, particularly the use of drum machines and samplers, and Scratching. Samplers are typically used as a sort of "intelligent" turntable, using looped sections of records to replace the tedious cueing of a disc. This has given the music a certain courtroom notoriety as the unauthorized use of sampled sections of copyright material has led to legal proceedings in many cases. The music is also eclectic in its borrowing from Hispanic and other musical forms. Typical artists include Interboro Rhythm Team (IRT), Whiz Kids, the B Boys, Derek B, double D and Steinski.

Hook

In popular music, a short melodic idea or "catch-phrase" designed to be instantly memorable. It is often used for the chorus of a song, as well as providing material for a Fade [2].

Horns

A term used in jazz and popular music to refer to the brass section in general which, in fact, seldom includes the horn in these types of music. *See also* Reeds, Rhythm Section.

Hot

In a Balanced Line transmission system, the conductor which carries the in-phase component of a signal. In the UK, this is pin 2 of an XLR (pin 3 is Cold and pin 1 is Earth).

House Music

A form of popular music used for dancing. As with much pop music, quadruple time with emphasized backbeats (second and fourth beats) is the order of the day, but in a very intensified manner. It could perhaps be thought of as heavy disco. In a very general sense, there is a tendency to align the pitch qualities of instruments with divisions of the bar, such that bass instruments tend to play two to four times a bar, while high pitched instruments tend to play eight to sixteen times a bar.

Howlround

Also known as Howlback. Oscillation which can occur in a device or system that has its output presented to its input, causing a vicious circle of over-amplification. Typically it occurs in PA systems if the microphone(s) are able to pick up the output of the loudspeakers, or in a tape machine if the output is fed into the input during recording. *See also* Feedback.

Hum

An undesirable, constant low-pitched sound which appears in some audio systems usually because of poor earth arrangements involving earth loops. It is derived from the AC mains frequency of (in the UK) 50 Hz. However, this frequency is rather low to be prominent and the hum that is usually heard most clearly is the second harmonic of this fundamental: 100 Hz. It is one of the types of Noise. *See also* EMI [2] and Earth Loop.

Hunting

A term used to describe the action of a tape transport or disk drive when some expected data is missing and the mechanism constantly searches backwards and forwards for it. Hunting can occur in synchronized tape recorder systems if timecode information, such as EBU, has been corrupted or erased, or if an incorrect Offset has been entered by the user.

Hypercardioid

A microphone which has a similar response to a figure of eight microphone, but is asymmetrical, in that it has greater sensitivity to sound arriving at the front of the capsule than to sound arriving at the rear. *See also* Cardioid, Omnidirectional.

Hypertext

A type of computer Database which has a user interface that allows so called "interactive" access to the data. In practice this might mean that the user does not have to approach the stored data in any sequential way, but can hop intuitively from one area to another. It might also mean that data is presented in a hierarchical manner, such that the most obvious bits are presented first and the user can then request that a particular section be expanded to provide more information about that specific area. The interface may present pictures as well as text. As an example, a user might access a database section called "Sports". Browsing through, he or she might find a page of information on fishing with a picture of a fishing rod. The user may go on to the next page, or might wonder what types of fish are caught in this way. By selecting the image of the fishing rod (perhaps with a mouse click), the current page will have a new page superimposed upon it which lists the various piscine species regularly slaughtered in the pursuit of human entertainment. The user may then click on a particular fish to view further details about it.

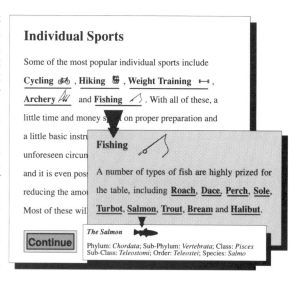

Individual Sports

Some of the most popular individual sports include

Cycling, **Hiking**, **Weight Training**,

Archery and **Fishing**. With all of these, a little time and money spent on proper preparation and a little basic instruction...

Fishing

A number of types of fish are highly prized for the table, including **Roach**, **Dace**, **Perch**, **Sole**, **Turbot**, **Salmon**, **Trout**, **Bream** and **Halibut**.

The Salmon

Phylum: *Chordata*; Sub-Phylum: *Vertebrata*; Class: *Pisces* Sub-Class: *Teleostomi*; Order: *Teleostei*; Species: *Salmo*

[Continue]

Hz
See Hertz.

IC
See Integrated Circuit.

Icon
A form of graphics where a picture is used by a computer to symbolize some job carried out by the program. For example, there may be a picture of a wastebasket on the Monitor[3]: objects placed over the wastebasket will be deleted. In general, any picture which can be manipulated as a unit is an icon.

ID Number
The data bytes (up to three) which follow a SOX (Start of Exclusive) status byte in a MIDI System Exclusive message. The number defines which manufacturer has originated this particular message and allows equipment from other manufacturers to ignore it. USA manufacturers have numbers in the range 1–31, European manufacturers have numbers in the range 32–63 and Japanese manufacturer's numbers start at 64. Because all the USA numbers have already been assigned, two additional bytes can be used to increase the range. A first data byte of value 0 indicates that the following two data bytes contain the manufacturer ID. Three ID numbers are set aside as the Universal System Exclusive codes. 125 is for non-commercial or academic use, 126 is for non-real time use and 127 is for real time use.

IEC
Abbreviation of International Electrotechnical Committee. An international body which agrees standards in the electronic field. CCIR and NAB are subcommittees of the IEC.

IEC Characteristic
The European pre-Emphasis and De-Emphasis equalisation standard for magnetic tape recording.

Imagesetter
See Printer.

IMD
See Intermodulation Distortion.

Impedance
The property of opposition to the flow of alternating current, measured in Ohms (Ω). Unlike resistance (which uses the same unit), there is no conversion of energy to heat: the opposition to current flow is the result of the Reactance of the component. Usually encountered in documents which describe the requirement of "impedance matching" of equipment, where low impedance outputs must be connected to low impedance inputs in order to avoid distortion or signal loss. Likewise, high impedance outputs should be connected to high impedance inputs. Line level inputs and outputs are usually high impedance. Low impedance is typically less than 1 kΩ while high impedance is typically greater than 20 kΩ.

Imperfect
See Cadence.

Import
In a computer, the act of placing data generated by another program into the current program. This will be possible only if the imported data is formatted in a way the current program can understand. This leads to a number of standardized file formats, such as ASCII (for text), the Sample Dump Standard and Standard MIDI File formats.

Improvisation
In music, a performance which is executed without the benefit of an explicit score or memory of one. Essentially music made up on the spot, although more often than not, done to some sort of given framework such as the 12-bar blues progression or the continuo part in baroque music. The realm of improvisation also includes the alteration or variation of an existing piece of music. The ability to

improvise has always been highly praised. For an engaging tale about improvisation (and the nature of patronage) readers are encouraged to find out the story behind J. S. Bach's "Musical Offering" (Musikalisches Opfer). Improvisation is less common in modern performances of art music. Even in concertos where an "improvised" cadenza appears it is usually worked out in advance by the soloist or may even be the work of another musician entirely. However, improvisation is a common feature of jazz and much rock music, where the term Jamming is often preferred. Mostly this is of the variation type, but there are musicians (Keith Jarrett is one) who will construct long solo pieces on the spot.

Increment

Terse word for increase by one, although sometimes used with larger values "increment by ten". *See also* Decrement.

Indie

Abbreviation of Independent, used with reference to record companies which are not part of large corporations. They often specialize in some minority musical interest and have a reputation for giving their artists more artistic freedom than the market-orientated multi-national companies. In practice, however, Indie labels are often bought out by a bigger company the moment they show any substantial profit. Thus, the latter gains a stake in new markets while maintaining a pretence of independence by allowing the newly acquired company to continue trading under its old name. The sight of the Indie company's former directors suddenly driving Porsches is usually a dead giveaway that independence has been compromised.

Indirect Sound

Sound which reaches a microphone after reflection from one or more surfaces. As the indirect path is invariably longer than the direct path, the indirect signal appears delayed in time. In some instances this can cause Cancellation of certain frequencies.

Inductor

An electronic device which presents a low impedance to DC (it allows it to pass) but an increasing impedance to AC as frequency rises. Inductance is measured in Henrys, although milliHenry is more common. It has the opposite characteristic to a capacitor. Physically a coil of wire, sometimes with a ferrite core. Often used in crossovers and filters generally. Any length of wire has some inductance.

Infrasonic

Pertaining to sounds whose frequencies are below normal human hearing: i.e. below about 20 Hz.

Inkjet

See Printer.

In Line

A configuration for input channels on a mixing desk, where the Tape Returns are connected via a parallel and additional line input to the channel. This obviates the need for a separate tape monitoring section on the desk, hence the tape returns are said to be "in line". The advantage is that during remix the input channels are all available as inputs allowing, say 24 tracks of tape to be mixed with 24 channels of audio from synthesizers etc. on a 24 input desk. Thus, in line operation effectively doubles the number of inputs on a mixing desk.

Input

The point of entry of a signal into a system. e.g. a section in a mixing desk where the signal is introduced. Used as a verb ("will you input that for me") and as a noun ("the change in input"). It stands to reason that an input on one device will be connected to an output of another. Also used with reference to computers to describe the point or means of entry of data into a system, for example "keyboard input".

Insert Point

On a mixing desk and some other equipment, a point where a signal may be diverted through a socket. If no plug is inserted, the signal bypasses the socket and is not diverted. Inserting a plug breaks the bypassing connection and makes a new connection through the plug to the outside world. There may be two sockets involved with a "Normalized" connection (one marked Send and the other Return) – or just one Breakjack in which one terminal is the Send and the other the Return. On a mixing desk, the input might be connected to the send terminal of an insert point for sending the signal to a device such as a compressor, which then returns the modified signal back into the channel. If no such unit is plugged in, the signal bypasses the Insert Point.

Insert Tape

A pre-recorded tape with a number of programme items on it, such as jingles and advertisements, assembled in order ready for playing at various points in an otherwise live radio production.

Instruction Set

A complete set of all possible instructions that a microprocessor can carry out. In the early years of microprocessor design the emphasis was on producing a wide variety of powerful and extended instructions, but it was found that programmers tended to use a small number of basic (forgive the pun) instructions to do almost every job. The recent fashion in certain applications has been to restrict the number of instructions to these basic functions, as the fewer instructions a microprocessor has, the faster it can execute any given instruction. This approach is particularly suited to microprocessors built into a product that has a specific purpose, such as a sampler. A microprocessor using this approach is described as a RISC (Reduced Instruction Set Computer). However, if the microprocessor is going to live in a general purpose machine like a personal computer, where versatility takes precedence over speed of execution, it is better to have a more complex instruction set: a microprocessor using this approach is described as a CISC.

Insulator

A material which has the property of inhibiting the flow of electricity: most plastics have this property. Insulators are used to separate conducting parts of an electronic circuit. A cable can be considered to be a conductor encased in an insulator.

Integrated Circuit	Essentially a complex electronic circuit compacted into an absurdly small space. This is achieved by etching large numbers of diodes, transistors and other components onto a Semiconductor substrate, usually silicon. Rough divisions of scale (i.e. how many devices are present) are indicated by the letters SSI, MSI, LSI, VLSI (Small, Medium, Large and Very Large Scale Integration). The components are joined by tiny tracks which are separated by distances comparable to wavelengths of light; this is the reason it is sometimes possible to see rainbow-like reflections off the surface of an IC. The complete assembly is typically only a millimetre or two square and is extremely fragile. In order to make the IC easy to handle and more robust it is generally encased in plastic resin, the complete package commonly being called a "chip". The circuitry is connected to the outside world by tiny single-strand wires, much thinner than a human hair, welded to flat pins arranged in rows on the sides of the package. All manner of useful circuits, from amplifiers to computers are available in this form.
Integrated Package	A suite of computer programs combining the most common types of business software (usually database, word processor and spreadsheet). The package should be designed so that data from one program can be easily transferred to another within the package. This allows, for example, a standard letter to be keyed into the word processor, leaving blanks for personal names and addresses which can be added automatically from the database during printing. Junk mail can thus be given a nausea-inducing, pseudo-personal touch.
Intellectual Property	*See* Copyright.
Intensity	Of sound (sound pressure level). *See* dB SPL.
Interactive	In computing and media-speak, a two-way communication process which has the features of interruptibility (one participant can interrupt the other without having to wait until the end of the current topic) and infinite destination – the direction of the interaction can lead anywhere, not just to pre-programmed destinations. A lecture is not usually interactive, a conversation with a friend often is. Humans are very good at interaction, computers currently are not. Although interactive is a vogue word at the moment, few computer systems are properly interactive in the above sense. Some CD-I systems feature city maps which at first glance are very impressive. The user can "navigate" up a street, turn left (or right) into another street at will and see the correct buildings going past. Entering buildings is not however possible as the CD does not contain information about them. Such a system is interruptible, but has finite destinations, so it is not truly interactive. But it is a start, I suppose. The projected big area for interactivity is computer-aided learning. *See also* Virtual.
Interface	That which joins, or the point of connection of two joined things. Usually used to refer to electrical connections and their associated data structures such as MIDI. More abstractly, in the sense of user interface, the environment in which a human communicates with a machine – graphic images on a computer monitor, front panel switches, a keyboard, etc.
Interference	*See* EMI [2].
Interlaced Scan	A method of generating the picture on a computer monitor. In the higher quality, non-interlaced system, the electron beam scans every line of Pixels on the screen to form the image for a single frame. Interlacing involves scanning only alternate lines on each pass of the beam– say, the odd-numbered lines on the first pass and the intervening lines on the second. As there is a persistence effect in both the human eye and the phosphor dots that make up the screen, the image appears intact, given a suitably fast Refresh Rate.
Interleaving	A method of arranging or rearranging data according to some systematic rule, to increase the efficiency of a data storage device, or so that the data may be protected during transmission. In digital stereo systems such as CD, the term is used specifically to describe the way in which audio data is arranged as alternate left and right samples. *See also* Error Correction.
Intermodulation Distortion	A form of Distortion in which Partials in an audio signal have the effect of modulating one another to produce unwanted audio components. This is most likely to occur in active devices, such as amplifiers, which process the signal in some way. A comparable effect can occur in a video signal, resulting in colour aberrations or worse.
Interpretation	The expression of personal insights and emotions in music by a performer, or group and (in the case of a large ensemble) its conductor. In the case of written music, interpretation fills the gap between notation and performance and partly explains why different musicians can produce very different results when playing from the same score. In cases where notation is sketchy or non-existent, such as folksong or improvised music like jazz, it is the larger gap between the bare structure of the music and its elaboration in performance. The interpretation may simply reflect the performer's experience and response to the music on that particular occasion; it may (especially in art music) involve study and communication of the composer's original intentions, the performance conventions in force at the time of its composition, and so forth; or it may be a deliberate attempt to re-interpret an earlier piece in terms of later styles, such as synthesized Bach, a Cover Version of an existing song, or an opera updated to modern times. *See also* Feel.
Interrupted	*See* Cadence.

Interval

The word is used in two senses: either the distance described by counting the number of scale divisions between two pitches, or the distance (however it is counted) between two pitches. Thus a fifth interval describes two notes five scale divisions apart, while an interval of three semitones is what it says. Scale intervals fall into the categories of Perfect (fourths and fifths) and Major or Minor (seconds, thirds, sixths or sevenths), and may be additionally augmented or diminished by a semitone.

Scale Intervals (based on the note Middle C):

| Major 2nd | Major 3rd | Perfect 4th | Perfect 5th | Major 6th | Major 7th | Octave |
| Minor 2nd | Minor 3rd | | | Minor 6th | Minor 7th | |

Making a Major or Perfect interval one semitone bigger produces an Augmented interval:

Making a Minor or Perfect interval one semitone smaller produces a Diminished interval:

| Augmented 2nd | Augmented 4th | Augmented 5th | Diminished 2nd | Diminished 3rd | Diminished 5th | Diminished 7th |

Semitone Intervals:

Whereas scale intervals count the lower note as "1", semitone intervals start from "0" and count-in all of the intervening semitones.

2 semitones (= a tone)   4 semitones

Intro

A section at the beginning of a piece of music (usually a song) which can serve to set the mood of the piece (both for singer and listener) by establishing the key and tempo – and possibly by giving a flavour of the main melody, which is often that of the chorus. *See also* Outro.

Inversion

1. A transformation of an interval which can occur in two ways. In "intervallic inversion", where two notes are played together, the lower note of the original interval is played an octave higher (or the upper note is played an octave lower). This causes an interval of a fifth to become a fourth and vice versa, an interval of a third to become a sixth and vice versa, and so on. It is an arithmetic phenomenon that the sum of the original interval and its inversion always comes to nine. In "melodic inversion", the interval between one note in a melody and the next note is inverted, so if the melody originally rises by a third, the inverted melody will fall by a third. Inversion is a possible form of transformation of a subject in a fugue.

Intervallic Inversion

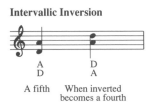

| A | D |
| D | A |

A fifth   When inverted
becomes a fourth

Melodic Inversion

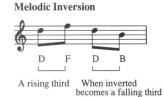

D F   D B

A rising third   When inverted
becomes a falling third

Inversion of Chords

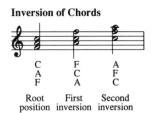

C	F	A
A	C	F
F	A	C

Root   First   Second
position   inversion   inversion

2. A transformation of a chord through intervallic inversion such that the original bass note no longer remains the lowest note of the chord. A major or minor triad (3-note chord) can appear in three positions: root position, where the chord consists of two intervals of a third on top of one another; first inversion, where the chord consists of a third with a fourth on top of it; and second inversion where the chord consists of a fourth with a third on top of it. *See also* Root, Triad.

IO Device

Input / Output device: *see* Peripheral.

Ionian

See Mode.

IPS

Abbreviation of Inches per second. *See* Tape Speeds.

IRCAM

Acronym from the French *Institute de Recherche et de Coordination Acoustique / Musique*. Founded in Paris, where it is housed at the Pompidou Centre, this body (as its name suggests) organizes and provides facilities for research into music and acoustics as well as composition and performance. It has several studios and performance spaces, equipped with state-of-the-art music production systems. The composer Pierre Boulez was appointed director in 1977.

Isolating Transformer

A transformer with (usually) equal primary and secondary coils used to provide power to a piece of electrical or electronic equipment. The lack of a direct connection between the primary power source and the secondary load improves the safety factor for the user of the equipment. *See also* Transformer.

IT

Abbreviation of Information Technology. A generic term for devices and software used in data processing and storage, and (particularly in education) the study of their operation and application.

Jack

A connector in the form of a socket into which jack plugs may be inserted.

Jack Field

See Patchbay.

Jack Plug

A cable-mounted connector, consisting of a screening ring with one or more consecutive concentric rings mounted around a central pole. The standard forms are mono, having one pole and one ring, and stereo, with one pole and two rings. The mono form is used for line level (either –10 dB(v) or +4 dB(v)) unbalanced line connections, while the stereo form is either used for mono balanced line connections or stereo unbalanced connections.

Jack Strip

A panel bearing a line of jacks. Several of these may be used to form a patchbay.

Jamming

Collective improvisation carried out by a group of pop or jazz musicians.

Jazz

A family of popular music forms which originated in the southern states of USA (often specifically attributed to New Orleans, Louisiana) at the end of the 19th Century. The word is thought to have been derived from the French creole word *jaser* meaning to gossip. It was (and is) largely improvisational and expressive in form. Originally it was popular among the Afro-American population, and the earliest practitioners were all Afro-Americans. Gradually its popularity increased with the white (wealthier and media-controlling) population which ensured a wider audience. Jazz shares with existing forms of African music elements of improvisation, polyphony, antiphony (in the form of call and answer songs) and social music making, the use of "blue notes" indicating a common ancestry with the Blues. Like any evolving artform there are many subspecies including Ragtime, Bebop, Swing, Dixieland and Boogie Woogie. Many art music composers including Stravinsky, Satie and, more famously, Gershwin, have composed in jazz-like styles or have included jazz idioms in their work, and some jazz fan(atic)s assert that it is the father of all popular music forms. *See also* Standards.

Jitter

In a synchronous system, a form of instability in the Clock signal which results in early, late, absent or multiple clock pulses. If a digital audio device is slaved to such a clock, this may cause audio signal degradations such as Wow and Flutter.

JMSC

Abbreviation of Japanese MIDI Standards Committee. A body which represents the interests of Japanese equipment manufacturers with regard to the development and implementation of the MIDI standard. *See also* MMA, UKMA.

Joystick

A hand operated stick-like control which has simultaneous movement in two axes (X and Y) and which allows the user (by waggling the stick) to define a unique position within the limits of movement of the control. Most commonly encountered on games computers, but sometimes used instead of a mouse or tracker ball to position a cursor on the screen. Also used on some synthesizers where it allows simultaneous control of two parameters, such as pitch bend and modulation. On some quadraphonic equipment, a joystick is used as a two-dimensional pan pot.

kb/s

Abbreviation of kilobits per second. *See* Data Rate.

KBD

See Keyboard.

kc/s

Abbreviation of kilocycles per second. However, the SI Unit, kiloHertz (kHz) is to be preferred.

Key

The tendency of tonal music to gravitate towards a "home" or key note, called the tonic. Key is established by the use of a fixed scale of notes based on this tonic note and can be emphasized by other, related notes and by Cadences. The tonic note or chord assumes greater importance than the others and leads, by extension, to a hierarchy of chords with the dominant (based on the fifth note of the scale) of particular significance. *See also* Key Signature.

Keyboard

1. The collection of keys, arranged in groups of twelve (usually seven white and five black) that are individually assigned to the semitones in each octave and form the main means of controlling a range of musical instruments from organs, harpsichords and pianos to synthesizers.

2. A collection of keys in a staggered but broadly rectangular pattern, which are differentiated by symbols, and which forms a means of input of data into a computer. *See also* QWERTY.

Keyboard Amp

An amplifier and loudspeaker combo optimized for use with keyboard and other Line Level instruments. Used for live performance, and for recording when Direct Injection is not preferred.

Keyboard Lab

A facility found in educational establishments which is designed to allow a group of students simultaneously to acquire keyboard instrument skills under the supervision of a single tutor. It normally consists of a number of Electric Keyboards, equipped with headphones, which are connected to a central point from where the instructor can monitor each player's progress and offer suggestions. More sophisticated versions use MIDI to record students' performances for subsequent analysis. Thought by some to be piano lessons on the cheap, such a system offers potential for "distance learning", in which the tutor can be aided (or even replaced) by computer software to undertake the more tedious aspects of repetitive instruction and assessment.

Keyboard Shortcuts

Keys, or particular combinations of keys, on a computer keyboard which have the same effect as using a mouse to select a function from a menu in a WIMP environment. Usually they will be mnemonic. For example, pressing the Control and "S" keys simultaneously may have the same effect as selecting "Save" from the File menu.

Keyboard Tracking

In a synthesizer or sampler, a facility for adjusting the degree to which a parameter, such as the filter cut-off frequency, can be controlled by the keyboard. *See also* Breakpoint, Scaling.

Keymap

The assignment of different sounds to a synthesizer or sampler keyboard, i.e. which key or range of keys will trigger particular sounds. This is useful for Drum Kit voices, where each note on the keyboard can control a totally different percussion sound. There is a more or less widely adopted keymap of drum sounds which was instigated by Roland.

Key Signature

The group of sharp or flat symbols placed on the stave at the beginning of a piece of music, and on every subsequent stave, to indicate the Key. These sharps or flats are presumed to be active for the duration of the piece or section, unless cancelled either temporarily (for one bar or part bar) by an accidental, or more permanently, by the placing of a new key signature.

Kilo

Prefix meaning thousand. Multiple of SI Units. Its symbol is a lower case "k".

Kilobyte

1,024 bytes. Not 1,000 as you might expect, but the nearest power of 2 which is close to a thousand. This is a result of the influence of binary numbers in computing.

Kunstkopf

See Dummy Head.

Label

Short for record label. A way of referring to recordings produced by a particular company: e.g. "you can find Bridge Over Troubled Water arranged for bagpipes on the Nurdy label". *See also* White Label.

Laptop

A generic term for a type of computer system claimed to be easily portable. All of its components (screen, computer, disk drive, keyboard and batteries) are packaged in a box small enough to fit on the lap. The box opens up, like a book held sideways, to reveal the screen and keyboard. The portability of laptops is somewhat compromised by the heavy weight and short life of their batteries, although new battery technology will hopefully ameliorate these problems. Even smaller versions, called Notebook computers, are lighter, but their size necessitates the use of tiny screens and often non-standard keyboards. *See also* LCD.

Larghetto

A slightly faster tempo than Largo.

Largo

From the Italian for broad. A slow or stately tempo. 48–60 MM.

Laser Printer

See Printer.

Latin American

A term used to refer to the music of Central and South America and, on occasion, to the Carribean. It covers a very broad range of musics including elements of African, native South American, Portuguese, Spanish and other European traditions. In a more narrow sense, it refers to the rhythmically vital dance forms of Samba, Rumba, Bossa Nova, etc. (see overleaf), and to the variety of percussion instruments (Congas, Cuica, Cabasa, Guiro, etc.) used in this music.

Some characteristic Latin American rhythms

Lavalier   A method of suspending a microphone around the neck of a person.

Layering   The simultaneous use of more than one distinct sound to make a composite timbre on a synthesizer.

LC Concept   The name of a French company and the system they have developed for implementing digital audio for cinemas. The system relies on the presence of an optical timecode on the film which is used to synchronize the digital audio soundtrack stored on a separate magneto-optical disc reader. In other words, the film carries no sound data at all. This is an elegant (and lateral) solution to the age old problem of fitting high quality audio onto cine film. It has the additional advantage of allowing multilingual presentation from the same film print – one can imagine a Eurocinema with headphone-equipped seats, allowing the audience to select from a variety of different languages while watching the film. However, it poses equipping problems for many cinemas, so there has been some resistance to the system. This resistance is being reduced by grants from the French government.

LCD   Abbreviation of Liquid Crystal Display. A type of display screen used on some computers (particularly portables) and very many items of music technology, as well as on digital watches, calculators, etc. Generally monochrome, but there have been advances in technology which allow colour display.

Leader   Plastic tape in different colours, fixed to the beginning or end of a film or magnetic tape, for the purposes of identification or protection. *See also* Spacer.

Leading Note   *See* Scale.

Lead Sheet   An abbreviated musical score, consisting of a melody line with chord names or symbols, and sometimes including lyrics. Used by buskers and improvising musicians (particularly in jazz).

Least Significant The rightmost value in any numbering system. In the decimal number 5463, three is the least significant number as it contributes least to the total value. *See also* LSB.

LED   Acronym from Light Emitting Diode. A diode which emits light when conducting current. Widely used for indication purposes on control panels and metering devices.

Legato   Smoothly, without obvious gaps between notes. Often shown by curved lines over the notes concerned.

Legato Footswitch One of the defined MIDI Controller messages with a status byte in the range 176–191 and a first data byte of 68. It has the effect, when on, of forcing a MIDI device into monophonic mode. Any Note On message subsequently received will be voiced without re-triggering the Envelope Generator through its attack phase, causing this note to join smoothly to the one before. When off, the device will return to its former Reception Mode.

Leger Line   Also spelt ledger line: *see* Stave.

Leggiero   Italian for lightly.

Lento   Italian for slowly.

Leslie Cabinet   A type of loudspeaker cabinet, developed by Don Leslie in the late '30s and used in electronic (especially Hammond) organs. The sound from fixed transducers is dispersed via a rotating horn or (for bass speakers) an aperture in a rotating chute. This causes a continuously varying Doppler shift of the pitches in the audio signal, which mixes (with some Cancellation) to give a swirling, chorus-like effect.

Leslie Simulator An effects unit which is intended to create the effect produced by a Leslie Cabinet. It is similar to a Chorus unit, but produces a richer effect.

Level   *See* Amplitude.

LFO   Abbreviation of Low Frequency Oscillator. An oscillator which functions at frequencies below, or at the lower end of, the audio range, e.g. in the range from 0.01 Hz to, say, 30 Hz. It is generally used as a Modulation[2] source on synthesizers and other equipments.

Librarian   1. A computer program which is able to store and organize all the Patch parameters needed for a particular synthesizer. Particularly useful if you have more patches than can fit in the synthesizer at any one time. Some sequencer packages include a librarian as an additional feature.

2. A mild-mannered local authority employee whose function is to tell people to be quiet and to explain in minute detail the limitations of the computer system and therefore why you are now being fined 43 times the original cost of a paperback book which you returned to the library five years ago.

Lick　A short (and sometimes difficult) musical phrase played on an instrument in a soloistic manner. Typically used with reference to guitar playing.

Limiter　A Compressor with a high compression ratio, typically more than 20:1. Used to ensure that the output of a system cannot over-modulate the recording or broadcast medium.

Line　In audio, a route in the programme chain.

Linear Potentiometer　*See* Potentiometer.

Line Input　An input for Line Level signals. Normally high impedance and thus not suitable for most microphones.

Line Level　A nominal signal level which is set at −10 dB(v) for domestic, and +4 dB(v) for professional equipment.

Line Printer　*See* Printer.

Line-Up　The procedure carried out to ensure that equipment works in the best possible manner. It consists of systematic adjustment of the equipment according to a schedule and may involve specialized test apparatus such as a multimeter, tone generator or oscilloscope.

Line-Up Tone　A sinewave tone at one of a range of standard frequencies (usually 100, 1000 and 10,000 Hz). It is set to zero level and is intended to be used during a line-up procedure.

Lip Ribbon　A ribbon microphone with a guard which is placed on the upper lip. The proximity of mouth and microphone makes it useful in situations with high background noise: e.g. battlefields or boxing matches.

Lip Sync　In TV and film, the precise correlation of the physical movements of speech or song with the recorded sound generated by those movements. The term was once used to describe the common practice of pop singers miming on camera to their own recordings. Nowadays it more usually refers to the over-dubbing of a foreign-language recording in which the translator and actors attempt to produce the effect of the original characters speaking the translated script: it is in the nature of language that even the skilled use of the technique is seldom convincing for long.

Live　**1.** In electrical systems, a conductor carrying current. Paradoxically it is used to describe the terminal in a mains supply that is likely to make you dead if you touch it.

2. Said of a broadcast which is transmitted as it actually happens.

3. Cynically said of a pre-recorded broadcast performance to which the performers actually mime.

4. Said of the acoustic in a building with many reflective surfaces.

Live Side　The side of a microphone which is most sensitive to sound.

Load　An impedance offered by a device (e.g. a loudspeaker) to a source of electrical energy (e.g. an amplifier).

Local Control　A Channel Voice message, specifically a Controller Change message, with a status byte value in the range 176–191 and a data byte value of 122, which effectively breaks the connection between a synth's keyboard and its voicing circuitry. The keyboard will still transmit data from the MIDI Out socket, and the voicing circuitry will still respond to Channel Voice messages received at the MIDI In socket. The message requires an additional data byte set to 0 for off and 127 for on. Sometimes called Local Off, it is used to break the Loop[4] that can cause notes to be sounded twice when recording with a sequencer that outputs all incoming data as you play.

Locrian　*See* Mode.

Long Word　*See* Word.

Loop　**1.** A section of tape with the two free ends joined, used for creating repeated sounds. A feature of early Electro-Acoustic music, tape loops were also used in the first Delay units, where a short tape circulated around a system consisting of a record head followed by a series of replay heads to pick up the increasingly delayed signal. The substantial build-up of noise, caused by continually re-recording the tape, ensured that such units quickly disappeared after the arrival of their electronic equivalent.

2. An analogous process to Loop[1] but referring to a digital sampler, where a section of memory containing sound data is continuously read between two points known as loop points. In a digital system a loop may be as short as a single cycle of the waveform (fractions of a millisecond), and may be read forwards or backwards or both.

3. A wire or cable system which has at least two ends joined together. With the exception of mains supplies, this is generally an undesirable situation, particularly so in audio where earth loops can result in problematic EMI[2]. *See also* Earth Loop.

4. The situation where a device has a connection from its output back to its input.

Loop Points Request

A Universal System Exclusive message of the Non-Real Time type, within the Sample Dump Standard, which allows a receiving device (e.g. a sampler) to request that a transmitter (e.g. a computer) should send information about the two sample numbers between which a loop will occur. It is a 10-byte message comprising the SOX status byte; an ID number data byte of 126 indicating this is a Non-Real Time System Exclusive message for the whole system; a sub-ID#1 with a value of 5 indicating a Sample Dump message; a sub-ID#2 with a value of 2 indicating a Loop Point Request message; two bytes for each of the two loop points; a byte for the Loop Type and finally the EOX status byte.

Loop Points Transmit

A Universal System Exclusive Message of the Non-Real Time type, within the Sample Dump Standard, which allows a transmitting device (e.g. a computer) to send to a receiver (e.g. a sampler) information about the two sample numbers between which a loop will occur.

Loop Type

1. In a sampler which allows a section of a sound to be repeated or looped, two types of looping are common: forwards only, and forwards and backwards.

2. A data byte in a Sample Dump Standard message which defines Loop Type [1]. A value of 0 is forwards only, 1 is forwards and backwards, and 127 indicates that no loop is used in this sample.

Loudness

The human perception of the intensity of a sound. It should be remembered that humans have an unequal frequency response, which favours certain frequencies over others, so the "loudness" of a sound is a quality distinct from its Amplitude. Loudness is measured in dB(A).

Loudspeaker

A device usually consisting of a box fitted with one or more Transducers, used to convert electrical audio signals into changes in air pressure, by which we can hear the audio information the signal represents. The transducer normally takes the form of a coil suspended in a magnetic Field[3] and connected to a cone shaped piston. The audio signal is fed into the coil which then moves relative to the magnetic field, thus moving the piston which compresses or rarefies the air in front of it. The various transducers are optimized for reproducing different parts of the audio spectrum – "tweeters" for frequencies above about 5–6 kHz, "mid-range" for frequencies between about 200 Hz and 3–5 kHz, and "woofers" for frequencies of below about 200 Hz. The principal difference between transducers is one of size. Lower frequencies require larger transducers and may even be housed in separate boxes ("sub-woofers"). It is sometimes necessary to distribute the signal to the transducers via a Crossover[1]. The word speaker is sometimes used to refer to the individual transducers. Other types of loudspeaker, not using moving coils, have been developed, of which the most popular has been the Electrostatic.

Low Pass

See Filter.

LP

1. Abbreviation of Long Playing. Records which play at 33⅓ revolutions per minute.

2. Abbreviation of Low Pass: *see* Filter.

LSB

Abbreviation of Least Significant Bit. The rightmost bit or column of a binary number. So called because it has the least effect on the result of any sum involving the number. Occasionally, in 16 bit or more (i.e. multi-byte) systems, it may be taken to stand for Least Significant Byte when referring to the rightmost byte for similar reasons. LSN is Least Significant Nibble.

LSI

Abbreviation of Large Scale Integration. An Integrated Circuit which contains about 1000 – 90,000 active elements. *See also* MSI, SSI, VLSI.

LTC

Abbreviation of Longitudinal Time Code. A method for recording Timecode onto tape. *See also* VITC.

Lydian

See Mode.

M

Abbreviation of Middle. The components that come from the middle of a stereo field. *See also* S.

M & S

Abbreviation of Middle and Side. A microphone technique which normally utilizes two microphones of different response pattern (Cardioid and Figure of Eight) placed at right angles to one another, with the cardioid facing the soundfield. The figure of eight output is split to two channels, one of which has reversed phase. These two channels are panned left and right and the cardioid to centre. The nett effect is to enhance, by exaggeration, the stereo image. The relative levels of the middle and side channels determine the extent of the effect. It gives good mono compatibility as the figure of eight microphone cancels completely when summed, leaving only the cardioid. Some consider it a special effect not for serious recording, while others acclaim it as the only true stereo recording method.

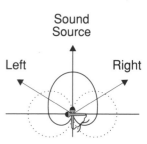

Machine Code
In a computer, the numbers which represent individual instructions which can be executed by the CPU in a small number (1–4) of clock cycles. It is the lowest level at which a human programmer can work (inside a microprocessor there is a lower level, called microcode, which the chip uses to perform the specific function – this is built into the chip during manufacture and is transparent to the programmer).

Machine Room
In audio, the soundproofed room which houses the more noisy electromechanical equipment, such as tape recorders, hard disks or devices fitted with fans like computers and power amplifiers. It is usually adjacent to the control room, this arrangement being an attempt to ensure that the background sound level in the control room is kept to a minimum. Sometimes incorrectly called Plant Room.

MADI
Acronym from Multi-channel Audio Digital Interface. In digital audio, a serial data interface proposed by AES / EBU, which can carry up to 56 channels of audio information through a single coaxial cable.

Maestoso
Italian for majestically.

Magnetic Field
See Field [3.]

Mainframe
A type of computer (strictly speaking of the third generation) which was first introduced in the mid 1960s and which took advantage of the then new SSI and MSI technologies. Machines of this type include the ICL 1900 series and IBM 300 series. More generally the term is used for a physically large computer which is located centrally to a network of users, each with their own Terminal [2]. These tend to be used in large business corporations, universities and specialist facilities such as IRCAM. It is a mistake to assume that physical size is necessarily correlated to performance. In fact many current microcomputers perform as well as, or better than, some mainframes. This is simply a manifestation of the increasing miniaturization of the ICs which do the work.

Mains
Commercially supplied AC electricity. In most domestic situations in the UK this supply is at a potential of 240V and is single-phase. In industrial situations there may additionally be a 415V, three-phase mains supply. On building sites which use electrical equipment out of doors, the supply may be converted to 110V by an isolating transformer.

Mains Adaptor
See PSU.

Major
See Scale, Diatonic.

Manual
1. The book which accompanies a piece of hardware or software, and which purports to explain its operation. The combination of technical obscurity, jargonese and ruthlessly literal translation from the Japanese has been so successful that an entire industry producing alternative guides, handbooks and magazines has been spawned off the back of these generally woeful publications.

2. The keyboard(s) on an organ or harpsichord played by the hands, as opposed to the Pedalboard, which is a keyboard played with the feet.

Marcato
Italian for "marked" – played with accents.

Mark/Space Ratio
In a pulse wave, where immediate transitions occur between "high" and "low" levels, mark is the time in one cycle occupied by the high level while space is the time in the same cycle occupied by the low level. The ratio of mark to the whole determines the timbre of the sound represented by the waveform. When the ratio is 1:2 this means that half of the cycle is mark and half is space. If the ratio is 1:3, $\frac{1}{3}$ of the cycle is mark and $\frac{2}{3}$ of the cycle is space. Also known as duty cycle, in which the mark is expressed as a percentage of the whole.

Masking
See Auditory Masking.

Mass Storage
A device or system for storing large amounts of data, although the meaning of mass in this context has changed. Ten years ago a computer might have had mass storage of only 100 Kilobytes. Now, mass probably means at least 10 Megabytes, as even the smallest hard disk has at least this capacity.

Master
In a system of devices it is sometimes useful to have one which governs the operation of the others (particularly for generating a timing reference, for example). This device is nominated the "master" while the others become "slaves". *See also* Master Clock.

Master Balance
A means of controlling the balance between the left and right outputs of a multi-timbral synthesizer (particularly one of the General MIDI type) in preference to adjusting individual channel balance (Controller 8). It is a Universal System Exclusive message of the Real Time type, with a Sub ID#1 value of 4, indicating a Device Control message, and a Sub ID#2 value of 2, followed by the LSB and then the MSB: 0,0 is full left and 127,127 is full right.

Master Clock
Some MIDI devices, such as sequencers and drum machines, require timing information which they normally generate for themselves. When such devices are combined in a MIDI network it is necessary for them to operate on common timing information if they are all to stay in synchronization. For this to happen, one device is nominated as a "master" and its internal clock is transmitted to the rest of the network. All other devices are told to look for an external clock, and thus become "slaves".

Master Controller
In a MIDI network, the device which a musician plays in order to control other devices in the network. Frequently this is a keyboard, but could just as well be drum pads, guitar or wind-type MIDI generators.

Master Fader
A fader to which the Groups [1] or Channels [1] in a mixing desk are connected. It normally controls the level of the stereo output from the desk.

Master Keyboard
In a MIDI network, a keyboard which a musician plays in order to control other devices in the network. A synthesizer may be used as a master keyboard, although high-quality keyboards without any sound-generating circuitry of their own are made specifically for the purpose of controlling synthesizer modules. Sometimes paradoxically known as mother keyboard.

Master Tape
The approved, final stereo mix of a recording from which CDs, cassettes, etc, will be produced – although a production master, including special equalisation or other processing for the particular medium required, will also often be needed. The master tape is sometimes called an original master. A duplicate of it, called a safety master, may be made for backup reasons.

Master Volume
A means of controlling the overall volume of a multi-timbral synthesizer (particularly one of the General MIDI type) in preference to adjusting individual channel volumes (Controller 7). It is a Universal System Exclusive message of the Real Time type, with a Sub ID#1 value of 4, indicating a Device Control message, and a Sub ID#2 value of 1, followed by the LSB and then the MSB: 0,0 is silent and 127,127 is full volume

Matrix
A term used to describe any system which allows devices to be connected as though they were arranged along the two axes of a grid. Clearly seen on the VCS range of modular synthesizers, where the outputs of the various modules are connected to the left edge of a grid of holes, while their inputs are ranged along the top edge. Connections are made by inserting a conducting pin at the appropriate junction of row and column – a neater system than the Patch Cord method employed by other manufacturers. Electronic versions of the matrix are implemented in software, particularly for ease of viewing or making complex relationships between sets of data that can similarly be arranged in rows and columns.

MCPS
Abbreviation of Mechanical Copyright Protection Society: *see* Copyright.

MD
1. Abbreviation of *Mano Destra:* indicates that the right hand should play any passage thus marked.

2. Abbreviation of Mini Disc. A system, devised by Sony, for recording a digital audio signal onto an erasable optical disc similar to a CD but just over half the size (64mm diameter as opposed to 120mm). Because the format stores a similar duration of music to CDs, the data rate has to be reduced below that ordinarily required to achieve CD-quality performance. To compensate for this, a data compression system known as ATRAC is employed which means that good audio quality can be achieved at one-fifth of the normal data rate. *See also* ATRAC, DCC and PASC.

3. Abbreviation of Musical Director.

Measure
In music, the American term for bar: e.g. "the fourth measure" = "the fourth bar". *See* Bar.

Measured Music
Any music which has sections with a well defined sense of pulse, and which can therefore be easily notated within bar lines. Almost all western art music between about 1600 and 1900, as well as most popular music, is of this type.

Mediaeval
See Musical Periods.

Mediant
See Scale.

Mega
Prefix meaning million. Multiple of SI Units. The term is also used to indicate that something is large or powerful. Its symbol is an upper case M.

Megabyte
1,024 Kbytes or 1,048,576 bytes. Not 1,000,000 as you might expect, but the nearest power of 2 which is close to a million. This is a result of the influence of binary numbers on computing.

Mellotron
A keyboard instrument, designed in the early '60s and based on a set of pre-recorded tones on tapes. Each key has its own short tape which, when the key is pressed, is brought into contact with a replay head: in effect, a sort of keyboard-controlled tape player or (in more modern terms) an analogue sample replay system. The tapes had up to four tracks, enabling a choice of timbres to be selected using a rotary switch. Mellotrons were very popular with groups such as Yes and Tangerine Dream in the late '60s and early '70s, but suffered from certain disadvantages. The tapes, which were not looped, ran out after eight seconds and took a little time to re-wind, and the entire machine with its racks of tapes was monstrously heavy, treating many a roadie to the delights of an inguinal hernia. Some Mellotrons were adapted for theatre use, offering different sound effects, rather than musical pitches, on each key.

Memory
An area in a device such as a computer, where programs and data are permanently stored (ROM: Read-Only Memory) or can be loaded and manipulated (RAM: Random Access Memory and WORM: Write-Once Read-Many). Memory is usually in the form of Integrated Circuits, although storage devices such as magnetic tape, CDs and floppy or hard disks can be seen as an extension of it.

Meno
Italian for "less", as in *Meno Mosso* – less movement, or slower.

Menu
In a computer program, a list of options from which a choice may be made.

Meta Events
See Standard MIDI File.

Metal Tape   A form of magnetic recording tape which has a coating of pure metal pigments fixed to a polyester carrier. It has superior characteristics to both Ferric Oxide and Chromium Dioxide types.

Meter   Device for indicating the level of a quality such as voltage, current, etc.

Metronome   A mechanical or electronic device which produces "click" or "beep" sounds at a regular and adjustable rate, so that a performer can listen to this pulse and play at the required tempo. This is described by an indication at the beginning of the score, in the form of MM = 72 or ♩ = 72, meaning 72 crotchet (quarter note) beats per minute. MM stands for Maelzel's Metronome (Maelzel being the German inventor of the device) although it is nowadays often referred to as simply the "Metronome Mark". MMs which describe crotchet beats are equivalent to the more technological notion of beats per minute (BPM) produced by the "metronome" on devices such as sequencers. The metronome has even been used as a musical instrument by Ligeti in his *Poème symphonique, 100 metronomes* of 1962.

Mezzo   Italian for half or between. Often used as an abbreviation for Mezzo Soprano – a voice halfway between Soprano and Contralto in range.

Mezzo Forte   Italian for moderately loud, usually abbreviated to *mf*.

Mezzo Piano   Italian for moderately soft, usually abbreviated to *mp*.

Mezzo Soprano   *See* Mezzo.

mf   *See* Mezzo Forte.

MIA   Abbreviation of Music Industries Association. A body set up to allow a forum for discussion among members of the UK music industry.

Micro   Prefix meaning one millionth. Sub-multiple of SI Units. Often symbolized by μ. The term is also used to indicate that something is small.

Microcomputer   A desktop-sized computer based on a microprocessor and which usually includes a Keyboard[2] and Monitor[3] with the package. The term is roughly synonymous with personal computer.

Micron   A unit of length equal to one millionth of a metre and denoted by the symbol μ. Now obsolete, having been rationalized into the SI Units system as the micrometre (symbol μm). Commonly encountered in descriptions of magnetic tape thickness, dimensions of integrated circuits, etc.

Microphone   A Transducer which converts mechanical energy into electrical energy. Its primary function is to convert changes in air pressure into electrical signals, and it is often the starting point of the programme chain. Many types are available and some are known by more than one name: *see* Bidirectional, Capacitor, Cardioid, Condenser, Electret, Electrostatic, Figure of Eight, Gun, Hypercardioid, Lavalier, Lip Ribbon, Omnidirectional, Pressure Gradient, PZM, Radio, Ribbon, Rifle, Unidirectional.

Microprocessor   An integrated circuit (usually LSI) which functions as the central processing unit (CPU) of a computer. It is the mass production, and therefore comparative cheapness, of these ICs which has contributed to the huge growth in computing and music technology since the mid 1970s.

Microtonality   The exploitation of intervals which lie between the semitone steps of traditional western pitch systems. This allows the use of new scales and non-western tunings and modes. This important and underestimated facility is at last becoming available on synthesizers.

Middle Eight   Originally an eight-bar section of contrasting material in the middle of a song, but later applied to a linking section of any length. The term bridge is now more often used. *See also* Break.

MIDI   Acronym from Musical Instrument Digital Interface. An internationally agreed standard of electronic hardware, along with a language of commands, which allows suitably equipped devices to be interconnected (via MIDI Sockets) and thereby remotely controlled. Primarily intended for musical equipment, it has more recently been extended to the control of other devices, such as lighting. MIDI can also be defined as a system for encoding a musical performance digitally in such a way that it can be stored and replayed by a computer, where the data can also be manipulated and edited. However, it should be understood that only the instructions necessary to carry out the performance are encoded and not the sound of the performance itself.

MIDI Adaptor   Hardware which can be fitted to an existing synthesizer, computer, etc., to equip it with MIDI facilities. Such Retrofits are particularly useful for upgrading synths which pre-date 1983.

MIDI Choke   Colloquial term for a condition which can occur in a MIDI network where data is being output at a faster rate than the interface can accommodate. Most likely to occur when a large number of messages (particularly controller data) is being sent from a single output, and can result in notes being delayed, lost or not turned off. Equipment with multiple MIDI ports is less likely to suffer from MIDI Choke, since the load on any one output can be reduced. Alternatively, MIDI filters or some judicious editing can usually thin the flow of data without noticeably affecting the musical result. *See also* MIDI Delay[2].

MIDI Clock   A System Real Time message with a status byte value of 248. It is transmitted by the device which is master in a MIDI network and ensures that any slave devices stay in synchronization with the current tempo. Usually only implemented by drum machines and sequencers. It is a relative time clock and should not to be confused with MTC which is an absolute time system. *See also* Active Sensing, Continue, Reset, Start, Stop.

MIDI Controllers

1. Devices which generate MIDI messages and which (usually) resemble conventional musical instruments, such as keyboards, guitars, etc. MIDI was originally conceived as a keyboard-related system, but manufacturers soon started to produce MIDI controllers which could be used by non-keyboard players. MIDI controllers are available in the following instrument types, amongst others: guitar, woodwind, wind valve, drum kit, xylophone, piano accordion, violin family and, of course, keyboards. Other types of instrument and singers can use a Pitch to MIDI Convertor, which will generate MIDI data from a microphone input. More esoteric input devices exist, such as Jean-Michel Jarre's laser harp and the MIDI "wand" which can be used by dancers and other performance artists.

2. MIDI Controller Messages. These are a type of Channel Voice message designed for adjusting individual controls, such as pan position or channel volume, on equipment in the MIDI network. In order to offer the greatest flexibility, the MIDI Specification never anticipated standardization of the full range of controller numbers. However, since it is more than a little frustrating to find, for example, that a carefully edited change in pan position for one synth is interpreted as a change in modulation rate on another, certain conventions have emerged. The table below gives the typical allocation of the more common controller numbers, although most instruments implement only a selection of these. Controller messages can be a simple on-off type, called Switched Controllers (e.g. numbers 64-90) or can contain a range of values (Continuous Controllers). Controller messages 0–31 take one additional data byte, and can therefore carry values in the range 0–127. However, these can be paired with controllers 32–63, in order to provide two data bytes of resolution (e.g. Controller 4 is paired with Controller 36). When this is done, the controller in the range 0–31 takes the MSB and its "pair" in the range 32–63 takes the LSB, the two together offering any of 16,384 possible values, although such high resolution is seldom needed for most controllers. Most Continuous Controllers carry values ranging upwards from 0, although physical controllers that centre around zero (balance, pan, pitch bend) may be implemented so that their associated Controller message carries values centred on the mid-range point (64 or 8,192).

Controller Nº and function	
0	bank select MSB
1	modulation wheel
2	breath controller
4	foot controller
5	portamento time
6	data entry MSB
7	channel volume
8	balance
10	pan
11	expression controller
12	effects control 1
13	effects control 2
16–19	general purpose 1–4
32–63	LSB for Nos. 0–31
64	sustain pedal
65	portamento
66	sostenuto
67	soft pedal
68	legato footswitch
69	hold 2

(Controllers 0–13, 16–19, 32–63: Continuous Controllers)
(Controllers 64–69: Switched Controllers)

Controller Nº and function	
70–79	sound controllers 1–10 (*manufacturers may implement these as desired. The first 5 default to:*
	70 sound variation (synths) exciter (effects units)
	71 harmonic content (synths) compressor (effects)
	72 release time (synths) distortion (effects)
	73 attack time (synths) equalizer (effects)
	74 brightness (synths) expander (effects)
	The others are currently undefined for synths)
80–83	general purpose 5–8
91–95	effects depth 1–5 (*originally assigned to specific effects such as chorus, phaser, tremolo, etc.*)
96–101	data controllers
120	all sounds off
121	reset all controllers
122	local control
123	all notes off
124	omni mode off
125	omni mode on
126	mono mode on (poly off)
127	poly mode on (mono off)

(Controllers 120–127: Channel Mode messages)

See also: Controller Change, Continuous Controllers, Switched Controllers.

MIDI Delay

1. A facility provided on some sequencers to allow a track to be fractionally delayed or advanced relative to others. Particularly useful for synthesizer voices which speak rather late or to give a part a sense of urgency by being played very slightly ahead of the beat. Also called offset.

2. Noticeable delay in the transmission of MIDI data is rare, but when it happens it is caused by MIDI Choke. Delays generated by the response time of instruments in the network are ususally too slight to be a problem and claims that the material or length of a MIDI cable can cause a perceptible delay are total nonsense. The propagation of an electronic signal through any conductor is about ⅔ the speed of light: to produce a one millisecond delay you would need a MIDI cable more than 100 miles in length – not likely to be stocked by your local music store. However, a cable longer than the 15 metres allowed by the MIDI specification may degrade the signal to the extent that it never arrives – a sort of infinite delay. See MIDI Choke.

MIDI Device

Any device equipped with MIDI. This includes sequencers, drum machines, synthesizers, samplers, master keyboards, wind instrument controllers, drum pads, computers, effects and even lighting units.

MIDI Echo

A facility offered on some MIDI devices whereby information received at the MIDI In socket is repeated at the MIDI Out socket. Sometimes called a "soft thru" connection.

MIDI Filtering

There are occasions when some of the data flowing through a MIDI network is redundant. Its presence may slow down the flow of other, more useful data. For example, a sequencer may be transmitting Aftertouch information to a synth which does not implement this feature. In such a case, it would be desirable to ensure the sequencer filters out the recorded aftertouch messages (output filtering), or does not record them in the first place (input filtering).

MIDI Implementation

The chart usually supplied with a MIDI device which purports to describe how the MIDI Specification has been implemented on that device: unfortunately, these are seldom without error.

MIDI In

See MIDI Socket.

MIDI Interface

See Tautology.

MIDI Machine Control

A protocol within the MIDI Specification to allow for the control of mechanical devices such as tape recorders via MIDI.

MIDI Mapping

The process of translating one type of MIDI message into a different type of MIDI message, according to a set of rules determined by the user. This might be to overcome a communication problem caused by variable interpretation of the MIDI specification by different manufacturers: for example, early Yamaha synths implemented Aftertouch as a Continuous Controller instead of using the Channel Key Pressure message – a MIDI mapper could be used to convert every Controller message into an aftertouch message. Mapping may be used for purely creative effect, such as generating a C major triad (the notes C, E and G) whenever a Note On message for Middle C is received. It can also be used to add new features to existing equipment, e.g. to make a keyboard split – all received note numbers below and including 60 should be retransmitted on MIDI Channel 2, allowing the bottom half of the keyboard to use a different sound from the top.

MIDI Merge

The process of combining MIDI messages transmitted from two or more MIDI devices into one coherent MIDI data stream, so that the messages appear to have been generated by only one device. This is not simply a case of joining the MIDI cables together, as MIDI messages are structured and this structure needs to be preserved. If two MIDI messages, such as Note On, arrive simultaneously at the two inputs, the merge device will have to store one of them temporarily in a buffer, while letting the other pass through. The message in the buffer can then be sent. Because MIDI messages are variable in length, and because Real Time messages have to take priority, the merge device must be able to identify and distinguish between different data. This generally requires a microprocessor to be used, making a MIDI Merge unit considerably more expensive than a plain MIDI Thru Box.

MIDI Message

A full instruction consisting of at least one status byte, and frequently with one or more data bytes, which causes a MIDI device to perform one of the functions defined in the MIDI Specification. MIDI Messages conventionally fall into the following categories:

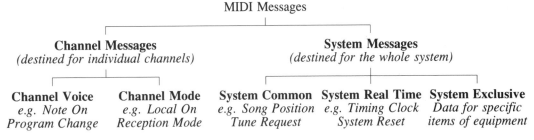

MIDI Mode

See Reception Mode.

MIDI Network

A term for a collection of MIDI devices connected together in such a way that MIDI messages can pass between them. The most common network is the Daisy Chain (each device connected to the next in line), although the MIDI specification also allows for a Star Network, where each device is connected to a central point.

MIDI Out

See MIDI Socket.

MIDI Patchbay

Essentially a patchbay for MIDI signals. Passive patchbays simply present MIDI In and Out sockets conveniently on a front panel and allow patchcords to join them together. Active patchbays will generally have MIDI sockets on the rear panel, switches and displays on the front panel and will also have a memory which allows commonly used patches to be set up with switches and recalled instantly. These, in turn, may be triggered by specific MIDI Program Change messages sent to the unit. As all this requires intelligence (usually provided by a microprocessor), an Active patchbay will often perform other functions such as MIDI Merge or MIDI Mapping.

MIDI Port

A means of overcoming the 16-channel limit on MIDI by using an Interface with multiple MIDI sockets that carry totally independent signals and effectively provide separate networks that function in parallel. Typically, there may be four such sets of sockets, designated A–D. Port A can then be used for channels 1–16, Port B for channels 17–32 and so on. Such interfaces, which are generally used as the hub of a large MIDI Network, are occasionally built into master keyboards. However, more typically they are add-on hardware devices for a computer and will often only operate in conjunction with sequencing software from the same manufacturer.

MIDI Processor
A device which translates one MIDI message to another. *See* MIDI Mapping.

MIDI Show Control
A protocol within the MIDI Specification which allows the control of lighting and other equipment via MIDI so that lasers, stage effects, projectors, etc., can be automated and controlled from the same source as musical events. As it facilitates the integration of visual and aural events, it can be seen as the implementation of MIDI in MultiMedia.

MIDI Socket
The MIDI Specification describes two connector types, XLR connectors and 5-pin DIN sockets, although only the latter type is commonly used on MIDI equipment. The sockets have three functional types: MIDI In allows a device to receive MIDI messages, MIDI Out allows a device to transmit MIDI messages, while MIDI Thru simply relays everything received at the MIDI In socket and is there for connecting additional equipment. A given MIDI device only needs to have those sockets which are appropriate to its function: for example, a MIDI reverb unit might require only a MIDI In socket, through which it can receive program changes, etc.

MIDI Specification
1. The internationally agreed document which defines the MIDI hardware and language standards. First described in October 1982 and formalized as version 1.0 in August 1983. Some other aspects have since been added to it as MIDI devices have become more sophisticated. Such adjuncts include the MIDI Sample Dump Standard, Standard MIDI File, File Dump Standard, MIDI Show Control and MIDI Machine Control.

2. Incorrectly used to refer to the implementation of MIDI on a device: *see* MIDI Implementation.

MIDI Thru
See MIDI Socket.

MIDI Thru Box
A device fitted with at least one MIDI In socket and a number of parallel MIDI Thru sockets. Any MIDI message appearing at the MIDI In will simultaneously appear at each MIDI Thru socket. Parallel wiring reduces the opportunity for degradation of the MIDI signal which might otherwise appear in a long Daisy Chain connection. In boxes that have more than one MIDI In, there will be a switching arrangement to select which is connected; due to the nature of MIDI messages it is not possible simply to combine the inputs unless the box contains some intelligence such as a microprocessor. *See also* MIDI Merge.

MIDI Time Code
Essentially the implementation of SMPTE in MIDI, allowing data representing absolute real time locations (in hours, minutes, seconds and frames) to be transmitted through a MIDI network for synchronization purposes. It is preferable to, and should not be confused with, the relative time locations provided by MIDI Clock. There are several messages related to MTC: MIDI Time Code Quarter Frame, MIDI Time Code Full Message, User Bits, Set Up and Real Time MTC Cueing.

MIDI Time Code Full Message
A System Exclusive message incorporating MTC information in a packet of ten bytes, which is used to update a MIDI network when devices on it are in fast forward, rewind, etc. It comprises the SOX status byte; a data byte of 127 indicating a Real Time System Exclusive message for the whole system; a sub-ID#1 with a value of 1 indicating an MTC message; a sub-ID#2 with a value of 1 indicating a full message; four bytes for hours, minutes, seconds and frames; and the EOX status byte.

MIDI Time Code Quarter Frame
A System Common message generated by a device in play (but not rewind or fast forward), with a status byte value of 241 and a data byte. This pair of bytes is transmitted as a string of eight messages which describes the number of frames, seconds, minutes, hours and SMPTE type, updating the time every two frames. The data byte is split into a three-bit nibble and a four-bit nibble. The three-bit section (the most significant) describes the message type: i.e. a value of 0 indicates that this byte represents the number of frames, while a value of 1 is the number of tens of frames and a value of 5 is the number of tens of hours, etc. The next four bits (least significant nibble) describes the actual value. Thus a data byte 1010010 indicates that this message represents 20 hours. *See also* the related MTC messages: MIDI Time Code Full, Set Up and User Bits.

Mid Range
1. *See* Loudspeaker.

2. In acoustics, frequencies in the 200 Hz to 3–5 kHz range.

Milli
Prefix meaning one thousandth. Sub-multiple of SI Units.

Miniature Score
A pocket-sized version of a Full Score.

Minicomputer
See Computer.

Minim
Note (♩) or rest (‑) whose duration is a half of a semibreve. Also known as a half-note.

Minimalism
A term taken from a description of a movement in the fine arts during the late '60s which stressed a "less is more" approach, and which is now perhaps more commonly applied to a related style of music. At that time the music was described as "systems music" and has also been known as "process music" and "solid-state music". It is minimal in that the focus is often upon the gradual working-through of very small changes in the music – sometimes only one parameter at a time. Minimalism is characterized

(certainly in early works) by almost stationary harmony and repetitive rhythmic patterns. It is the result of a number of influences particularly from Indian, African and Gamelan musics. The main exponents include John Adams, Cornelius Cardew, Philip Glass, Michael Nyman, Steve Reich, Terry Riley and La Monte Young.

Minor

See Scale, Diatonic.

MIPS

Acronym from Million Instructions Per Second. Invariably prefixed by a number (e.g. 400 mips) and intended to give some indication of the performance of a computer (usually one in the supercomputer class). However the indication can be misleading, as it does not take account of factors such as access time to memory or storage devices. As a result some computer engineers wryly explain it as "Meaningless Indicator of Performance Speed". As technology improves GIPS is becoming more common (Giga is 1,000,000,000 or a billion).

Misterioso

Italian for mysteriously.

Mix

1. The particular combination of a number of signals output from a mixing desk at any given moment. Alternative mixes of the same material are sometimes made for different purposes, such as the soundtrack of a film, the album of the same soundtrack and a disco version of one of the individual numbers. Re-mixes are also made to give old records a new lease of life, both artistically and commercially. *See also* Foldback Mix.

2. The main stereo or L–R mix bus on a Mixing Desk.

Mixer

See Mixing Desk, Vision Mixer.

Mixing Desk

A device for processing and combining audio signals from a number of channels, ultimately to produce a single stereo output. Each signal passes through a Channel [1], the controls for which are arranged vertically, as shown right, in the order (from top to bottom) in which the signal passes through the various facilities on the desk. Mixing desks provide from as few as six to as many as sixty or more such channels, each with a similar set of controls arranged side by side.

The Input section allows selection of the audio source: either Microphone or Line Input (for electronic instruments connected by a Direct Inject input or other audio sources such as tape tracks or a record deck). A Trim control allows this input to be matched to the requirements of the system, particularly to enable the signal level to align with those on other channels. Equalisation controls will almost certainly include High and Low Frequency Gain, plus adjustable Mid-Range EQ: more elaborate facilities are common. The Auxiliary section provides connections to Foldback and external Effects units: usually with gain controls for the amount of signal to be sent. These can be switched to operate Pre- or Post-Fader. The Routing section allows the signal to be sent to whichever tape track you wish to use, or to be Panned left or right in a stereo mix. The section nearest the operator provides a Fader to control the channel's volume – the relative heights of an array of faders give a rough impression of the mix. This section will also include switches to Mute or Solo the channel for monitoring purposes.

In addition to the individual channel controls, there will be (at the side or centre of the console) master faders for the entire mix and facilities for monitoring the recording, including VU or LED meters to check that output levels are satisfactory. Other aids may include a Talkback system for communicating with performers in the studio, master controls for the auxiliary Sends and Returns, and technical features such as generators for Line Up Tones. The rear panel of a mixing desk will contain many inputs and outputs, in the form of Jacks, XLRs, etc., some of which will have Insert Points for connection to other equipment. Some modern desks offer automated operation, enabling complex settings to be stored by a microprocessor and called up as required. The advent of digital recording has prompted the more recent development of fully digital mixing desks which allow the signal to be processed entirely in the digital domain.

Mixing Desks are used both for multi-track recording and for the subsequent re-mixing of these tracks into a stereo Master Tape, as well as for broadcasting. Smaller units are also used for balancing sounds in live performance and recording. Similar equipment for mixing video signals is properly called a Vision Mixer. *See also* Automation.

Mixolydian

See Mode.

MM

Abbreviation of Maelzel's Metronome or Metronome Mark. *See* Metronome.

MMA

Abbreviation of MIDI Manufacturers' Association. The representative body of manufacturers involved in the development of MIDI equipment and MIDI as a standard. *See also* JMSC, UKMA.

MMC *See* MIDI Machine Control.

MMU Abbreviation of Memory Management Unit. *See* DMA.

Mode 1. Essentially a seven-note scale. There are seven principal modes, each of which can be found by starting on the notes A to G and playing up the white notes (only) on a piano to the corresponding note an octave higher. They are named Aeolian (A–A), Locrian (B–B, but very rare), Ionian (C–C), Dorian (D–D), Phrygian (E–E), Lydian (F–F) and Mixolydian (G–G). These can be transposed to start on different pitches – the interval pattern between notes is the essential feature. Modes are most commonly encountered in folk and ethnic music and were the foundation of almost all composition until around 1600. The modern major and natural minor scales correspond to the Ionian and Aeolian modes respectively, and formed the basis of most western art music written in the following 300 years. Twentieth century art music, jazz and some popular music have been much influenced by the folk and art music of other cultures in rediscovering the possibilities inherent in a wider range of modes and scales.

2. *See* Reception Mode.

Modem Acronym from MOdulator / DEModulator. A device which allows digital data to be transmitted and received via a telephone line. It is essentially uses FSK as a means of converting the digital data into an audio signal suitable for line transmission. The maximum data rate is often limited to about 2400 Baud, although faster speeds are possible.

Moderato A moderately fast tempo: about 95–115 MM.

Modular Synthesizer A synthesizer where the individual sound generators or processors such as oscillators, filters, amplifiers, envelope generators, etc., are physically separate units which are connected together by the user. This is usually achieved by linking one unit's output to another's input, using a patchcord. The earliest synthesizers were of this type and this is the origin of the term Patch to describe the parameter settings on modern synthesizers which no longer use this arrangement. Modular synthesizers were made by Moog (Series III), Roland (System 100 and 700) and Korg (MS 10, 20, etc.). These systems were very flexible and led naturally to creative experimentation, but were expensive to manufacture and market. This resulted in a newer generation of synths which were easier to use but which provided less flexibility, having a more predetermined signal path. There has recently been a revival of interest in modular synthesizers and there are still manufacturers such as the English company, Digisound, making them.

Modulation 1. The rapid changing in some quality such as pitch or volume, usually generated by imposing the output from a Low Frequency Oscillator on a signal, and having the musical effects of vibrato (pitch) or tremolo (volume).

2. In music, a change of key.

3. The superimposition of one signal on another: e.g. in radio transmissions the audio signal is used to modulate a radio frequency Carrier. Two types of modulation exist: AM (Amplitude Modulation) and FM (Frequency Modulation).

4. The variation in the normally geometric groove on a record, which encodes the audio signal.

Modulation Wheel One of the defined MIDI Controller Change messages with a status byte value in the range 176–191 and a data byte value of 1. Physically it most often appears as a wheel at the left side of a keyboard. When operated it will introduce some effect such as vibrato to the sound. Its precise function varies from device to device and can often be programmed by the user.

Modulator *See* FM Synthesis.

Module *See* Tone Module.

Molto Italian for much or very: e.g. *molto vivace* – very lively.

Monitor 1. To listen to (or occasionally measure) a signal at some point in the programme chain. By extension, the loudspeaker(s) in the control room, through which the signal is heard.

2. A section on a mixing desk for adjusting aspects of the monitoring process.

3. The visual display unit (VDU) used for a computer or video system. *See also* Dot Pitch, Interlacing, Pixels, Refresh Rate, Resolution[2].

Monitor System A system comprising at least one amplifier and one loudspeaker for mono (two channels of these for stereo) which allows one to hear, or monitor, audio signals.

Mono Abbreviation of monophonic: an audio signal that is carried by a single channel. The number of microphones or loudspeakers that are used to generate and replay the sound is irrelevant, what counts is that the various signals are mixed to one channel. *See also* Stereo.

Monophonic Said of any instrument that can play only one note at a time and of music that consists of only an unaccompanied melody. Most monophonic synthesizers follow a rule to deal with occasions when two notes appear. It might play the most recently received or it might play the note with the highest pitch.

Some MIDI Controllers[1] require synthesizers that can work monophonically across a number of channels – six, in the case of a MIDI guitar. Thus, although the synthesizer may be Polyphonic, it is working monophonically on each Channel[2]. If you think about it, a real guitar can be considered to be six monophonic string instruments. *See also* Polyphonic.

Moog

Allegedly pronounced to rhyme with rogue. The tradename of an American company, founded by Robert Moog, which made synthesizers from the late '60s to the early '80s. At one point, the word Moog was virtually synonymous with synth, in much the same way that vacuum cleaners are called Hoovers. The most famous were the Series III modular synthesizer, used by Keith Emerson and Walter (now Wendy) Carlos, and the Minimoog, used by just about everyone else.

MOR

Abbreviation of Middle of the Road. A very broad spectrum of popular music that is not going to offend too many people.

Mordent

See Ornamentation.

Most Significant

The leftmost value in any numbering system. In the decimal number 5463, five is the most significant number, as removing it would make the greatest difference to the value. *See also* MSB.

Mother Keyboard

See Master Keyboard.

Motif

Also called Motive. In music, a short but memorable melodic or rhythmic idea. Often used as building blocks for longer melodies, or even complete movements. Motifs tend to remain recognizable as a binding force in the structure even when transposed, inverted or otherwise altered. Perhaps the most famous motif of all is the first four notes of Beethoven's 5th Symphony.

Moto

Italian for movement: e.g. *con moto* – with movement.

Mouse

1. A hand-operated control which is a useful adjunct (sometimes essential) to many computer programs. In its most common form, a mouse consists of a frame holding a ball which rolls when the mouse is moved. Movement of the ball in two dimensions is transmitted to sensors which send signals to position a Cursor on a computer monitor. It is usually fitted with one or more switches, the pressing of which will select or activate an area of the screen currently under the cursor. Other forms of mouse have no ball, but work optically by shining a pulsed LED at a semi-reflective surface. Lines printed on the surface decrease the intensity of the reflected light and this interference in the pulse rate is interpreted as movement. *See also* Tracker Ball.

2. A small member of the order *Rodentia,* which frequently lives in a commensal relationship with man.

Moving Coil

A coil of wire suspended in a magnetic Field[3], such that the field will repel the coil when a voltage is flowing through it, or that the coil will generate a voltage when it is moved in the magnetic field. This is used to convert an electrical signal into mechanical movement or vice versa. In a moving coil microphone (also called a dynamic microphone), sound pressure waves cause a diaphragm and its attached coil to vibrate, inducing voltage in the coil. In a moving coil loudspeaker, audio signals are fed into the coil which then vibrates, causing sound pressure waves. *See also* Voice Coil.

mp

See Mezzo Piano.

MS

Abbreviation of *Mano Sinistra*, Italian for left hand. Indicates that the left hand should play any passage thus marked.

MSB

Abbreviation of Most Significant Bit. The leftmost bit or column of a binary number. So called because it has the most effect on the result of any sum involving the number. Occasionally in 16-bit or more (i.e. multi-byte) systems it may be taken to stand for Most Significant Byte when referring to the leftmost byte for similar reasons. MSN is Most Significant Nibble.

MSC

See MIDI Show Control.

MSDOS

See Operating System.

MSI

Abbreviation of Medium Scale Integration. An integrated circuit which contains about 100–900 active elements. *See also* LSI, SSI, VLSI.

MTC

See MIDI Time Code.

MU

Abbreviation of Musicians' Union: a UK body which represents the interests of performing musicians and negotiates fees and working conditions, including those for recording sessions.

Multicore

An assembly of cables or wires, often used to convey several channels of audio signals between two points. The most commonly encountered form consists of several sets of cables of screened, twisted-pair wires for Balanced Line connections. Each cable in the multicore may have a differently coloured sheath to help identify it. Multicore is sometimes called "snake" or "rope".

Multi-Effects Unit

A device which can simultaneously provide a number of different effects, such as Gated Reverb with Chorusing. It is intended to replace a number of separate units, although it is argued that the latter actually offer better quality and greater flexibility.

MultiMedia The simultaneous use of text, visual images and sound by a computer or other system, or the integration of music, picture and other effects during a performance.

Multimeter An electronic device for measuring and displaying absolute values for a number of different qualities such as voltage, current, resistance, frequency, capacitance, etc.

Multiple Loop Points A category of message in the Sample Dump Standard, which allow loop points to be determined or changed within a sampler independently of the sample itself i.e. without having to retransmit the entire sample. Loop Points Request and Loop Points Transmit are two such messages.

Multiple Loops The ability of a sampler to handle more than one Loop[2] in any given sample. Some machines allow only two loops per sample, while others allow as many as eight.

Multiplexer A device which switches an input sequentially (or in some other pre-set order) between multiple outputs, or vice-versa. Some digital mixing desks use a Multiplexer to compensate for having only one Analogue to Digital Convertor between, say, eight inputs. In such a case, the ADC will perform one sample of each input in turn, but will run at eight times the normal sampling rate to ensure that each input receives appropriate attention.

Multistage EG *See* Envelope Generator.

Multisync The ability of some computer monitors to adapt (often automatically) to a variety of different video signal standards, sometimes even from different types of computer.

Multi-tasking A much abused phrase intended to suggest the ability of a computer to carry out more than one job simultaneously. In fact, almost all current computers (even the largest) can execute only one instruction at a time. At best, all you can say is that the separate jobs are done sufficiently quickly that a human perceives them to be simultaneous. The term multi-tasking is frequently used to describe a process whereby, once loaded, different programs can co-reside in a computer, allowing the user to switch instantly from one task to another. However, in such cases, the previous task is either suspended or shares "time slices" with the current operation.

Multi-timbral The ability of a sampler or synthesizer to produce more than one tone colour (timbre) at a time, allowing the user to generate a number of simultaneous parts (e.g. drums, bass, strings, sax, etc.).

Multi-track A tape recorder with more than two tracks. 4, 8, 16 or 24 tracks are standard on analogue machines and 24, 32 or 48 tracks are standard on digital machines. The intention is that each track carries a recording of an instrument or group of instruments, recorded at an optimum level, so that the various tracks can be mixed in volume, equalized, panned, etc., on a Mixing Desk.

Music Difficult to define without excluding some aspect of human endeavour in the field, and thus the source of much philosophical debate. "The intentional organization of sound" is often suggested as a possible formula. It is sufficiently broad to include most human musical activity, but it encompasses ordered sounds, such as a knock on the door or a chime over an airport PA system, that have a purely functional, signalling purpose. "The intentional organization of sound for intellectual or aesthetic stimulus" homes in more precisely, but excludes the work of composers such as John Cage who strive towards the Zen notion of "no intention". It also excludes the sounds of nature, such as bird-song or waterfalls, which might be considered music to the ears of some, although most would probably say that the word music is used more as a metaphor in such a context. This highlights a significant difference between the adjective "musical" and the noun "music" – hitting two stones together may produce a musical sound (i.e. a sound with qualities such as pitch and tone), but this act does not necessarily produce music unless there is an intention so to do. In fact, *intention* is a key element in the definition, since the vocabulary of music includes many sounds (cannons and typewriters are but two well known examples) which in other circumstances might be the antithesis of music.

Any attempt to define music should also refer to its rôle as a means of communication independent of words. This gives it a certain universality, unfettered by the multiple forms and dialects of world languages. However, claims that music is a "universal language" are greatly exaggerated and often result from the assumption of western imperialism that the rest of the globe has now absorbed its culture. Those making such a claim tend to think of music only in the context of Europe, America and their spheres of influence, and would find themselves at a total loss to understand the musical language of, say, the *duudlaga* of Mongolian shamanic song. Unlike languages using words, numbers or signs, which have evolved to convey generally very precise meanings, the ideas expressed by music are often impossible to capture in words – doubtless one of the reasons for its very existence in every human culture – and can "mean" very different things to different people, or even to the same person on different occasions. Music may be divided into various generalized types: *see* Art Music, Folk Music, Jazz, Popular Music.

Musical Periods Music history divides the last millennium into a number of stylistic periods. This is not to imply that there was no music before 1000 AD. However, it is not until around this date that reliable systems of notation began to appear, without which it is impossible to know how earlier music sounded. These periods are not just convenient divisions of time, but also reflect aesthetic movements in music and the arts in general:

Mediaeval	(up to about 1430)
Renaissance	(between about 1430 and 1600)
Baroque	(between about 1600 and 1750)
Classical	(between about 1750 and 1810)
Romantic	(between about 1810 and 1900)
20th Century	(since 1900)

These dates are slightly arbitrary, and obviously many composers will straddle two periods. There are also various transitional styles and artistic movements within these periods (and particularly in the twentieth century) that have been separately identified with names of their own. It should be noted that the term classical has a formal meaning which is much more limited in scope than its common usage to describe any "art" music. To avoid confusion, it has been suggested that the classical period be termed the Enlightenment, as its dates correspond to the so-called "Age of Enlightenment". However, since this "enlightened" age also saw an explosion of wars and revolutions to right the injustices of the past (and create new ones), even this might be thought a misnomer for the period and its music.

Music Therapy

The use of music to alleviate medical and other conditions as diverse as psychopathy, ligament strain, stress and autism. It is thought that rhythm is most probably the prime mover in therapeutic uses of music. The use of music to accompany meditation is sometimes grandly described as music therapy.

Music X

See University Music Systems.

Musique Concrète

A type of Electro-Acoustic music associated particularly with the French composers Pierre Schaeffer and Pierre Henry. Typified by compositions based on the use of sounds that do not normally have a musical connotation, assembled in "concrete" form on tape. *See also* IRCAM.

Mute

1. A switch on a mixing desk which silences a Channel [1], and effectively removes it from the mix. A similar function is provided to silence tracks on a sequencer. *See also* Solo [1].

2. A device placed on or in a musical instrument with the intention of reducing its volume or altering its timbre. *See also* Sordino.

NAB

Acronym from National Association of Broadcasters. A body involved in the specification and development of technical standards in the American audio and broadcasting industry.

NAB Characteristic

The pre-emphasis and de-emphasis equalisation standard for magnetic tape recording adopted in USA and Japan.

NAB Spool

The 10-inch metal tape spools used on professional tape recorders.

Nak

Acronym from Not AcKnowledged. One of the characters transmitted for the purposes of Handshaking in a data transfer. It is sent back to the transmitting device by the receiving device to inform it that a block of data has not been received without error and that it should be retransmitted. It also occurs as part of the Sample Dump Standard as System Exclusive message of the Non-Real Time type with a Sub ID#1 value of 126. *See also* Ack.

Natural

A symbol (♮) which is used to cancel the effect of a Sharp or Flat.

Natural Frequency

The rate of vibration which an object will inherently adopt given suitable excitation: e.g. a bowed violin string or a suspension bridge in a gale force wind. Also called the normal mode. *See also* Resonance, Wolf Note.

Network

1. A configuration of components in an electrical circuit.

2. An arrangement of interconnected devices (computers or MIDI devices) to form a system which allows a degree of communication between them. Computer networks allow information, or some other resource such as a printer, to be shared by other devices in the system.

New Age

Essentially the background "mood" music of the '80s, harmlessly offering a gentle blend of soft rock and synthesizers with elements of jazz and Minimalism. Promoted as an alternative to hard rock and the commercialism of the pop charts, it was often associated with socio-political causes, such as "Save the Whale". Although dominated by small, independent companies and often sold by mail-order or through alternative outlets such as health food shops, both the music and the production had such a flawless slickness that it became almost wearisome. Mike Oldfield's *Tubular Bells* (1973) and Brian Eno are often seen as the harbingers of New Age music. The style also encompasses the synthesizer-based "space music" of Jean-Michel Jarre, Kitaro, Tomita and Vangelis.

New Romantics	A flamboyant and short-lived popular music (and dress) style of the early '80s. Particularly developed in London night clubs. Centred around the personalities of Steve Strange and Rusty Egan, a flourish of whose flouncy shirts and velvet make-up bags revealed such bands as Culture Club, Adam Ant, Spandau Ballet, Soft Cell, Wham, Ultravox and Visage.
New Wave	A term used to describe a wide variety of music that bubbled up in the wake of Punk Rock in the late '70s. The music, which replaces the rawness of punk with a certain finesse, encompasses such diversity as Elvis Costello, The Jam, Blondie, The Cars, Police and Talking Heads.
Nibble	In computers and digital systems, a group of four Bits, i.e. half a Byte (haven't computer folk got a wonderful sense of humour). In MIDI Channel messages the channel number is described by the least significant nibble of the status byte. Some data bytes in MIDI (e.g. MTC Quarter Frame messages) are also split into nibbles but, as a MIDI data byte has only seven bits, the most significant nibble is only three bits long. Sometimes eccentrically spelt nybble.
NICAM	Acronym from Near Instantaneous Companded Audio Multiplex. A television broadcasting standard that allows transmission of digital audio data alongside video, giving improved audio quality and stereo operation.
Noise	Unwanted sound, in particular that which masks or corrupts wanted sound information. In audio, noise may include electrical disturbances, hiss, rumble, hum, general studio background noise and external events such as passing aircraft.
Noise Gate	A device which will not pass low-level signals but which allows through signal levels above a certain predetermined threshold. Such a device is useful for suppressing unwanted background noise, spill or tape hiss. It is also used for creative effects such as Gated Reverb, etc.
Noise Reduction System	A method of limiting inherent noise in tape recording and some other transmission systems. This is most commonly achieved by compressing the signal before recording or transmission and then expanding it on replay. Some systems also make use of psychoacoustic effects such as Auditory Masking. *See also* Dolby, DBX.
Nominal Level	*See* Output Level.
Non-Interlaced Scan	*See* Interlaced Scan.
Non-Linear	Said of any system whose output fails accurately to reflect the profile of its input. Also used in the context of Reverberation, with the specific meaning that the decay is artificially cut short (perhaps by Gating) or reversed, etc.
Non-Real Time	**1.** The situation where events can occur at any time, independently of other events and without the need for synchronization *See also* Real Time. **2.** *See* Universal System Exclusive.
Non-Volatile Memory	In a computer system, a type of memory whose contents will be retained during the time that the system is unpowered. This is either due to the presence of an alternative or back-up source of power such as a battery (especially in the case of semiconductor memory), or because the memory is magnetic and does not require power to maintain its contents.
Normalized	The condition where an input socket and output socket (or Send and Return) are connected together unless a plug is inserted into one socket to divert the signal. It is a common feature of Patchbays and Insert Points. For example, the group outputs of a mixing desk might normally be connected to the inputs of a tape recorder. If, instead, you wish to use the group output as a foldback mix send, inserting a plug into the normalized group insert point will divert the signal.
Normalling	A method of wiring two jacks together so that a circuit is broken when a plug is inserted.
Note	A symbol representing an individual musical sound and, by extension, the sound itself.
Notebook Computer	*See* Laptop.
Note Number	The value which appears in the first data byte of a MIDI Note On or Note Off message. It determines which note will be turned on or off. 128 notes (more than 10 octaves) can be described, with note number 60 being middle C. *See also* Pitch for a list of MIDI note numbers.
Note Off	A Channel Voice message with a status byte value in the range 128-143, which causes a device to stop playing the note defined in the message. It comprises three bytes: the Note Off status byte which includes the Channel[2] number, the Note Number data byte (i.e. which note to turn off) and the Release Velocity data byte (i.e. how quickly the note is to be turned off). True Note Offs are seldom used, except on those devices that implement release velocity sensing, the preferred method being to send a Note On message with zero velocity. This allows the use of Running Status to reduce the amount of data transmitted. *See also* Pitch for a list of MIDI note numbers.
Note On	A Channel Voice message with a status byte value in the range 144–159, which causes a device to sound the note defined in the message. It comprises three bytes: the Note On status byte which includes

the Channel[2] number, the Note Number data byte (i.e. which note to turn on) and the Velocity data byte (i.e. how quickly the note is to be turned on – in practice this usually determines how loud the note should be). A Note On with a velocity of zero is frequently used as a method of turning notes off: *see* Running Status and Note Off. *See also* Pitch for a list of MIDI note numbers.

Nyquist Sampling Theorem	*See* Sampling Rate.

OBU	Abbreviation of Outside Broadcast Unit. A team of technicians responsible for recording or broadcast away from a studio.
Octave	The distance between two frequencies which are related by the ratio 2:1. Thus 880 Hz is an octave above 440 Hz. It is called an octave because western music has traditionally divided this distance into a scale of eight notes of various patterns of tones and semitones. Two notes an octave apart tend to sound very similar due to the simple relationship between their frequencies.
Oersted	Unit of magnetic field strength, such that 2 Oersted is the strength of a field at the centre of a circular coil of wire 1 cm in radius carrying a current of 10 amperes. If that means as little to you as it does to me, you will be pleased to know that the unit is now outmoded and has been replaced by the SI Unit "ampere per metre" which is a bit easier to understand.
Offbeat	*See* Beat[1].
Off Line	In a network, the condition of any device which is unable to receive or transmit a signal.
Offset	In a synchronizing system, the relative distance in time between the pre-recorded timecode tracks on the master and slave(s), or between the start times of the timecode on tape and a song on a sequencer. Also used more generally for any event that has been shifted slightly from its expected position.
Ohm	The SI Unit of impedance, reactance and resistance. Its symbol is Ω.
Ohm's Law	A mathematical expression describing the relationship between electrical voltage (V), current (I) and resistance (R). Usually expressed as the equation $V=IR$: in everyday language, the voltage equals the current (in amps) multiplied by the resistance (in ohms). It can be applied to circuits carrying DC, and to AC circuits with virtually no Reactance.
Omnidirectional Microphone	A microphone which is uniformly sensitive in all directions. *See also* Cardioid, Figure of Eight, Hypercardioid.
Omni Mode	**1.** A condition in which a device on a MIDI network receives and responds to all Channel messages regardless of the specific Channel[2] to which it is set. **2.** A Channel Voice message (either Omni On or Omni Off) which selects the condition described in Omni Mode[1]. *See also* Reception Mode.
Ondes Martenot	Also called *Ondes Musicales* (musical waves). An electronic musical instrument (arguably a synthesizer) invented by Maurice Martenot about 1925. Similar to the earlier Thérémin, its basic form consisted of a metal rod which could detect the position of the right hand, using this information to determine the basic pitch of a modulated oscillator. The left hand operated a control which determined the timbre by altering filters through which the basic pitch was passed. A continuous Portamento was a feature of this type of *Ondes Martenot*, but keyboard versions were also developed. These were notable for an Aftertouch facility where sideways motion of the key after it had been depressed altered the basic pitch by microtonal amounts. It was Monophonic, like the Thérémin, but its greater precision of control and wider timbral range made it inherently more interesting to contemporary composers such as Messiaen, Honneger, Varèse and Milhaud, all of whom wrote works in which it features – the most famous, perhaps, being Messiaen's "Turangalîla-symphonie" of 1948.
One Legged	A term which describes a broken electrical connection. In a Balanced Line connection, a symptom is the loss of gain and low frequency content in the signal. In an unbalanced line connection the signal will probably disappear altogether. *See also* Open Circuit.
On Line	**1.** In a network, the condition of any device which is able to receive or transmit a signal. **2.** In a system of synchronized devices, the condition of a slave device which is waiting for a particular timecode value to be reached before it will play or record, etc.
Open Air Acoustic	In a studio, the simulation of an open air acoustic is achieved by the use of screens to surround the sound source and a microphone. This ensures that much of the sound energy which travels away from

the microphone is absorbed and is not reflected back to it. This absence of reflection makes the source sound appear to be located out of doors. *See also* Anechoic, Dead.

Open Circuit

A circuit through which an electrical current cannot flow, perhaps because a component has failed or a connection has been removed. *See also* One Legged, Short Circuit.

Operating System

The part of a computer's software which looks after housekeeping tasks such as updating the Monitor[3], opening and closing disk files, checking the Keyboard[2] for key presses, etc. – the really mundane stuff. The OS is either stored in a chip in the computer or has to be loaded from disk, or some combination of these. Without an operating system, the computer will not normally run any software. Sometimes programmers speed up the operation of their software by writing their own routines to by-pass the Operating System, although this can lead to incompatibility problems if the proper OS is upgraded by its manufacturer. GEM (Graphic Environment Manager), TOS (Tramiel Operating System, exclusive to Atari computers), MS-DOS (MicroSoft Disk Operating System, for PCs), Unix and the Apple Desktop are all operating systems.

Operator

The basic unit of sound generation in FM synthesis as implemented by Yamaha. It consists of an oscillator followed by an amplifier which is controlled by an envelope generator. The oscillator has pitch control and modulation inputs, and the amplifier also has modulation inputs. In early machines like the DX7, the oscillator only produced a sinewave, so two were required to produce more complex waveforms. To be strictly accurate, there is always at least one operator which can produce more complex waveforms on its own, but only because it has its output fed back to the input and thus modulates itself. Later machines like the DX11 featured operators with oscillators which could produce a range of complex waveforms, while the most recent generation can replay digital recordings of sounds (Samples). Yamaha's instruments have four or six operators per voice, depending on machine.

Optical Track

A method of recording an audio signal in the emulsion of a film alongside, and in synchronization with, the picture frames. *See* Film Soundtrack.

Opto Isolator

An electronic component that can pass a signal via a light path, thus avoiding a direct electrical connection between two separate circuits. This will prevent voltage spikes generated in one piece of equipment from finding their way into another, and stops earth loops forming. The unit consists of a light source (an LED) and a light detector (a phototransistor) enclosed in a sealed box, the whole package looking just like a normal IC. The part of the MIDI Specification that deals with hardware requires that all MIDI In connections use an opto isolator.

Original Master

See Master Tape.

Ornamentation

The decoration of a musical idea, usually by the introduction of extra notes. The form of the ornament is often indicated by a symbol in the score, although un-notated embellishment is an important feature of baroque music, as well as many jazz styles.

Trill   Lower Mordent   Acciaccatura

Three common types of ornament

OS

See Operating System.

Oscillation

The behaviour of an oscillator: i.e. cyclic changes in voltage. In practice, any electronic system can be prone to oscillation (*see* Feedback, Howlround), and it is sometimes said that design engineers spend half their time stopping amplifiers from oscillating, and the other half stopping oscillators from merely amplifying. Also used to describe cyclic motion in mechanical systems.

Oscillator

An electronic device for generating cyclic waveforms. The primary source for sound generation in synthesizers and also used for test purposes, such as generating Line Up Tones in Mixing Desks.

Oscilloscope

A device which allows voltage to be plotted against time and displayed on a CRT so that periodic phenomena, such as waveforms, can be examined. It may allow several channels to be displayed simultaneously so that any time delay between them can be measured. Some may also be able to store "snapshots" of data.

Ossia

Italian for "or". Usually used to indicate an alternative version of a musical passage.

Ostinato

Italian for "obstinate". A short melodic and/or rhythmic idea which is continually repeated, often in the bass. Usually known as a Riff in popular music.

Output

The point of exit of a signal from a system, e.g. a section in a mixing desk or other device where the signal is transmitted. Used as a verb ("will you output that for me?") and as a noun ("the change in output"). Also used with reference to computers to describe the point of exit of data from a system, e.g. to output data to a computer monitor or printer.

Output Level The voltage that a system outputs under a specified load. Normally expressed in dB(v). In recording, two output levels are common: the domestic or "semi pro" level of -10dB(v) and a level for professional equipment of +4dB(v). Also known as the Nominal Level.

Output Power The power level that a system outputs under a specified load. Expressed in VA (or watts) RMS.

Outro A term which derives from Intro (Introduction) and which refers to a section at the end of a piece of music; used in popular music in preference to the classical term Coda. It leads to or replaces (in the case of a fade-out) a definite ending.

Out-takes In recording, the unwanted parts of a tape (often containing mistakes and other accidents) that are left over after editing. A whole comedy industry has arisen around the concept of embarrassing performers by the broadcast of such clips – although few seem sufficiently embarrassed to forgo useful publicity by refusing permission for the use of their out-takes.

Overdrive A characteristic guitar sound of Heavy Metal and other hard rock music, in which a guitar amplifier (preferably a valve type) is overloaded to the point of Clipping and complete Distortion. A similar result can be provided by an Effects [2] unit of the same name. Not to be confused with Fuzz, in which the distortion is introduced before the amplification stage.

Overdub The addition of new material to an existing recording, either by a mixing and re-recording process or by adding a new track in multi-track recording. Used by sequencers to refer to the recording of MIDI data on an existing track without erasing material already there.

Overflow MIDI devices invariably have a limited amount of polyphony: any attempt to exceed this (by sending too many simultaneous notes) will result in an overflow of data. If a device has an overflow facility, Note On messages beyond its total polyphonic capacity are passed out to a second device for it to voice.

Over Modulation A situation which occurs when the amplitude of a signal exceeds the limits of the recording or broadcasting system. This causes distortion and can, in exceptional circumstances, damage equipment through which the signal passes.

Oversampling The principle of sampling a signal at an integer multiple of the normal Sampling Rate. The factor can be as little as 2 times, although it may be much more. The effect is to distribute a fixed level of Quantization [2] noise over an ultrasonic frequency range, thus "diluting" the noise in the audio bandwidth and improving the signal-to-noise ratio. *See also* Quantization Error, Shannon Channel Capacity Theorem.

Overtone American term for Partial, usually with the implication of Harmonic Partial.

p *See* Piano.

Pa *See* Pascal.

PA **1.** Abbreviation of Public Address. The distribution of audio signals to loudspeakers for an audience.

2. A system of equipment, including mixing desk, amplifiers, loudspeakers etc., assembled for the implementation of PA [1].

Pad **1.** *See* Attenuator.

2. A sustained chord part which provides harmonic padding in a piece of popular music.

3. *See* Drum Pads.

PAM Acronym from Pulse Amplitude Modulation. The first stage in digital sampling, in which pulses of fixed width have their amplitude modulated by an analogue signal (i.e. the height of the pulse is determined by the amplitude of the signal). It is followed by an encoding stage known as PCM.

Pan One of the defined MIDI Controller Change messages with a status byte value in the range 176–191 and a data byte value of 10. It is assigned to the parameter in a synthesizer which determines the stereo position of a sound, effectively making that controller a Pan Pot.

Panning The process of controlling the relative position of a sound in a stereo field during mixdown or recording using a pan pot. Also, a similar process on synthesizers, sequencers, etc., using a pan control. Usually this is not completely effective as panning alters only the relative amplitude of the sound left to right and not the crucial aspect of delay. *See also* Haas Effect.

Pan Pot

Abbreviation of Panoramic Potentiometer. A device on a mixing desk, etc., which increases the amplitude of an audio signal in one channel while simultaneously reducing the amplitude of that signal in another channel. Most commonly the two channels would be the left and right components of a stereo output. The effect is to give some impression of the signal being at one side of a stereo image or of moving across it. However, the effect is not the same as true stereo placement which also relies on time delays. *See also* Haas Effect.

Parabolic Reflector

A dish-shaped structure used to focus sound waves onto a microphone. The reflector faces the sound source and the microphone is mounted "backwards" – i.e. pointing towards the centre of the parabola. Particularly used to gather sound in outdoor locations, such as in wildlife recording. A satellite receiving dish for television uses a similar principle to focus incoming electromagnetic waves.

Parallel Interface

A means of outputting computer data, in which all bits in a digital Word are sent simultaneously. This is generally more expensive, as the connectors involved have to have a pin for each bit plus a few pins for ground, handshaking, etc. However, the time taken to transmit each word is less than for serial data.

Parameter

In technological usage, a quality which can be varied by the user. On a synthesizer, the settings which determine a sound (filter cut off, oscillator amount, modulation, etc.) are often called parameters. The word has a related and specific use in the context of Parametric Equalizer

Parametric Equalizer

A type of equalisation device which provides the user with control over three parameters: Cut Off frequency, Bandwidth and Gain (positive or negative, boost or cut).

Partial

A single-frequency, sinewave component of a sound. Almost all sounds are composed of a number of partials. There are two classes of partials, Harmonic and Enharmonic. *See also* Sound.

PASC

Acronym from Precision Adaptive Sub-band Coding. A method of data compression, originally intended for use in the digital audio broadcast standard, developed by Philips for use in their DCC system. It exploits the way the human ear and brain work – particularly the phenomenon known as Auditory Masking, where tones which are quieter than others in the same or adjacent frequency bands are ignored. PASC divides the audio signal into 32 frequency bands, each 750 Hz wide. In sampling the sound, PASC does not use a full 16 bits for every sample, but instead distributes the bits so that only the most active bands are sampled. This means that periods of silence generally use no bits at all, unlike conventional sampling processes where all 16 bits are employed all of the time. The data compression ratio achieved in this way is approximately 4:1 when averaged out, and this enables Philips to run DCC at a quarter of the data rate normally required for CD-quality digital audio. In some ways this method is similar to ATRAC, a method developed by Sony for use in MD.

Pascal

1. The SI Unit of pressure (Pa). Sometimes used as an absolute level of sound pressure. 20 µPa (20 millionths of a Pascal) is considered to be 0 dB SPL, the threshold of hearing. The threshold of pain (140 dB SPL) is approximately 200,000,000 µPa (200 Pa).

2. A high level language for computers.

Passive

Electronic circuits are commonly divided into two classes: active and passive. In rough terms, any circuit which contains only resistors, capacitors or inductors (coils, transformers, etc.) can be called passive while circuits which contain valves or semiconductors (transistors, diodes or integrated circuits) can be called active. The definition is sometimes considered from the aspect of gain. Generally, semiconductor (active) circuits are able to increase the gain of a signal, while those without semiconductors (passive) are not.

Password Protection

A method of preventing access to a computer system or program by requiring users to enter a word which (in theory) is known only to authorized personnel. The degree of protection offered is often very limited, posing no real challenge to the hacker. Passwords are often short or familiar enough to be guessed or, if longer, defeat the memory of the genuine user. More elaborate numerical systems (such as those involving the factoring of prime numbers) require substantial processing power to generate in the first place. *See also* Dongle, Hacking.

Paste

In a computer, a command which places a section of text or picture, previously placed in the Clipboard, at the currently selected position. *See also* Copy, Cut.

Patch

1. Originally synthesizers looked like telephone exchanges with separate modules linked by Patchcords. Quite soon, any configuration of these modules including the relative settings of all the knobs became known as a "patch". This usage has survived, even though synthesizers look quite different now, and is used to describe the configuration of all parameters necessary to make a particular sound on a synthesizer. The MIDI specification uses the word Program (i.e. program change) to have the same meaning.

2. Of a patchbay, used as a verb ("can you patch the reverb in for me?") or noun ("the compressor patch"). The physical connection of an input and output on a patchbay using a Patchcord.

Patchbay

A device in a recording studio consisting of a number of sockets arranged in rows and columns on a panel. These are connected to sockets at the rear of the panel which may be linked to the various inputs and outputs of equipment such as the mixing desk, effects units, etc. The patchbay allows easily visible connections to be made between any two pieces of equipment, using a Patchcord. Patchbays usually come in 19" rack format or are fitted into one side of the mixing desk. The sockets are usually jack (the term jackfield is sometimes used) or bantam for audio signals, or BNC for video/digital audio signals. In some cases (e.g. insert points) it may be desirable to have two sockets connected together as the normal condition, but for the connection to be overridden when a patchcord is plugged into a socket. This is called a Normalized connection.

Patchcord
A short cable, fitted with a plug at each end, used to make a connection on a patchbay.

Patch Mapping
The Program Change message is limited to only 128 values, while some synthesizers can store as many as 1000 distinct programs or patches. This would mean that you could only access the first 128 via MIDI. Patch mapping is a process whereby a given program change number received by a MIDI device can be linked to any one of the available patches. This is determined on a patch map – a table set up by the user with entries such as: 1=43, 2=2, 3=984, etc. Any 128 programs can thus be selected. To get beyond this total, the MIDI Continuous Controller message, Bank Select, has been defined for selecting different "banks" of sounds prior to sending a program change number. *See also* Bank Select.

Pattern
On a drum machine, a small section (usually a single bar) which can be repeated or alternated with other such patterns, to form a complete drum part. Sequencers use and extend this principle to musical material of any type or length, allowing patterns to be moved, copied, repeated and sometimes individually named for ease of identification.

Pause
An instruction to linger on a note or rest, more commonly known by the Italian term Fermata in the USA. It is notated with the symbol $\frown$ colloquially known as an "eyebrow".

PA Version
Abbreviation of Public Appearance. A pre-recorded tape of just the instrumental backing of a song, with which a solo vocal artist can sing during public appearances to promote a record.

PC
See Microcomputer.

PCB
See Printed Circuit Board.

PCM
Abbreviation of Pulse Code Modulation.

1. A method of encoding an analogue signal into binary words of fixed length, once it has first been through a PAM sampling process. Used in digital audio devices.

2. A prefix used by a number of manufacturers to denote digital audio equipment, such as the Sony PCM 3324.

Peak
1. The highest signal level in a recording or broadcast. It should ideally coincide with 0 dB(v).

2. A term used to describe the extreme points of a Waveform.

Ped
In piano music, an indication (usually printed $\mathcal{P}ed.$) to use the Sustain[2] pedal.

Pedal
1. A foot-operated lever on a musical instrument. *See* Pedalboard, Soft Pedal, Sostenuto[1], Sustain[2], Swell Pedal.

2. Strictly, pedal point. A sustained, or continually repeated, note that occurs throughout a passage of changing harmonies. Commonly on the Dominant note, where it creates a feeling of tension, or on the Tonic, where it creates a sense of repose. It often occurs in the bass: if it is placed above the other parts, it is known as an inverted pedal. Known as a drone in folk music.

Pedalboard
A large and widely-spaced keyboard designed to be played by the feet, commonly found on organs, although also available as a type of MIDI Controller[1]. Generally used to play bass notes.

Pentatonic
A scale in which the octave is divided into five notes: *see* Scale.

Perdendosi
Italian for dying away.

Perfect
See Cadence, Interval.

Perfect Pitch
The ability to identify the pitch of sounds as specific note names without use of a reference point such as a piano and, as a consequence, the ability accurately to sing the pitch of any given note. Although sometimes described as a "gift", it is no more remarkable than the ability of a child to name a colour and, like that skill, can be learnt by children and even some adults: it is a much rarer skill simply because it is not practised. Many professional musicians get to memorize the standard tuning-note A, and can work out other pitches from this – the first stage, perhaps, in acquiring perfect pitch. The term "absolute pitch" is often used as a synonym for perfect pitch, but it more properly refers to the rarer ability to identify a note as, say, a fractionally flat C#. This is the aural equivalent of identifying a pot of paint as "Kentucky Green". Here, too, the term "gift" seems misplaced – such people even experience discomfort at the slight irregularities in musical pitch which go unnoticed by the majority. Interestingly, such enhanced aural awareness is more common among autistic children; it has also been noticed that deprivation of one of the senses, such as the sudden onset of blindness, is matched by a rapid increase of acuity in the remaining senses which can be directed towards, for example, greater pitch awareness.

Peripheral

An adjunct to a computer, including output devices (printer, monitor, etc.), input devices (mouse, keyboard, scanner, etc.) and combined input/output (IO) devices such as disk drives and modems.

Perspective

The effect of front-to-back depth in an audio signal. This may be inherent in the stereo image or may be artificially achieved by varying the amount of direct and indirect signal. The indirect signal may be obtained from microphones placed some distance from the source, or may be generated by a reverberation unit.

Pesante

Italian for heavily.

Phantom Powering

A method of providing a DC supply voltage (typically 48 Volts) to electrostatic (condenser) microphones, via the wires that carry the audio signal. The signal is decoupled from the DC at each end by capacitors and to that extent the signal never "sees" the DC – hence phantom. Effectively the signal forms an AC "ripple" component of the DC supply, or conversely, the AC signal can be understood to have a DC Offset.

Phase

1. Relative delay between two cyclic signals, expressed in terms of angle. 180° is a delay of half a cycle while 360° is one full cycle.

2. By extension from Phase [1], the positive or negative half cycle of an AC signal.

3. In a Balanced Line, the two legs are said to be "in phase" (hot) or "out of phase" (cold).

Phase Coherent

1. The ability of an audio processor to pass a signal without causing Phase Shift.

2. The property of a stereo signal which has the correct phase relationship between both channels.

Phase Modulation

Also known as Phase Shift. An alteration of the Phase [1] of Partial components in a signal. Virtually all signal processing devices will cause a certain amount of phase modulation: this may be regarded as a form of distortion in EQ and amplification, but equally may be used for creative effect as in Phasers, Flangers, etc. Like other forms of modulation, it can be used in synthesis.

Phaser

1. An Effects unit which uses a short delay to introduce phase differences into an audio signal. This produces a characteristic "swirling" effect.

2. Originally one of the defined MIDI Controller Change messages with a status byte value in the range 176–191 and a first data byte of 95. It is assigned to the parameter in a synthesizer which alters the depth of the effect described in Phaser [1]. More recently this message has been reassigned as one of five generalized Effects Depth messages. *See* Effects Control.

Phase Reversal

1. This will occur if the connections in one channel of a stereo signal are reversed. This is most likely to occur at the loudspeaker and will result in Cancellation, particularly in the bass.

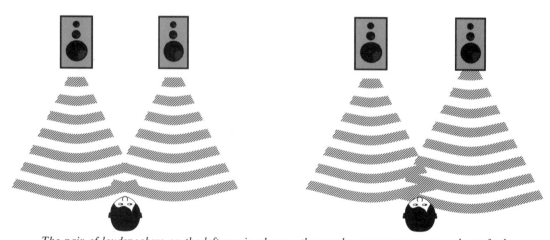

The pair of loudspeakers on the left are in phase – the speaker cones compress and rarefy the surrounding air in unison. Those on the right are out of phase, causing the air compression generated by one speaker to be cancelled by the rarefaction generated by the other.

2. A similar effect can occur in a Balanced Line if the hot and cold lines become crossed.

Phase Shift

See Phase Modulation.

Phon

A unit which takes account of the ear's non-linear response to the loudness and frequency of a sound. The phon uses a logarithmic scale based on the level of intensity of a given sound that corresponds to the dB rating of a pure tone at 1000 Hz subjectively judged to be of the same loudness. An increase of one phon is about the smallest increment in loudness that can normally be noticed. The scale practically ranges from 0 to 130, and its logarithmic nature means that a rise of 3 phons approximates to a doubling in intensity. Thus, one flute playing loudly might produce 60 phons but another joining in on the same note, and at the same volume, will only raise the level to about 63 phons.

Phono

Sometimes called RCA Jack, a type of connector consisting of a single pole with a concentric Screen [2]. They are often used for unbalanced, domestic line level (-10 dB(v)) inputs and outputs on audio equipment.

Phrasing

The division of music (usually melody) into coherent sections, broadly parallel to the phrases and sentences of language. Sometimes indicated in notation by a curved line over the notes to be grouped together. Phrasing implies, for the performer, a subtle manipulation of articulation and shaping of dynamic levels, and sometimes even minute shifts in tempo. *See also* Articulation.

Phrygian

See Mode.

Pianissimo

Italian for very soft, usually abbreviated to *pp*.

Piano

Italian for soft, usually abbreviated to *p*. The number of marks indicates the degree of quietness: *pppp* is about as soft as possible.

Pick Up

1. A transducer fitted to a steel-strung guitar. It consists of a coil or pair of coils placed under each string. The movement of the string in the magnetic field of the coil induces a small electrical signal which can then be amplified. When the strings are not of steel, a microphone-type pick up is required.

2. A transducer fitted to the tone arm of a record player, which converts the bumps in the groove into an electrical signal which can then be amplified. *See also* Cartridge.

Pilot Tone

See Line-Up Tone.

Pinchwheel

In a tape recorder, a freewheeling rubber roller which presses the magnetic tape against the Capstan, ensuring enough friction to drive the tape past the heads.

Ping Pong

1. A stereo effect generated by an autopanner or some multi-effects units, whereby a sound is made to appear in rapid alternation at the extreme right and left of the stereo field.

2. *See* Track Bouncing.

Pink Noise

A form of noise covering a wide range of frequencies, but weaker at the higher end of its spectrum than at the lower. It can be approximated by passing White Noise through a -3 dB/octave low pass filter.

Pitch

Broadly speaking, the musical equivalent (expressed in note letter names) of the technical term Frequency, which is expressed more precisely in Hertz. Pitch levels have tended to rise over the centuries, evidenced by tuning forks and organ pipes that have survived from previous ages. Thus, the note A above middle C, which is now standardized at 440 Hz, would have sounded much lower to earlier generations.

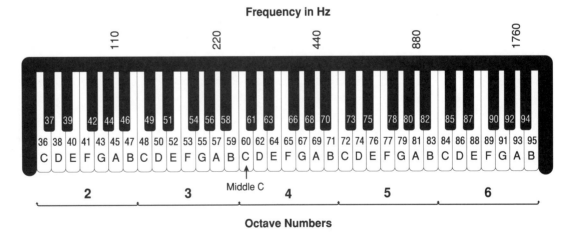

MIDI Note Numbers are shown on each key

The relationship between pitch and the more technical term "frequency".
The upper numbers show the frequency of the note A at different octaves. Octave numbers are used on synths and sequencers to allow precise identification: here, A4 = 440 Hz. Unfortunately, this benefit is considerably lessened by a lack of standardization in the numbers used for each octave.

Pitch Bend

A deviation in the pitch of a note used for expressive effect, particularly by singers, saxophonists and guitarists in jazz and popular music. Also, the MIDI Channel Voice message with status byte values in the range 224-239, which causes a device to bend the pitch of currently active notes up or down. The message requires 2 data bytes, although many manufacturers use only the second byte for operational data.

Pitch Shifter	An Effects unit which will output a version of the input signal shifted to a different pitch. This may be mixed with the original to provide a harmony line, and the term "harmonizer" is often used. The harmony will either be at a fixed and constant interval, or at varying intervals determined by each Note On message received at a MIDI In socket. This effect has only become practicable with the advent of digital technology.
Pitch to MIDI Convertor	A device for producing MIDI data from pitched sounds picked up by a microphone. It is essentially a MIDI Controller [1] for Monophonic acoustic instruments (such as the flute) and solo singers. The process of isolating and converting sounds into the unambiguous realm of MIDI is complex, and such devices are seldom able to operate without occasional glitches.
Più	Italian for "more", as in *Più forte* – more loudly.
Pixels	Derived from Picture Cells: the individual dots which form an image on a computer monitor.
Pizzicato	Italian for plucked – an instruction to players of bowed string instruments that they should pluck the strings rather than use the bow. The effect is cancelled by the instruction *Arco*.
Plagal	*See* Cadence.
Plant Room	A room which houses utility equipment, such as air-conditioning and power distribution, for a building. In studios, sometimes incorrectly used instead of Machine Room.
Plate Reverb	*See* Reverb Plate.
Platform	**1.** A stage or other elevated area in a performance hall or railway station. **2.** A generic term for a range of computers rather than specific models. For example, an application may be described as running on the "Mac Platform", while an operating system like UNIX, which can run on many different types of computer, may be described as "Multi-Platform".
Playlist	**1.** A list giving the chronological order in which a number of pieces of music or sound effects are to be played. The list will often describe the start time, duration and finish time of each item. **2.** In editing (particularly digital audio editing) a list similar to Playlist [1] which gives the order in which sections from various recording Takes will be used. It will usually include timing information which may be locked to timecode, as well as information about type and duration of crossfades, etc. Also known as EDL.
Poco	Italian for little, as in *poco crescendo* – getting slightly louder.
Poco a Poco	Italian for little by little, or gradually, as in *poco a poco accelerando* – gradually getting faster.
Point	A typographical measurement, approximately equal to $1/72$ of an inch. Used to refer to the vertical size of letters in DTP and Scorewriter programs. This text is set in 10-point Times Roman.
Polar Diagram	*See* Response Pattern.
Polyphonic	**1.** Music which simultaneously has more than one independent melodic line. **2.** The ability of a synthesizer or sampler to play more than one note at a time: not to be confused with Multi-timbral. The opposite of Monophonic. A monophonic instrument presented with polyphony will generally be programmed to select which of the simultaneous notes to play.
Polyphonic Key Pressure	A Channel Voice message with a status byte value in the range 160–175, used to implement Aftertouch on each note independently. Thus you can play a chord, pressing into the top note, and have only this note modulated, without affecting the others. Somewhat expensive to implement, so rarely seen. The message requires two data bytes, the first being the note number.
Popping	Distortion caused by over-modulation of a microphone, usually as a result of placing it too close to the sound source. It commonly occurs with the plosive sounds "b", "p" and "t".
Popular Music	Music intended for a broad range of consumption. Popular means "of the people" – it doesn't mean that everybody likes it. Popular music can be said to include folk, jazz and all kinds of light and commercial music, as well as pop music itself. However, it is often used in a narrower sense (strictly, "pop") for music which features in the singles and album charts. Although, to some extent, popular music excludes art music, there have been many examples of orchestral and operatic arrangements which have made the Crossover to the popular domain. Some forms of pop music, like folk and jazz, are heavily dependent on an aural tradition. However, commercial and chart music invariably has a composer, is notated, and indeed much money is made from its publication. Much western pop music is in $\frac{4}{4}$ time, with a strong accent on the second and fourth beats of the bar.
Port	An input or output socket on a device such as a computer, as in Parallel port or Serial port.

Portamento

1. A continuous movement in pitch from one note to another without step. Instruments with notes of fixed pitch, such as the piano, are unable to do this, but the human voice, fretless instruments (violins, etc.) and instruments fitted with slides (trombones, swanee whistles, etc.) can. It is a different effect from, and should not be confused with, *Glissando.*

2. Also called Glide. A parameter on a synthesizer which implements Portamento [1]. The parameter usually adjusts the time taken to move from one note to the next. *See also* Portamento Time.

3. One of the defined MIDI Controller Change messages with a status byte value in the range 176–191 and a first data byte of 65. It switches a synthesizer's Portamento on or off.

Portamento Time

One of the defined MIDI Controller Change messages with a status byte value in the range 176–191 and a data byte value of 5. It is assigned to the parameter in a synthesizer which determines the time taken for portamento to occur.

Portastudio

Acronym from PORTAble STUDIO. Originally a trade name used by Tascam for a four-track cassette recorder combined with a mixing desk in the same unit, but now used generically to refer to any device of this type irrespective of manufacturer. Currently, up to eight tracks can be recorded on standard cassettes (although not necessarily at the standard 1⅞ ips), and up to twelve on proprietary cassettes.

Post-

1. After. Generally, the situation after some process has been carried out: post-fader, post- equalisation, etc. A point at which a signal may be monitored.

2. Binding post. A connector, consisting of a threaded shaft and nut, for terminating bare wire. Used on loudspeakers, etc.

Post-Production

1. In audio, a term used for tasks which have to be done after the Master Tape has been made. These include further editing, grouping of individual tracks into an album and, for CD, the addition of Subcode.

2. The addition of a soundtrack (dialogue, music or sound effects) to an edited film or video.

PostScript

A computer language (specifically a page description language) designed for high quality printing of text and graphics. Encountered in DTP, Scorewriter and various graphics programs. These generate PostScript files automatically from the user's input, either for interpretation by a printer or for embedding in some longer document (*see* EPS). However, it is possible to program directly in the language to produce special graphic and typographic effects, since it is based on simple ASCII files. An important aspect of PostScript is that the quality of printed output depends only on the Resolution of the printer used: the better the device, the more impressive the result.

Post Sync

A recording of music, effects or dialogue (e.g. a translation of a foreign-language film) made to synchronize with an existing film or video tape. *See also* Lip Sync.

Pot

See Potentiometer.

Potential Difference

The difference in electrical potential between two points in a circuit. It is measured in Volts and this leads people to substitute the word voltage, which is strictly incorrect. *See also* Electricity.

Potentiometer

A type of variable resistor. In audio, the term is generally confined to rotary controls. Some potentiometers have the resistive element arranged in a straight line and are known as linear potentiometers (or "sliders"). These are commonly encountered as the main level controls of a mixing desk, where they are known as Faders.

Power

1. The rate of doing work, measured in Joules per second. Its SI Unit is the Watt.

2. A source of energy (power supply).

Power Amplifier

An amplifier used to drive an electromechanical load such as a loudspeaker, and thus found in hi-fi and monitoring systems. Due to the requirement to deliver power into the load it will have its own power supply, and in fact can be considered to be an audio-controlled power supply.

Power User

A self-congratulatory term used by, and less frequently of, a person who can use a computer for more than ten minutes without looking at the manual. Power Users tend to scorn useful implements such as a mouse, preferring instead to memorize hundreds of keyboard shortcuts and arcane commands. The computer equivalent of a train spotter and therefore best avoided. *See also* WIMP.

pp

See Pianissimo.

PPM

Abbreviation of Peak Programme Meter. It indicates peak levels present in an audio signal, usually by means of an LED display. PPMs have a very fast response to changing levels, and thus may allow the top LED reached by a peak to stay illuminated for a while, as a reference for the user.

PPQ

Abbreviation of Pulses Per Quarter-note. An indication of the timing resolution of a sequencer – effectively, the number of "time slices" into which a quarter-note (crotchet) is divided. The greater the number, the higher the resolution of the sequencer.

PQ Codes

In digital audio systems, particularly CD, a name for the eight Subcode bits that are interleaved with the audio data. So called because the bits are identified by the letters PQRSTUVW.

Pre-

Before. Generally, the situation before some process is carried out: pre-fader, pre-equalisation, etc. A point at which a signal may be monitored.

Pre-Delay

In reverberation, the delay before any reflected sound is heard. This is the main aural clue to the size of the space in which a sound occurs. When a person claps their hands in a centre of a room, the sound waves will travel away at approximately 334 metres per second. If there is a pre-delay of 100 milliseconds before the reflected sound is heard, the walls of the room must be approximately 15 metres away – i.e. the sound has taken 50 milliseconds to travel out, hit a wall, and 50 milliseconds to travel back to the listener, a total distance of approximately 30 metres.

Pre-Fade

A fade-out starting at a predetermined time, so that it finishes precisely at the end of a recording.

Pre-Fade Listen

A monitoring point placed before a fader on a mixing desk, so that the signal can be monitored before being faded up for recording or broadcasting. *See also* Solo.

Pre-Production

A term used for those tasks which can, or need to, be done before the actual recording is made. A pre-production suite may be provided for the programming of synths and preparation of samples and sequences for use during the session.

Presence

The enhancement of frequencies in the upper mid-band of a sound, around 2-8 kHz. A facility found on some Equalizers and domestic hi-fi amplifiers, to give the effect of bringing the affected range forward in the sound field. Over-use of presence can add a harsh, metallic quality.

Preset

On Hammond organs, synthesizers, etc, a single control (often a push button) for recalling a complex combination of timbres and other parameter settings. Often used as a synonym for Patch.

Pressure Gradient Microphone

A directional microphone with a diaphragm which is exposed to sound on both faces. Cardioid, Figure-of-eight and Hypercardioid are examples of this type.

Pressure Sensitivity

See Aftertouch, Channel Key Pressure, Polyphonic Key Pressure.

Prestissimo

Italian for as fast as possible: 200+ MM.

Presto

Italian for very fast: 168–200 MM.

Printed Circuit Board

A means of supporting electronic components and allowing connections between them, by means of an insulating board (typically fibre glass) laminated with metal foil. The foil is etched in a photochemical process to leave areas called "tracks" which run between areas called "pads" or "lands". These are drilled through so that component leads can be soldered into place. The board may have foil on both sides to increase the density of tracks and make the job of layout somewhat easier as connections can then be made on either side. Multilayer boards may have as many as sixteen foil laminations bonded into a single board.

Printer

An output device used by a computer to render text and graphics onto paper, film, etc. A number of technologies are available. Impact printers, such as Dot Matrix, use a print head consisting of individually controlled pins (typically 9 or 24) that can be fired through an inked ribbon to form a fairly low resolution image on the paper. Other technologies spray ink (Ink Jet) or explode tiny ink bubbles (Bubble Jet) onto the paper and can achieve higher resolution and colour operation. Laser printers use a modulated laser beam to generate an electrostatic image on a revolving drum. As it rotates, dry toner powder is attracted to the charged areas and paper passing over the drum picks up the particles of toner. Heat then fuses this toner to the paper to form a permanent image. Although capable of high quality, the resolution partly depends on the size of the toner particles, and these cannot be made small enough to make the individual dots of the image totally unnoticeable. Typically, laser printers offer 300-600 dpi (dots per inch) resolution. Imagesetters are used mainly in professional printing and graphics work. These also use a laser, but it is fired directly onto photosensitive paper ("bromide") which can accurately reproduce a resolution of 1200-2400 dpi. This is then developed by a similar chemical process to that used in photography.

Because visual quality is so important in printing, manufacturers make ambitious (and sometimes misleading) claims about the resolution of their equipment. A 24-pin dot matrix printer may technically produce 360dpi, but the splattering of ink generated by the impact process will not give the quality of a 300dpi laser printer. Equally, a 1200dpi "high resolution" laser will not give the same results as a 1200dpi imagesetter, since the fusing of toner particles similarly causes a small degree of spread in the image on paper.

Print Through

In analogue tape recording, a phenomenon whereby a strong magnetic pattern in one layer of a spooled tape imposes a residual magnetic pattern on the layer next to it. The effect is to make a lower amplitude copy of the sound from one layer to the next. This is the cause of so called tape pre-echo or ghosting. For this reason it is best to store spooled tape "end out" i.e. played through onto the right hand tape spool with the end of the music on the outside of the tape. Thus, any loud event in one layer will always print through onto a later section of the tape, where it will often be less offensive. Some bulk tape copying systems actually exploit print through by passing the copy tape, in contact with a strongly recorded master tape, through a pair of rollers without the need for any electrical signal transfer.

Process Music   *See* Minimalism.

Processor   **1.** A device which alters a signal in some predetermined manner.

2. The part of a computer that alters data according to a rule or function. *See also* Microprocessor.

Pro-Digi   A family of formats for recording digital audio data onto open-reel tape. Developed by Mitsubishi but also used by other manufacturers. Its rival is Sony's DASH family.

Producer   The person responsible for the aesthetic or non-technical aspects of a recording or broadcast, working in conjunction with the sound engineer. In recording, the producer will often supervise the session, planning and advising on editing decisions to ensure that both artistes and record company are happy with the end result. *See also* Executive Producer.

Production Master   *See* Master Tape.

Profanity Delay   *See* Delay.

Program   A set of instructions that can be loaded into a computer. *See* Software.

Program Change   A Channel Voice message with status byte values in the range 192–207, which causes a device to change to a different patch or configuration. The message requires 1 data byte. *See also* Patch Mapping.

Programme   In audio, the signal which is being processed or recorded.

Programme Chain   The sequence of components or equipment which are used to process a signal. It usually starts with a microphone and ends with loudspeakers, incorporating a mixing desk, tape recorder, etc.

Programmer   **1.** A person who writes software for computers.

2. A person who creates new sounds, etc., on synthesizers and samplers, or who operates MIDI devices in a studio. The rôle of the programmer emerged during the '70s and '80s, and came to rival the engineer's in importance.

PROM   Acronym from Programmable Read-Only Memory. A form of memory that can be programmed once only, usually by the manufacturer, and not erased by the user. *See also* EPROM, ROM, WORM.

Propagation   Movement through a material: e.g. the movement of sound waves through air.

Propagation Delay   The time taken for a signal to pass through a system. *See also* MIDI Delay [2].

Proximity Effect   The increased sensitivity to low frequency Partials in a Pressure Gradient Microphone placed close to the source of a sound. Sometimes called "bass tip-up".

PRS   Abbreviation of Performing Rights Society: *see* Copyright.

PSU   Abbreviation of Power Supply Unit. A device, usually including a Transformer and Rectifier, for converting an AC mains electrical supply to the low-voltage DC needed by many items of electronic equipment. It may be built into the equipment, or it may be housed separately. Low current PSUs small enough to be incorporated into a mains plug are often called mains adaptors.

Psychoacoustic   Pertaining to the way in which audio information is processed by the brain. Humans have developed a number of techniques for processing sound. These techniques allow information to be recovered even when obscured by considerable noise (the Cocktail Party Effect), and allow the brain to disregard unwanted information. *See also* Auditory Masking.

Public Domain   Things "in the public domain" can generally be freely used by the public, either because any copyright has expired or has been relinquished by its owner. The latter is common with computer software, and is done to encourage wider access or to fulfil some personal political agenda. The author will usually still place certain restrictions on its use, to prevent alteration or distribution for financial gain. Note that Shareware is not in the public domain. *See also* Copyright.

Pulse Code Modulation   *See* PCM.

Pulse Wave   A family of geometrical waveforms typically generated by an oscillator. They are all rectangular in shape but can have any possible Mark/Space Ratio. A square wave is a special case of pulse wave with a mark/space ratio of 1:2. The harmonic partials present in a pulse wave are reflected by the right hand number of its mark/space ratio, with the harmonics which are multiples of this number being absent. Thus, a pulse wave with a mark/space ratio of 1:3 will not have the 3rd, 6th or 9th harmonics of the fundamental. The amplitude of other harmonics will depend upon their proximity to these absent harmonics. When the ratio becomes very large (i.e. the pulse becomes very narrow), the timbre becomes correspondingly brighter like the thin and nasal sound of an oboe or harpsichord. *See also* Ramp Wave, Sine Wave, Square Wave, Triangle Wave.

Punch In / Out   *See* Drop In, Drop Out [3].

Punk Rock   A form of popular music. Originally the term was used in America to refer to certain types of "garage band" (do-it-yourself guitar groups which were often obliged to rehearse in places where automobiles are normally parked) during the early and mid '60s. The more common usage refers to a movement (some would say a bowel movement) in British rock during the early to mid '70s. It is normally described as having started with the "punk festival" at Oxford Street's "100 Club", but this simply marks the beginning of its exploitation, most notably by Malcolm McLaren. British punk rock owes its origins to a combination of influences ranging from Velvet Underground to the heavy metal of Led Zeppelin. Musically, it is simply good old rock and roll played at very high speed and without any great care. Many of the bands were proud of their musical inability and this is typical of the behaviour which has earned the style its "iconoclastic" label. Other cultural features include clothing with a surfeit of zips and straps, near symbolic use of the safety pin and the application of epoxy adhesive as a hair treatment. Unfortunately, being a generally white phenomenon and having a tangential relationship to the skinhead "Oi" music, what was otherwise a fun time for all was tainted by Neo-Nazism. It died in labour in the '80s, having given birth to "New Wave" and "Goth Rock".

PZM

Abbreviation of Pressure Zone Microphone. A microphone designed to be mounted very close (less than 3mm) to a flat surface (often a plate that is joined to the microphone housing). The complete unit can be placed on the floor, or taped to the wall, of a studio. The microphone's proximity to a reflecting surface minimizes the delay between direct and reflected sound paths which can cause Cancellation. First developed by Crown, but much copied. Sometimes called Boundary Effect microphone.

Qawaali

A form of religious music in the Islamic tradition, associated with Sufi communities in India, Pakistan, Britain and elsewhere. It has features derived from the systems of Raga and Tala common in Indian music (Indian in the sense that the systems predate the political divisions of 1947), and can be considered as a popular form of traditional Indian art music. Qawaali is encountered at the singing competitions known as "ghazals", and is based on mystical and devotional texts which may be in Hindi, Pharsi, Punjabi, Urdu or other of the regional languages of the subcontinent. The texts are often articulated in alternating patterns of slow, free time singing and fast, highly rhythmic singing. It also features group singing and hand clapping. The overall effect is of exciting and uplifting emotion and, despite obvious cultural and technical differences, may be likened to Gospel music in expression, if not content.

Q-Factor

See Resonance.

Quad

1. Quadraphony. An attempt to model a live acoustic using four audio channels to give the effect of sound arriving from different parts of the listening environment. Various systems have been tried, but none has been particularly successful.

2. Long-established company specializing in domestic Hi-Fi products, which are none the less frequently encountered in studios. *See also* Electrostatic Loudspeaker.

Quality

1. A parameter in a system: e.g. loudness is one quality in an audio signal, stereo position is another.

2. The degree to which a sound is accurately reproduced by a recording or broadcast medium. While it is technically possible to measure such things as frequency response or the amount of distortion, there is not always a direct correlation between the best technical specification and the best perceived sound quality. So, in the end, subjective judgments tend to be used.

Quantization

1. In sequencers, the facility to move a recorded event from one time slot to another nearby so that it will be in the most rhythmically useful position. Essentially, it is an automatic correction feature for events which aren't quite in the right place. In the upper diagram, four notes are shown on a typical sequencer display just as they were recorded. The lower diagram shows the effect of quantization to crotchets (quarter-notes): the first three notes have been nudged to their correct positions, but the fourth was played so early that it has been shifted to the 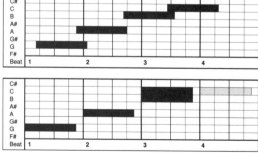 wrong beat entirely (its desired position is shown in grey). Most sequencers offer a range of quantization facilities, both for note starts and note lengths, and allow the user to specify variable degrees of correction. In fact, sequencers quantize events all the time, in the sense that they all have a finite resolution determined by their PPQ figure – in practice, this is large enough for few people to notice.

2. In digital systems, the PCM process whereby PAM samples are assigned a numeric value. It is this process which gives the word digital to the concept. *See also* Quantization Error.

Quantization Error	In digital audio, the number of bits a system uses to describe numbers (the Word size) defines the resolution of the system, and thus the maximum accuracy with which PAM samples can be described in PCM. With four bits it is possible to divide the amplitude of a signal into sixteen quantization steps. Thus, a signal whose peak amplitude was 2 volts would be described in steps 125 mV apart. Signal levels which fall between these steps are not recorded (the quantization error), and the signal is therefore distorted by the quantization process. This error manifests itself as noise for large signals and as harmonic distortion at signal levels close to zero. In practice, the resolution determines the Signal-to-Noise Ratio and, by extension, the dynamic range of the encoded signal. In general, the greater the number of bits used to encode the signal, the wider the dynamic range. As a rough guide, the dynamic range increases by 6 dB for each bit added to the word size. Thus eight bits gives a dynamic range of 48 dB, twelve bits gives 72 dB and sixteen bits gives 96 dB. *See also* Oversampling.
Quarter Frame	*See* MIDI Time Code Quarter Frame.
Quarter Track	A system of recording four channels in separate tracks on magnetic tape. For stereo use, tracks 1 and 3 are recorded in one direction, and tracks 2 and 4 are recorded in the other by reversing the tape spools. Similar machines are used for four channel multitrack, with each track able to record or replay independently.
Quaver	Note (♪) or rest (𝄾) whose duration is an eighth of a semibreve. Also known as eighth-note.
Quintuplet	A modification to the basic duration type of a note (crotchet, quaver etc.), whereby five notes are played in the time otherwise occupied by four of that type. *See also* Tuplet.
QWERTY	Acronym formed from the first six letters of the top letter row on most typewriter and computer keyboards. A term used to refer to the standard overall layout of keys. *See also* Keyboard [2].

R & B	*See* Rhythm and Blues.
Rack Module	*See* Tone Module.
Rack Mount	Standardized type of equipment case which can be mounted in a frame, or rack, with a width of about 19". The height of the front panel of such a case is determined by standard units (U) of 44 mm. Thus a 2U case has a front panel height of 88 mm. Many items of music technology, from synthesizer modules to effects units and synchronizers, are built in cases of this type.
Radio Frequency	Electromagnetic signals from 100 kHz to 30,000 MHz. The constant frequency of the Carrier [1] wave (the frequency which you tune into) falls within this range. This is then Modulated [3] by the audio (or other) signal, according to some scheme such as AM or FM. *See also* VHF.
Radio Microphone	A microphone with a built in radio transmitter, used instead of a cable connection to give a performer increased mobility. A receiver system picks up the transmitted signal for distribution to a PA, etc.
Raga	Also variously Raag, Rhag, etc. Strictly refers to the system of pitch groups (broadly equivalent to western scales and modes) common in Indian art music, but by extension the term also applies to a particular piece of music in a given scale or mode. Such pieces are largely instrumental improvisations around a basic formal structure, typified by a broad and slow free time introduction followed without break by much more rhythmic and faster playing. Sometimes these styles are alternated throughout a piece. The improvisations are not just melodic but also use Tala (the metrical or rhythmic cycles which are the temporal equivalents of raga).
Ragtime	A form of popular music (and the first to be exported internationally) that originated in America in the 1890s and reached its heyday in the period 1910-20. Its name and its syncopated melodies derived from the "ragged" rhythm of the banjo music, popular in 19th century "minstrel shows". This was superimposed upon the duple time, firm bass and clear-cut western harmonies of the equally popular march and its related dance music, such as the military two-step. From these came, too, the standard form of repeating and mildly contrasting "strains", usually of 16 bars in length. While best known as piano music, not least due to its refinement in the hands of Scott Joplin, there were also ragtime songs and rags for bands. The latter, particularly, became one of the sources of music used by the early jazz players in New Orleans. Although now clearly seen to be heavily dependent on existing techniques in European music, the rhythmic novelty of ragtime also inspired composers of art music, such as Debussy and Stravinsky.
Rallentando	Italian for becoming gradually slower.
RAM	Acronym from Random Access Memory. Essentially, any form of memory which allows you to write

new data into it at random locations, unlike ROM which can only be read. Generally used specifically to refer to semiconductor memory (chips).

Ramp Wave

A geometrical waveform, typically generated by an oscillator. It resembles a series of ramps placed nose to tail. It has all possible Harmonic partials (odd and even numbered) giving a powerful and brassy timbre. The amplitude of each harmonic is the reciprocal of its number in the series (e.g. the 5th harmonic is ⅕ the amplitude of the first). Ramp Waves sound the same whether they rise left to right (Ramp Up) or fall left to right (Ramp Down). Sometimes called Sawtooth Waves. *See also* Pulse Wave, Sine Wave, Square Wave, Triangle Wave.

Random Noise Generator

A device for generating an audio signal of random frequencies. The inherent logic of the digital domain is ill-suited to any form of randomness, although computers can generate patterns so complex that any underlying order is not apparent. The simpler method of reversing the current flow through certain types of diode until they "scream" can produce perfectly acceptable results. Noise generators can be useful for synthesizing sounds with many Enharmonic partials, such as wind, rain, snare drum notes, etc. *See also* Pink Noise, White Noise.

Rap

A form of popular music which developed among Afro-Americans during the late '70s. Essentially, rhyming speech declaimed over an elaborated disco beat. The lyrics are often boastful, scatological or obscene, and always forceful. It has its origins in, and incorporates, the verbal sparring matches known as "Signifying", "The Dozens" or "Toasts", which were a common means of expression among Afro-American youth. Muhammad Ali's poetic baiting of his opponents is a typical example of this. Rap developed amongst DJs improvising chants over the instrumental passages of existing records, often cutting between copies of the same record on two turntables in order to prolong the instrumental passages. This led to the development of Scratching, an important feature of the genre. In time it became the practice to put an instrumental version of a song on the B side of a 12" single. Gradually Rap became a musical form in its own right and many DJs became performers with their own (typically electronic) backing group. By this time, a double deck turntable had become an integral part of the instrumental line-up. Artists such as Afrika Bambaataa and Grandmaster Flash typify the early Rap style. The appearance of white rappers indicates the commercial appeal of the form. *See also* Hip Hop.

RCCB

Abbreviation of Residual Current Circuit Breaker. *See* ELCB.

RDAT

Acronym from Rotary-head Digital Audio Tape. A standard for digital audio recording, which employs a rotating head mechanism similar to that of video recorders. Two channels of 16-bit digital audio information, plus Subcode and track information, can be recorded onto a tape approximately 3 mm wide, travelling at a very low speed of about 50 cm per minute. The tape is housed in a case similar to a video cassette, though much smaller. RDAT machines offer three sampling rates: 32 kHz, 44.1 kHz and 48 kHz. Maximum continuous record time for a cassette is 2 hours at standard play and four hours at long play (with reduced quality). The diagram shows how the tape is wrapped around a rotating

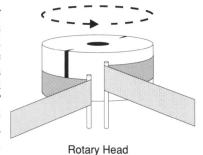

Rotary Head

head assembly. The head is represented by the vertical black line on the drum. This arrangement, and the skewing of the head relative to the tape, allows the head to write a large number of short "tracklets" of digital audio data at an angle across the tape, rather like a stack of fallen dominoes.

Reactance

A property of inductors and capacitors which presents a frequency-dependent impedance to AC.

Real Time

1. The ability of a computer or other device to carry out a process without noticeable delay, such as real time editing on a sequencer – making changes to the music as it is playing.

2. In a sequencer, the ability to record MIDI messages as they are played on a keyboard or other controller, i.e. to behave like a tape recorder. This is generally the method preferred by trained musicians. *See also* Step Time.

3. Events which have to occur at particular times to ensure synchronization between devices, as opposed to those (non-real-time) events which can occur at any time.

4. *See* Universal System Exclusive.

Real Time MTC Cueing

Messages similar to Set Up which contain information such as cue points, punch in/out points, event start and stop points and event names. Unlike conventional MTC set up messages which include details of the absolute times (in the future) at which events should occur, the messages are to be acted on when received. A family of messages of the Universal System Exclusive Real Time type, with a Sub ID#1 of 5, and a Sub ID#2 which defines the set up type.

Recapitulation

In a musical structure, the final return to themes from the main opening section (usually modified to occur in the home key). *See* Sonata Form.

Reception Mode	A Channel Voice message (specifically a Controller Change message) with data byte values in the range 124–127, which determines how a device will respond to future messages. There are four reception modes:

Mode 1	Omni On/Poly	Receive all channel voice messages irrespective of channel and play polyphonically (formerly called Omni Mode).
Mode 2	Omni on/Mono	Receive all channel voice messages irrespective of channel and play monophonically.
Mode 3	Omni Off/Poly	Receive only channel voice messages on the selected channel and play polyphonically (formerly called Poly Mode).
Mode 4	Omni Off/Mono	Receive only channel voice messages on the selected channel and play monophonically (formerly called Mono Mode).

Multi-timbral sequencing generally requires the use of Mode 3, or some proprietory adaptation of it, called Multi Mode on many synths The four modes are made up from a combination of the Channel Mode messages: either monophonic on (data 126) or polyphonic on (data 127), plus omni mode on (data 125) or omni mode off (data 124). Changing reception modes has the side effect of cancelling any notes which are currently sounding.

Reconstruction Filter In a digital audio system, a low pass filter, placed on the output of the DAC, which has the function of reconstructing or demodulating PAM samples to produce an analogue signal with none of the discrete steps of the sample data. Its cut-off frequency is set to slightly less than half the sampling rate, in accordance with the Nyquist Sampling Theorem.

Record Head In a tape recorder, an electromagnetic device for imposing magnetic patterns onto tape, according to the amplitude of a voltage representing the sound being recorded. In some systems, the same head is also used for replay of the tape.

Rectification The process of converting AC to DC using diodes. Various networks of diodes allow different degrees of rectification: half wave (where only one Phase [2] is rectified) or full wave (where both phases are rectified).

Reduction **1.** The mixing of a number of tracks of a multi-track recording to produce a mono or stereo master; also called mix down.

2. In music, an arrangement of a Full Score for performance by a smaller group of instruments or, more usually, by just piano. *See also* Vocal Score.

Reeds A term used in jazz and popular music to refer generally to the woodwind section, and specifically to saxophones and clarinets. Most woodwind instruments generate sounds by use of a single or double reed. The flute is an exception, but was often played (when needed at all) by a saxophonist – hence the all-embracing term. *See also* Horns, Rhythm Section.

Reflection A return of energy which results when a wave strikes a medium through which it cannot pass: e.g. a sound wave hitting a wall. *See also* Early Reflections.

Refrain A synonym for the chorus in a song: *see* Song.

Refresh Rate The number of times per second that the complete screen image is redrawn on a computer monitor or TV. The figure, also known as the vertical scan rate, is expressed in Hz. This continual redrawing is needed because the phosphor dots on the screen glow only for a fraction of a second when struck by the scanning beam of electrons. Refresh rates of below 60 Hz are likely to cause Beating with the AC mains supply, resulting in an uncomfortable flicker that can even be injurious to health.

Regeneration *See* Feedback [1].

Reggae A form of popular music which appeared in Jamaica during the mid to late '60s. The derivation of the word is not clear and is variously given as: a corruption of "regular" (a reference to its slow and hypnotic bass) or the related patois words "regge-regge" (talking back or impertinence) and "streggae" (rude) – both references to the "rude-boy" street gangs of the time. It probably evolved out of the local calypso style and the influence of American R & B radio broadcasts. An interim stage in its development was "ska", which featured strong offbeat guitar, organ or piano chords. As ska slowed down and became heavier in sound, it became known as "rock steady". The exaggeration of these tendencies and emphasis on a powerful bass resulted in the reggae style we now know, as well as variants such as "dub" – a form of poetry recited to a reggae backing. Reggae's best known (and perhaps greatest) exponent was Bob Marley and his band, the Wailers. Marley's death from cancer in 1981 ended the period of mass popularity, although it continues to develop in Jamaica and Britain, where the music is inextricably linked to the Rastafarian religion.

Register A specific part of the pitch range of an instrument, voice or melody: e.g. a cello in its "tenor" register.

Registration The choice of Stops (i.e. tone colours) in organ music.

Relay

An electro-mechanical device; essentially a solenoid-operated switch. Largely superseded by the transistor, except in certain high-current applications. One possible such use is in amplifiers, where a relay may break the connection to the loudspeakers before the usual thump, caused by turning off the power, has time to do any damage.

Relay Station

In broadcasting, a remote site with equipment to receive a signal, either through a telephone land line (sometimes called a "music line") or a microwave link, and re-transmit it for improved local reception.

Release Time

1. Of a Limiter or Compressor, etc., the time the device takes to respond fully to a change in the signal which takes it below the threshold.

2. Of an Envelope Generator, the time taken for the envelope to reach its minimum level from (usually) the sustain level, once the note is released or the gate signal removed. If the EG is being used to control an amplifier (VCA or DCA), it is the time taken to reach minimum loudness. In synthesis, the release is (usually) the end of the sound. It should be remembered that musicians are apt to refer to the end of a sound as decay.

Release Velocity

See Velocity.

Remix

See Mix.

Remote Keyboard

A keyboard which can be slung around the neck, like a guitar. It will transmit the performance through a MIDI cable or (occasionally) via a radio / infra-red transmitter matched to an appropriate receiver and MIDI module. Essentially, a type of MIDI Controller [1].

Renaissance

See Musical Periods.

Repertoire

1. Music which a soloist or group already knows – i.e. it does not require extensive rehearsal in order to make it ready for performance.

2. The catalogue of songs or performers that a publishing or record company has signed to it. *See also* A & R.

Replay Head

In a tape recorder, an electromagnetic device for converting magnetic patterns recorded on tape into a voltage whose amplitude is proportional to the pattern. On some systems, the replay head is also used as a record head, i.e. the replay head is driven rather than "listened to", and it may also be used as a Sync Head. The replay head is sometimes called a Repro Head.

Reprise

A repeat of a section of music, generally after intervening material rather than immediately.

Repro

See Replay Head.

Reset

See System Reset.

Reset All Controllers

A Channel Voice message which instructs a MIDI device to set all controllers to their inactive condition, effectively doing for controllers what an All Notes Off message does for notes. The message is actually a type of Controller Change message with a data byte value of 121. *See also* All Notes Off, All Sounds Off.

Resistance

The property of opposition to the flow of current, associated with the conversion of electrical energy into heat. Measured in Ohms (Ω). *See also* Impedance, Resistor.

Resistor

An electronic component which has constant resistance to a current, regardless of frequency. In principle, it converts electrical energy into heat – in fact any length of wire will do this to a greater or lesser degree. Potentiometers and Faders are variable resistors. A hair dryer can be regarded as an air-cooled resistor.

Resolution

In general, a guide to the limit of quality that might be expected from a system, expressed in terms of the maximum number of units it processes in a given time or space. On a scanner or printer, the units are usually Dots Per Inch, typically 300 dpi for a laser printer. On a computer monitor, the units are given in Pixels across the viewing area, typically 800 x 600 for a 14" screen. In digital audio, the time-based resolution is given by the Sampling Rate, and the amplitude-based resolution by the Word Length: 44.1 kHz and 16-bit, respectively, for CD. In MIDI, tempo resolution is indicated in pulses per quarter note, typically 192 or 384 PPQ, while the resolution of controllers such as Pitch Bend may be determined by the manufacturer or adjusted by the user. In general, the higher the number quoted for resolution, the better the quality. However, other factors must often be taken into account: the size of the dots (Dot Pitch) on a monitor, for example, play almost as important a part in determining picture quality as the claimed resolution.

Resonance

Strictly, the property of a mechanical or electrical system to support oscillation at a particular frequency, given suitable excitation. This frequency is called the Natural Frequency, and is determined by the mechanical or electronic design. In musical terminology, resonance is often regarded as the principle behind the natural amplification of almost all acoustic instruments: the reed of an oboe or the vibrating string of a violin would be near inaudible without the resonance of the semi-enclosed air space inside the tube or body of the instrument. The fact that this space cannot be altered by string players, and can be adjusted only imperfectly through the preset keys and valves of a wind instrument, leads to a pleasing variety of tone as different pitches move closer to or away from natural resonances. However, it also poses problems for players and instrument technologists, since notes right on the natural frequency, or its Harmonics, are more often disturbing than delightful. *See also* Wolf Notes.

Resonance is a property that can also be used to create a peak in gain around the Cut-Off frequency in a Filter, as shown right. This peak is measured by a unit simply termed Q. A high Q-factor in a filter can cause the whole circuit to oscillate at the Cut-Off frequency – an effect exploited in the tuning circuits of radio receivers. If the filter is a band-reject type (i.e. it removes a designated range of frequencies) the effect is to narrow the focus of rejection. This is ideal for taking out a specific frequency, such as 50 Hz mains hum. Filter resonance is a parameter which may be found in synthesizers and samplers for enhancing particular frequency bands.

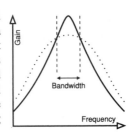

Response Pattern

The frequency/amplitude response of a microphone, loudspeaker or electromagnetic transmitters and receivers such as satellite dishes, radio and TV aerials. The response pattern relates frequency response to direction. A chart of such a response is called a polar diagram.

Retrofit

The process of upgrading a piece of equipment by fitting new electronics or firmware subsequent to purchase: this may be just a ROM, but is often a complete circuit board. A typical example of a retrofit would be to add MIDI to an old analogue synthesizer.

Retrograde Motion

The transformation of a musical idea so that it essentially appears backwards (last note first, etc). An important technique in Serialism and occasionally found in fugal music.

Return

A signal input to a piece of equipment, such as a mixing desk. Often implemented as a send / return pair on an Insert Point.

Reverberation

A complex of many reflected sounds occurring in an enclosed space such as a building or cave. The effect is often confused with echo which, strictly, is a clearly separate repeat of a sound rather than just its prolongation by reverberation. Any place where a sound can occur is likely to generate some reverberation, but the effect is most noticeable in very large buildings with many hard reflective surfaces at complex angles to one another, such as churches. Most people are able to associate particular lengths of reverberation with rooms of varying sizes. Thus, the degree of reverberation on a recording is important in suggesting the characteristics of the recording venue to a listener. Devices for artificially creating reverberation (sometimes called "room simulation") have been available for some time. Initially based on electromechanical means, such as reverb springs or reverb plates, these are now usually digital devices. Several distinct characteristics are present in a reverberative sound: *see* Pre-Delay, Early Reflections, HF Damping, Decay.

Reverberation Time

Also call Rt60. In a reverberant environment, this is the time a sound event will take to decrease in amplitude by 60 dB(SPL). In general, bigger spaces will have longer Rt60 times than smaller spaces, although there are other factors to consider, such as the damping effect of furniture, curtains or people.

Reverb Plate

A sheet of metal which is used to produce reverberations. One transducer causes it to vibrate and the reflected wave motions are picked up by other transducers.

Reverb Spring

A spring which is used to produce reverberations. One transducer causes it to vibrate and the reflected wave motions are picked up by other transducers.

RF

See Radio Frequency.

Rhythm

The time-dependent, rather than pitch-dependent, aspects of music. *See also* Accent, Beat[1], Time Signature.

Rhythm & Blues

A form of popular music created by Afro-American musicians during the '40s. As the name suggests it is related to Blues, but can be seen as a developmental strand in jazz. It emerged at a time when the Big Bands of the swing era were reducing in size, leading to a focus on the vocalist as central performer, set against a more powerful rhythm section. This reduction in numbers allowed bands to take advantage of smaller and more numerous venues. The vocalist was almost invariably a guitarist, and the emergence of R & B coincides with the development of the electric guitar. This new, amplified instrument allowed the guitarist to stand apart from the rhythm section, and adopt a more soloistic style. The style is best exemplified by musicians such as Muddy Waters, B. B. King and Chuck Berry.

Rhythm Machine

See Drum Machine.

Rhythm Section

In jazz and popular music, the group of instruments, including bass, piano (or keyboards), drums and guitar, which provide a rhythmic (and harmonic) backing. *See also* Horns, Reeds.

RIAA

Abbreviation of Recording Industries Association of America. An industry body set up to define standards and practice in the recording industry. In particular, its internationally accepted standard for the recording characteristic (involving emphasis and de-emphasis) for vinyl records.

Ribbon Microphone

A Pressure Gradient Microphone which uses a corrugated strip of aluminium instead of a Moving Coil.

Riff	A short and constantly repeating musical pattern. Used in popular music in preference to the art music term Ostinato, it probably derives from "refrain". A feature of R & B and other guitar-based rock. The bass line of a 12-bar blues often comprises a one-bar riff which is repeated and transposed as necessary.
Rifle Microphone	*See* Gun Microphone.
Ringing	The tendency of a device such as an amplifier to break into oscillation. *See also* Resonance.
Ring Main	A looped system of mains voltage distribution with a number of feeds to serve a room or building.
Ring Modulator	An electronic device that accepts two input signals and modulates one against the other to output a complex tone made up of the sum and the difference of the input frequencies. The resulting tone is thus rich in Enharmonic partials. If already complex waveforms are fed in at high levels, this output can range from screeching sounds to white noise. However, inputting simpler sine waves can produce interesting, bell-like sounds. The ring modulator was an important tool in the early days of Electro-Acoustic music, and the ease with which it produces enharmonic partials led to its adoption in analogue subtractive synthesis, effects units and some digital synths.
RISC	Acronym from Reduced Instruction Set Computer. Essentially a microprocessor which only implements a few instruction types and is thus able to operate much more quickly than a general microprocessor as there are fewer possibilities for it to look up. The increased speed of operation is very desirable for processing digital audio and video data, and these ICs are often used in effects units, synthesizers, samplers and graphics terminals, i.e. in devices which are factory-programmed to perform a specific function, as opposed to a general purpose computer such as a basic PC. *See also* Instruction Set, CISC.
Risoluto	Italian for resolutely or boldly.
Ritardando	Italian for becoming slower.
Ritenuto	Italian for held back or delayed.
Ritmico	Italian for rhythmically.
RMS	Abbreviation of Root Mean Square. A reasonably accurate way of determining the average voltage or current in a time-varying waveform. For a simple sinewave, such as a mains electrical supply, it is $1/\sqrt{2}$ (≈ 0.7071) times the peak value.
Rock & Roll	Or Rock 'n' Roll, if you insist. One of the forms of popular music which resulted from the adoption by white musicians of Afro-American music forms such as gospel, jazz and blues. It is most directly derived from R & B songs such as "Shake, Rattle and Roll", originally released by Afro-American singer Joe Turner. This was made available to a white audience (these were still the days of segregation in some states) in Bill Haley's more famous cover version. Indeed, many of the early rock & roll hits were covers of songs previously released by Afro-American artists. Typically it is up-tempo music in $\frac{4}{4}$ time, with a harmonic pattern of 12 bars derived from blues. The most important early exponents include Elvis Presley, Buddy Holly, Little Richard and Eddie Cochrane.
Rock Music	Used very broadly to include all the styles (R & B, Rock & Roll, etc.) which white musicians derived from the Afro-American genres of gospel, jazz and blues. It is also sometimes used to draw a distinction between commercial pop music (which is considered frivolous and disposable) and other supposedly less ephemeral styles. Most rock music is in a strongly accented $\frac{4}{4}$ time.
Rockwool	A stranded or fibrous mineral material with excellent sound and thermal insulation properties, which is often used to fill partition walls in studios to assist in sound-proofing. It is made by passing steam through the molten slag that is left over from the extraction of metal from ore. Rockwool is extremely nasty to work with, as the fibres tend to break into tiny particles which can cause itching and respiratory problems if protective clothing is not worn.
ROM	Acronym from Read-Only Memory. A form of memory which allows you to read information or data from it, but not to write or save new data to it. Thus, a standard CD is a type of ROM. Generally used specifically to refer to semiconductor memory (ICs). *See also* EPROM, PROM, RAM, WORM.
Romantic	*See* Musical Periods.
Rondo Form	A musical structure in which a principal passage subsequently appears in alternation with contrasting sections (called Episodes). It can be represented by the pattern "A B A C A D ... A". Rondo (also known in French as rondeau) has its origins in the baroque period and became well established during the classical period as the finale of multi-movement works by composers such as Mozart and Haydn.
Room Simulation	*See* Reverberation.
Root	The lowest note of an uninverted chord, and therefore the note which usually gives the chord its name. For example, in a Triad (3-note chord) it is the lowest note when the chord is arranged as two thirds on top of one another: C is the root of the chord of C (C, E and G) – an arrangement known as root position. If the root is not the lowest note, the triad is said to be inverted. *See also* Inversion, Triad.
Rotational Latency	*See* Access Time.

Rough Mix

A Mix of a recording in progress, either as it occurs or (in the particular case of a stereo mix down of a multi-track recording) one made at the end of a day's work for overnight audition.

Routing

1. The process of directing a signal from one point to another.

2. The pathway a signal takes, e.g. through which busses it passes on a mixing desk.

RSI

Abbreviation of Repetitive Strain Injury. An occupational hazard for musicians, athletes, computer operators and others who make repetitive awkward movements. The individual act of stretching to a high note on a violin, or to an extended finger position on a keyboard, is unlikely to cause pain by itself. It is the repeated use of such movements which results in damage, and it may thus be some time before any problem manifests itself. Twinges of pain, and possible associated symptoms such as headaches or itching, should always be heeded and investigated as early as possible. Taking care and specialist advice over matters such as posture, hand position and seating angle can help to avoid the injury in the first place.

Rt60

See Reverberation Time.

Rubato

Italian for "robbed", as in *tempo rubato* – robbed time. In the performance of music, the (usually slight) adjustment of note position, or even tempo, for expressive effect. The term "free" is more commonly used in popular music. When the sense of pulse should be absent in an extended passage, the term *senza misura* (without a strict beat) is sometimes preferred.

Rumble

Low-frequency noise caused when vibrations from the motor of a record deck (or even external sources such as passing traffic) are mechanically transmitted to the pick-up.

Running Status

A method of thinning out the MIDI data flow by not transmitting unnecessary status bytes. Normally MIDI messages begin with a status byte and are then followed by a variable number of data bytes. A three-note chord requires nine bytes to sound (a Note On status byte and two data bytes for each note) and, similarly, nine bytes to turn the notes off: 18 bytes in total. Under running status, the system assumes that any status byte remains in effect until replaced. Thus, all data bytes following a Note On status byte will be interpreted as new notes without the need for further status messages. Therefore, in the example above, we can reduce the first nine bytes by two, through sending just one Note On message instead of three. If Note On velocities of zero are used to turn notes off, the status does not need to be changed even to stop the notes sounding. The total bytes required for the chord, using running status, is thus reduced from 18 to 13, a saving of 27%.

S

Abbreviation of Side, the "difference" component of a stereo signal: i.e. the components which come from the side of the stereo field. *See also* M, M & S.

S & S

Abbreviation of Sampling and Synthesis. A term used to describe synthesizers which combine elements of these processes to produce their sound.

Safety Master

See Master Tape.

Sample

In digital audio, one instantaneous measurement of the audio signal. As the sample value is expressed in binary there is a correlation between samples and bytes. However the precise relationship depends on a number of factors, including the resolution of the converter and the number of audio channels to be simultaneously converted. For a 16-bit mono recorder, a sample is two bytes, for 12-bit mono it is 1.5 bytes, and for 16-bit stereo it is 4 bytes, etc. The term is also more loosely used to refer to the short digital recordings made by a sampler – each actually consisting of a very large number of individual samples. All digital recording, including CD and direct-to-disk systems, is based on the principle of sampling.

Sample and Hold

A device which samples the amplitude of a signal periodically, and retains the output at this level for the duration of the "hold" period. Thus, it can turn a smooth waveform into a stepped one. In analogue synthesis, an S/H circuit is often used to extract a series of random voltages from white noise, to use as a modulation source or to produce random pitch events.

Sample Dump Standard

A part of the MIDI specification which allows the interchange of digital audio data between samplers of different manufacture, or between samplers and other equipment such as computers, via MIDI. It is a set of Universal System Exclusive messages of the Non-Real Time type with an ID number of 126, followed by various Sub ID#1 numbers to determine the message type: i.e. Ack, Cancel, General Information, Loop Points Request, Loop Points Transmission, Nak, Sample Dump Extension, Sample Dump Header, Sample Dump Packet, Sample Dump Request, Wait.

Sampler

A device for making short digital audio recordings, often of single notes from live sources. These can then be triggered by a keyboard or other MIDI device to operate like a synthesizer voice. One sample will usually suffice for several different pitches, the electronics altering the sample replay rate as needed. Since some samplers can record at least 30 seconds of music, the commercial use of samples taken from existing CDs has raised interesting problems for copyright lawyers.

Sampling

See PAM, Sample, Sampler, Sampling Rate.

Sampling Rate

The rate at which PAM samples of an analogue signal are encoded or decoded by a digital device. The higher the sampling rate during the encoding process the greater the Bandwidth of signal it is possible to record accurately. This relationship is described by the Nyquist Sampling Theorem. For audio purposes it can be summarized as follows. For one cycle of a sinewave to be digitally encoded with sufficient accuracy to allow its reconstruction at the correct frequency, it must be subjected to at least two sampling events. This is normally misleadingly paraphrased as "the bandwidth is half the sampling rate", which is only correct if anti-aliasing filters are fitted to the encoder – in which case the bandwidth will still be slightly less than half the sampling rate.

SATB

Abbreviation of Soprano, Alto, Tenor, Bass – usually indicating a choir consisting of these voices. *See* Voice [3] and separate entries.

Sawtooth Wave

See Ramp Wave.

Scale

An ascending or descending series of notes that subdivide an Octave into various (usually unequal) pitch steps. Between about 1600 and 1900 western art music was centred on just the two scale patterns (major and minor) which form the basis of Diatonic harmony, although increasing use of the Chromatic scale (all 12 semitones of the octave) helped to break down this harmonic system. Before 1600, the major and minor scales had not assumed their pre-eminent importance; other scales, known as Modes, were also in common use and many of these survived in folk music to be given a new lease of life by twentieth century musicians. Many non-western cultures employ scales with different patterns of tone and semitone, and different tunings, such as the Pelog and Slendro of Gamelan music. Even closer-pitched divisions (microtonal intervals) are also used: Middle Eastern and Indian music, in particular, have very sophisticated scale systems. Other scale types include the Pentatonic (5-note), Whole Tone (6 equal divisions), and variants of major/minor such as the 'Blues scale', all of which have found their way into modern western music. Major and minor scales can begin on any note: those starting on C comprise the following notes (the technical name for each degree of the scale is shown below): *See also* Diatonic, Gamelan, Mode, Raga.

✱ Semitone steps

Tonic Supertonic Mediant Subdominant Dominant Submediant Leading Note Tonic

The scale of C major. Major scales starting on other notes still preserve this same pattern of steps. Minor scales have their Mediant a semitone lower and may also lower the Submediant and Leading Note.

Scaling

In a synthesizer or sampler, a method of relating a parameter to a control so that the degree to which the control effects the parameter can be adjusted. For example, a pitch bend wheel might be scaled to produce a semitone bend for a given amount of movement, or it might be scaled to give a whole octave. Non-linear scaling between control and parameter will produce an output corresponding to some sort of curve: for example, moving the control through positions 1 to 4 might take the output through values 1, 4, 9 and 16. If there is a stage on the curve where the output changes radically (perhaps reverses direction) this is often called the Breakpoint. The scaling of keyboard parameters is sometimes called keyboard tracking.

Scanner

A computer input device which, essentially, is the opposite of a printer. It is used for converting a printed image into binary data for processing on a computer, thus avoiding the need to enter the information manually. Scanning produces a Bitmap graphic so, if the document contains text, optical character recognition software must then be used to turn this graphic into characters that can be manipulated in a word processor. Such OCR programs are seldom 100% successful at this task, working best if the original layout is clear and simple.

Scherzo

Italian for joke. Originally a light or humorous madrigal, but later (in the classical period) the name given to a fast movement that was used as an alternative to the minuet. *Scherzando* means playfully.

SCMS

Acronym from Serial Copy Management System (pronounced "scams" or "scums"). A system employed in RDAT and DCC machines to ensure that, while an original recording can be digitally copied, no duplicates can be made digitally from the copies themselves. This prevention of "second generation" copying is achieved by the inclusion of a copy inhibit flag in the data stream. Unfortunately for the manufacturers, it quickly proved possible to by-pass this. Within a few weeks of the appearance of SCMS, the author saw a protection-defeating unit advertised in the back of a pro-audio journal. This device is transparent to all data it receives, with the exception of the copy inhibit flag which it conveniently strips from the data stream before retransmission.

Scorewriter

A category of computer software which allows a user to input, edit, store and print notated music (often called a Music Origination System). Essentially, it is to music what a word processor is to literature. Sequencers sometimes include this facility (in a rudimentary form), and scorewriters can often "play" (in a rudimentary manner) the score like a sequencer, but each is usually optimized to its own task. So it is sensible to record and edit a piece of music on a sequencer and then export the data to a scorewriter so that its appearance in notation can be edited separately.

Scratching

A technique employed by some DJs, consisting of the rapid back and forth movement of a record turntable to cause the pickup to produce the rhythmic scratching sound that is characteristic of much Rap and Hip Hop music. This is done manually, with the turntable drive disengaged (or on a special turntable made for the purpose) to accompany a track playing on another turntable or some other source. Sometimes the turntable will be spun in the correct direction after these manœuvres, allowing the sound of the disc to continue more or less correctly. Much of the DJ's art is in keeping the scratching creatively rhythmic. Many records now feature scratching as an integral part of the recording process. With the demise of vinyl records in favour of CDs, some CD players are becoming available with facilities for scratching and other effects beloved of DJs.

Screen

1. A panel with surfaces designed to reflect or absorb sound, used to alter the acoustic behaviour of an area in a studio, or to isolate one performer from another.

2. A metallic material which is wrapped around signal wires so as to provide a low impedance path to earth for any EMI[2]. Radiated interference prefers this route to the alternative, where it crawls to earth via your signal, manifesting itself as noise on the way. Also called a Shield.

3. The visual display of a computer monitor.

Scroll

A display facility on WIMP software that allows the user to move an image horizontally or vertically in order to access parts of it otherwise out of view. Usually activated by clicking or dragging the Mouse[1] on specific areas called scroll bars. Also used more generally in the sense of "to scroll through the text" or "to scroll to page 3".

SCSI

Acronym from Small Computer Systems Interface (pronounced "scuzzy"). An agreed standard of hardware and command language, which allows fast parallel data communication between components in a computer system. Primarily used for hard disk drives and CD ROM drives, but also used for scanners, etc.

SDAT

Acronym from Stationary-head Digital Audio Tape. A bi-directional cassette tape designed for domestic digital recording. It uses a stationary head as opposed to the rotating head of RDAT. The tape speed is very low compared to professional stationary-head systems, such as DASH. The required data rate for stereo operation is achieved by distributing the 16-bit data over 20 data tracks in each direction. The sample rates are industry standard: 32 kHz or 48 kHz for recording and 44.1 kHz for replay of pre-recorded cassettes. Interestingly enough, 4-channel recording is possible at 32 KHz with 12-bit, non-linear (i.e. companding) operation. It should not be confused with DCC which, while similar to the SDAT format, does not conform to the agreed SDAT standard. *See also* RDAT.

SDS

See Sample Dump Standard.

Second

The interval between one note and another, one semitone (minor second) or two semitones (major second) above or below it.

Seek Time

See Access Time.

Segue

Pronounced "seg-way": Italian for "follows". An instruction to continue from one piece of music to another without a break. By extension, a piece of music written to fill a gap, particularly in a musical or to link scenes in a film or TV programme.

Semibreve

Note (o) or rest (—) whose duration is the longest commonly found for a single symbol. Also known as the whole note. The breve, twice the length of the semibreve, is sometimes seen in early music.

Semiconductors

A class of materials which can function as either electrical conductors or insulators, depending on the level of impurities present in their basic material. The most common semiconductor is silicon – hence "silicon chip". Silicon dioxide (sand) is actually the most common mineral on earth. The placing of impurities into semiconductor material is called "doping"; a process that has to be very finely controlled. Typical materials used to dope semiconductors include boron, arsenic, gallium and phosphorus. Semiconductors are used to make transistors, diodes and integrated circuits.

Semiquaver

Note (♬) or rest (♯) whose duration is a sixteenth of a semibreve. Also known as sixteenth-note.

Semitone

One twelfth of an octave: the smallest pitch interval normally used in western music. Two semitones form a Tone.

Sempre

Italian for "always", pronounced "sem-pray": e.g. *sempre legato* = always smoothly.

Send
A signal output from a piece of equipment such as a mixing desk. Often implemented as a send/return pair on an Insert Point.

Sensitivity
A relative measure of the ability of a device such as an amplifier or transducer to process signals of varying magnitudes. A device with high sensitivity can process very small signals, but may be distorted by large ones, whereas one with low sensitivity can process large signals without distortion, but may add noise to a small signal. *See also* Velocity Sensitivity.

Senza
Italian for "without": e.g. *senza sordini* – without mutes, *senza misura* – without a strict beat.

Separation
In a multiple microphone set-up, the extent to which any one microphone is able to reject unwanted sounds intended to be picked up by other microphones. Separation is desirable if Cancellation is to be avoided, and can be increased by careful microphone placement and exploitation of the response patterns of different types of microphone. *See also* Microphone.

Sequence
A noun for the performance data recorded on a Sequencer (also known as a "song"), and a verb meaning to record such data (e.g. "I sequenced the drum track myself").

Sequencer
A device, or a category of computer software, which allows a user to input, edit, store, play back and (sometimes) print music, these days almost invariably using MIDI messages. In practice they generally behave like multi-track tape recorders, having a number of "tracks" and "transport controls". However, they record only performance instructions – not the sounds themselves, which have to be generated by a synthesizer or sampler linked to the sequencer. Drum machines and synthesizer Workstations generally combine sequencing and sound-generating capabilities.

Serial Interface
A means of outputting computer data whereby all bits in a digital word are sent one after the other. This is generally cheaper than using a Parallel Interface, as the connectors involved need only one transmit pin and one receive pin, plus ground. However, the time taken to transmit each word is greater than for parallel data. MIDI is a serial interface.

Serialism
Originally, a form of Atonal Music which took as its basic presumption the equal importance of all 12 pitches of the equally tempered scale, as a way of avoiding the perceived limitations of hierarchical tonal music. This is done by basing composition on the idea of a tone row, in which each of the 12 semitones is used only once. The whole piece is then constructed from this row, its Inversion, and Retrograde versions of both of these: either at the original pitch or transposed. This basic notion was introduced by Schoenberg in the early '20s. The concept of serial ordering of pitches was later extended to other musical elements, such as dynamics and note durations.

Session Musician
A professional musician whose career is mainly spent playing in the recording studio rather than in live performances. Usually recognizable by their pallid complexions and large bank accounts.

Set Up
A Universal System Exclusive message of the Non-Real Time type which defines a list of events which are to be carried out at given MTC times by the receiving device. The 13-byte message is comprised of the SOX status byte; an ID number data byte of 126, indicating this is a Non-Real Time System Exclusive message for the whole system; a sub-ID#1 with a value of 1 indicating an MTC message; a sub-ID#2 with a value in the range 3–14 indicating a Set Up message; eight bytes to describe the set up; and the EOX status byte. The eight set up bytes are also known as Additional Information and are regarded as a group of 16 nibbles. These nibbles determine such things as event name, start and stop, plus effect parameters and ASCII characters.

Seventh
The interval between a note and another that is seven scale steps above or below it: this will be either ten semitones (minor seventh) or eleven semitones (major seventh).

Sforzando
A sudden accent, usually abbreviated to *sfz*.

Shannon's Channel Capacity Theorem
The formula $DR_{max} = W \log_2 (1+SN)$, where DR is data rate, W is bandwidth and SN is signal-to-noise ratio. It expresses the relationship between these three variables in digital audio.

Shareware
Term used to describe software which can be tried without purchase and only paid for if found to be useful, essentially relying on the honesty of potential users. Unfortunately, many people abuse the system, which is a shame as it discourages the production of new shareware. In addition, the author will often forward improved versions of the program to those who have paid up and registered as users. Shareware is not in the Public Domain.

Sharp
The condition of a note which is, either deliberately or accidentally, raised in pitch. This might be by only a few cents or as much as a tone (double sharp). In music notation a sharp (raising the pitch by a semitone) is indicated by the symbol ♯ and a double sharp by the symbol ✕.

Shield
American term for screen: *See* Screen [2].

Short Circuit
A circuit in which some accident, such as the failure of a component or a piece of stray metal bridging two "live" points, has reduced the resistance, resulting in increased current flow. It can be said that a complete short circuit has zero resistance and consequently infinite current flow – at least until the PSU explodes. Hopefully, some weaker part of the circuit (preferably a Fuse) will disintegrate and cut the current before this sad state of affairs occurs. *See also* Open Circuit.

Sibilance

Excessive prominence of fricative consonants, such as "s" and "ch" in recorded singing or speech. It can sometimes be reduced by moving the microphone, or by a device such as a De-esser.

Sidebands

1. In FM broadcasting, the new frequency components of a composite signal produced when an audio frequency signal is used to modulate a radio frequency Carrier. Used in stereo transmissions.

2. In FM synthesis, the new sets of Partials generated by the modulated Carrier which gives it a timbre other than that of a sinewave.

Signal

1. A generic name for any one of a number of forms (magnetic orientation, voltage, etc.) which audio may take in the programme chain.

2. The information content of any transmission medium.

Signal Earth

A low impedance path to earth in the form of a metallic screen which sheathes the cable carrying an audio or data signal. Also a wide metallic track on a printed circuit board, surrounding a signal Track[4]. In both cases, the purpose is to help protect the signal from EMI[2].

Signal-to-Noise Ratio

The amount by which a signal exceeds the noise with which it shares a path. It is expressed in negative dB(v) with the peak signal at 0 and the noise (hopefully) some amount below. In a more general sense, it is the ratio between information and anything that masks or corrupts it.

Simile

Italian for similarly. Used to indicate that a style of playing (e.g. *staccato*) is to continue.

Simple Time

See Time Signature.

Simulcast

The simultaneous transmission of a stereo radio programme and a TV programme so that the radio broadcast provides the sound for the TV picture. It is intended to give better sound quality than the sound normally transmitted as part of the TV signal. This process has been made redundant by new TV broadcast techniques, such as NICAM, which include stereo sound.

Sine Wave

A geometrical waveform formed of a curve defined by the function y=sin x. In theory, it has no Partials and can therefore be considered as the basic component from which (by combination) all other waveforms are made: it is thus the building block of all sound. Sometimes used incorrectly to describe pure tones irrespective of their waveform. *See also* Pulse Wave, Ramp Wave, Square Wave, Triangle Wave.

Single Note Retuning Message

A Universal System Exclusive message of the Real Time type, with a Sub ID#1 of 8, which is intended to provide a performance control over the tuning of an individual note.

SI Units

The *Système International d'Unités* is an international system of units, designed predominantly for scientific use. It comprises seven base units plus two supplementary units (for geometry):

Quantity	Unit	Symbol
length	metre	m
time	second	s
luminous intensity	candela	cd
thermodynamic temperature	kelvin	K

Quantity	Unit	Symbol
mass	gram	g
electric current	ampere	A
amount of substance	mole	mol
plane angle	radian	rad
solid angle	steradian	sr

These base units are used to form a large number of derived units, including:

Quantity	Unit	Symbol
frequency	hertz	Hz
power	watt	W
potential difference	volt	V
resistance	ohm	Ω
capacitance	farad	F
electric charge	coulomb	C
temperature	°Celsius	°C

Quantity	Unit	Symbol
energy	joule	J
force	newton	N
pressure, stress	pascal	Pa
conductance	siemen	S
inductance	henry	H
magnetic flux	weber	Wb
magnetic flux density	tesla	T

For convenience, various prefixes are used for multiples and sub-multiples of these units. The complete list is as follows, although those marked with an asterisk are not normally used:

Multiple	Prefix	Symbol
10	deca *	da
100	hecto *	h
1000 (or 10^3)	kilo	k
Million (or 10^6)	mega	M
10^9	giga	G
10^{12}	tera	T
10^{15}	peta	P
10^{18}	exa	E

Fraction	Prefix	Symbol
tenths	deci *	d
hundredths	centi *	c
thousandths (or 10^{-3})	milli	m
millionths (or 10^{-6})	micro	μ
10^{-9}	nano	n
10^{-12}	pico	p
10^{-15}	femto	f
10^{-18}	atto	a

So, 1 μV (a microvolt) = 1 millionth of a volt, while 1 MV (a megavolt) = 1 million volts.

Sixth

The interval between a note and the one six scale steps above or below: eight semitones (minor sixth) or nine semitones (major sixth).

Ska

See Reggae.

Slapback

A type of Echo effect in which a sound is repeated once or twice only, with a short delay of about 40–60 ms.

Slave

In a system of devices, it is sometimes useful to have some which are subordinate in operation to one Master device (particularly for receiving a timing reference, for example). Such devices are nominated slaves.

SMF

See Standard MIDI File.

SMPTE

Acronym from Society of Motion Picture and Television Engineers (pronounced "simpty").

1. A body involved in the specification and development of technical standards in the film, TV and video industry, including the timecode standard defined below.

2. A timecode standard for the unique numeric identification of individual film and video frames, and to allow synchronization between two or more film or video devices. It was subsequently adopted by the audio industry, initially for audio to video synchronization and subsequently for synchronization of tape machines, sequencers, drum machines and other time-reliant devices. Timing is still defined in terms of hours, minutes, seconds and frames within each second: this information is carried in a unique 80-bit message for each frame. *See also* Drop Frame, EBU.

Soca

A form of popular music which appeared in Trinidad during the mid '70s. Essentially a combination of Calypso and Soul, later influenced by Reggae. Although maintaining the up-tempo speed of calypso and often exceeding it, the heavy bass and offbeat rhythms mark it as a more modern development. Its invention is generally credited to Garfield Blackman ("Shorty"). Other exponents include Lord Kitchener and Mighty Sparrow.

Soft Pedal

1. On a piano, a pedal for producing a softer sound. This is achieved by moving the action sideways so that fewer strings per note are struck: on cheaper instruments, all the hammers are moved closer to the strings instead. *See also* Tre Corda, Una Corda.

2. One of the defined MIDI Controller Change messages with a status byte value in the range 176-191 and a first data byte of 67. It is a switch assigned to the parameter in a synthesizer which reproduces the function described in Soft Pedal[1].

Software

A series of instructions, called a program, which determines how the hardware of a computer will function. Written by a programmer, who must analyze the problems to be solved, identify those parts of the computer's Instruction Set which will help provide a solution, and make use of these in the required order. Although the computer ultimately works only in terms of binary digits, the programmer is protected from working at such a low level by the use of increasingly sophisticated computer "languages" that provide the necessary translation into numeric form. For any given problem, there are often many routes to a "correct" solution: elegant programming is therefore something of an art, needing an intuitive feel for problem-solving as much as ruthless logic. Programs which do not work well can result from an incomplete definition of the problem as much as from poor programming. *See also* Firmware, Hardware, High Level Language, Public Domain, Shareware.

Solid State

Archaic term used to describe equipment incorporating semiconductor devices instead of valves.

Solo

1. A switch on a mixing desk which silences every Channel[1] except the one whose solo button was pressed. The effect is to allow monitoring of just one part of the mix. A similar facility is provided on sequencers. *See also* Mute.

2. A section of music which gives particular prominence to one musician. Also called a break in jazz and popular music.

Sonata

A piece of instrumental music, usually for solo performer and often accompanied by keyboard. The term was originally used simply to distinguish played music from sung music and described a single movement work, not necessarily for a soloist. During the baroque period it began to refer to a work, often in four movements, having contrasts of tempo. At this time, sonatas featuring two melodic instruments accompanied by continuo (Trio Sonatas) were popular. From the classical period onwards, the solo sonata gained supremacy, particularly for solo piano, and works of three movements became common in a fast, slow, fast arrangement. The first of these often used a structure that has become known as Sonata Form.

Sonata Form

One of the most important structures in classical music, particularly used for the first movement in longer works. Its essential feature is the concept of departure from, and return to, a home key. This invariably involves the contrast of two related keys in the first section, known as the Exposition. These keys are associated with two themes (or groups of themes) known as first and second Subjects, although their content may not necessarily be highly differentiated. The next section (Development) contains an exploration of this material over a wider range of keys. Finally, the Recapitulation restates the opening material but this time firmly centred in the home key. Various other sections (Bridge Passages, Codetta, Coda) can usually be separately identified. It is important to realize that Sonata Form is more of a principle than a textbook plan used by composers of the time, and can therefore be a very flexible structure – which partly accounts for its enduring popularity. The name, however, is rather unsatisfactory as the form is used in individual movements, not complete sonatas, and is anyway found in many other types of music, such as symphonies, overtures and chamber music. The alternative description, "First Movement Form" is similarly unhelpful, as the structure is also used (sometimes in modified form) for other movements.

Song

1. Strictly, a piece of solo vocal music, with or without accompaniment and often of quite short duration. In popular music, the term is also used for music sung by a group. The words of a song are called the lyrics, and are often not written by the composer – in art music, they may well be drawn from existing poetry. In stage works, the overall dramatic text is called the *libretto* in opera or the "book" in musicals – in the latter, this may well have been written by a third person.

Although songs can be written in any form, certain general patterns are often used. One of the most common is the strophic song – the same music fitted (or adapted) to different verses of text. An extension of this is the verse and chorus structure, in which a refrain (usually with similar text and music on each repeat) falls between each verse. Songs have, for many centuries, also used Ternary form: one particularly common variant of this being an AABA design (i.e. the first section is repeated). The middle (B) section was conventionally known as the Middle Eight in popular music, even when it did not contain eight bars, although the term Bridge is now often preferred. Various linking, contrasting and elaborating sections may fit around such a design. These might include an Intro, an "Instrumental", and either an Outro for a fade-out or a Coda for a definite ending. More elaborate structures are sometimes used in art music – and occasionally there may be very little repetition in the music, such "through-composed" songs relying more on the dramatic impetus of an unfolding narrative for their design. *See also* Aria.

2. A synonym for a sequence (i.e. the performance data recorded on a Sequencer).

Song Position Pointer

A System Common message with a status byte value of 242, which outputs the position in a song (sequence) from which a MIDI sequencer or drum machine should start playing.

Song Select

A System Common message with a status byte value of 243, which outputs the number of the song (sequence) which a MIDI sequencer or drum machine should play.

Soprano

A high, usually female, voice above the Alto in pitch, in the range from about middle C upwards for two octaves (on a good day). Boys voices in the same range are usually called Treble, although the castrated male soprano (*castrato*) was once popular in Italian church and operatic music, and a few male Falsetto singers can reach this range. By extension, instruments which operate in a similar range may also be prefixed by the term: e.g. soprano sax. The very highest instruments in a given family are sometimes called Sopranino: e.g. sopranino recorder. Soprano parts are notated using the treble clef. *See also* Alto, Baritone, Bass, Mezzo, Tenor, Treble, Voice [2].

Sordino

A Mute used by a string or brass player to produce a distant or muffled sound. Various mutes for special effects are used by brass players (e.g. Wa-wa).

Sostenuto

1. A pedal on a piano which has the effect of sustaining only the note(s) sounding when is pedal was pressed, subsequent notes being damped as normal. Usually the middle pedal of three.

2. One of the defined MIDI Controller Change messages with a status byte value in the range 176-191 and a first data byte of 66. It is a switch assigned to the parameter in a synthesizer which reproduces the effect described in Sostenuto [1].

Soul

A form of popular music, created by Afro-American musicians in the early '60s which combined aspects of Blues and Gospel. Strongly linked to the Detroit-based Motown record label: Detroit was the car-building capital of America and Motown appears to be derived from "motor town". Often attributed to the influence of Ray Charles, who first introduced the passion (suffering) of gospel music to R & B. Aretha Franklin, Isaac Hayes, Ben E. King and Wilson Pickett are typical of this tradition. In the '70s, the passion in soul music became less religious and more romantic, even sexual, with artists such as Barry White and others.

Sound

The experience caused by rapid cyclic changes in air pressure, or vibrations conducted through other materials. Most sounds are composed of many components, called Partials, which are sine waves of different frequencies. Sounds which contain a lot of Harmonic partials are generally perceived as having pitch, while those which are rich in Enharmonic partials are not. *See also* Audio Frequency, Frequency, Timbre, Waveform, White Noise.

Sound Check

A checking procedure carried out before a performance or recording, particularly when amplified instruments and/or a PA system are used, to ensure equipment is working and sound levels are satisfactory.

Sound Controller Messages	The ten defined MIDI Controller Change messages with status byte values in the range 176–191 and data byte values in the range 70–79. They are assigned to general-purpose parameters in a synthesizer or multi-effects unit and allow real time editing of sound quality and effects from the sequencer. *See* MIDI Controllers [2].
Sound Engineer	*See* Engineer.
Sound Module	*See* Tone Module.
Sound Wave	*See* Waveform.
SOX	Acronym from Start Of eXclusive. A MIDI message in the form of a status byte with a value of 240, used to indicate the start of a System Exclusive message.
Spaced Pair	A microphone system which uses a pair of microphones spaced some inches apart for recording stereo. If the microphones are separated by more than about two feet, the stereo image may appear to have no "middle".
Spacer	Plastic tape in different colours, used to separate sections of film or magnetic tape, for the purposes of identification or protection. *See also* Leader.
SPDIF	Abbreviation of Sony/Phillips Digital InterFace. Basically, an unbalanced version of the AES/EBU digital interface. It is implemented on domestic digital audio equipment such as CD players.
Speaker	*See* Loudspeaker.
Spectrum	The range of frequencies or partials present in a complex waveform, such as an audio signal.
Spectrum Analyzer	A device for displaying the relative amplitudes of frequencies in a Spectrum.
Spill	The tendency of a microphone to pick up sounds from sources other than those intended for it. *See also* Separation.
SPL	Sound Pressure Level: the intensity of a sound. This is not quite the same as Loudness, which is a more subjective measure. *See also* dB SPL.
Splice	A join in recording tape, made with the aid of a special adhesive tape (splicing tape). In a butt splice, the ends are cut at right angles – this is best used at a silence. When the sound spills past the edit point, splicing the tape at a shallower angle will help mask the join.
Splitpoint	In an electric keyboard instrument, a point on the keyboard which divides it into two playing areas, each of which can be assigned a separate sound, MIDI channel, etc. This is particularly useful in live performance to prevent having to play two synths stacked on top of each other.
SPP	*See* Song Position Pointer.
Spreadsheet	A category of computer software designed primarily to allow a user to generate tables of arithmetic calculations. Normally used for such things as keeping track of income and expenditure and making financial projections. It consists of a grid of "cells" for entering figures or labels. The user may relate these to each other by various mathematical formulæ. Thus, the cell at the bottom of a column might be called "total" and automatically display the sum of all numbers above it in that column. Having established a set of mathematical relationships (which might represent the cash flow for a company) it is then possible to alter specific values and immediately see the overall effect of that change. This is often called "What if...?", as in "What if we sack the accountant?". Zero would be placed in the cell for the accountant's salary and this decrease in expenditure will be reflected all the way down the balance sheet.
Spring Reverb	*See* Reverb Spring.
Square Wave	A special case of Pulse Wave, with a Mark / Space ratio of 1:2. Only odd-numbered Harmonic Partials are present and the amplitude of each is the reciprocal of its number in the series (i.e. the third harmonic is ⅓ the amplitude of the first). It has a hollow timbre similar to that of a clarinet. *See also* Pulse Wave, Ramp Wave, Sine Wave, Triangle Wave.
SR.D	A system developed by the Dolby company for placing a digital audio soundtrack onto cine film. The data encodes six audio tracks, five covering the full frequency range and one for low frequencies only. Using a data compression method derived from audio satellite techniques, it is possible to achieve a compact data rate of 320 kb/S. The data is printed onto the film between the sprocket holes. *See also* Dolby, Film Soundtrack.
SSI	Abbreviation of Small Scale Integration. An integrated circuit which contains about 10–90 active elements. *See also* LSI, MSI, VLSI.
Staccato	Italian for short or detached (often shown by dots above/below notes affected). The opposite of *legato*.
Staff	*See* Stave.

Stage Monitor	A wedge-shaped loudspeaker placed on stage close to a musician in broadcasting and live performance. It allows them to hear the general mix, or some specific part of it – for example, the bass player may particularly need to hear the drum beat.
Standard MIDI File	A part of the MIDI specification which allows the interchange of MIDI data on disk between devices, particularly different makes of sequencer, which might otherwise be incompatible. This method only works, of course, if the receiving device is able to read the physical format of the incoming disk. Sequence data is stored on disk in one of three formats. Type 0 packages all data into a single track, regardless of its original tracks. Type 1 retains the track layout, although the tempo and time signature of all tracks will be those of track one. Type 2 is the same as Type 1, except that each track keeps its own tempo and time signature, but is seldom implemented. The files include information called "meta events" about such things as track and instrument names, copyright notice, tempo change, SMPTE offset, lyrics and key and time signatures. The time between sequence events is encoded in "delta time" messages of between one and four bytes. *See also* File Dump Standard.
Standards	In jazz, a fairly small repertoire of pieces, many of them popular songs of the '20s, '30s and '40s, that form the basis for much jazz improvisation. *See also* Changes.
Star Network	**1.** A type of MIDI network in which a master unit is directly connected to all devices in the system, instead of linking them serially in a Daisy Chain. This obviates the need for MIDI Thrus, but requires the use of a device that has a number of parallel MIDI sockets. *See also* MIDI Port.
	2. In audio and other wiring systems, the practice of establishing only one central earth point, to which all screens and earth wires have a single direct path. This is considered good practice as other arrangements almost invariably lead to problems with earth loops causing hum, etc.
Start	A System Real Time message with a status byte value of 250 which will cause a MIDI device to start playing the current song. Usually only implemented by drum machines and sequencers. *See also* Active Sensing, Continue, MIDI Clock, Reset, Stop.
Start Bit	In serial data transmission (particularly Asynchronous), the use of an extra bit to precede the data bits and which serves to "wake up" the receiving device, in readiness for the data to follow.
Status Byte	Any byte with a value of 128 or greater, used in a MIDI message. It determines what type of instruction is described by the message, and is usually followed by one or more Data Bytes.
Stave	Also called staff. In notated music, the group of five horizontal lines upon and between which notes are written. The lines and spaces represent increasing pitch from bottom to top. The precise correspondence between line and pitch is determined by the Clef used. The stave will occasionally have short lines (leger lines) added above or below when needed for pitches which fall outside of the range of the stave. It is common to group staves of simultaneous music into "systems", by joining them with a vertical line at the left edge of the page and often by linking their barlines.
Step Time	In a sequencer, the facility to record without having to play rhythmically or in real time. MIDI messages can be input one at a time from a music or computer keyboard, front panel switches or by pointing and clicking with a mouse. *See also* Real Time.
Stereo	Abbreviation of Stereophonic. An almost universal form of audio reproduction, using two separate channels, which attempts to model human aural perception of live sounds. *See also* Monophonic.
Stop	**1.** A System Real Time message with a status byte value of 252 which will cause a MIDI device to stop playing the current song. Usually only implemented by drum machines and sequencers. *See also* Active Sensing, Continue, MIDI Clock, Reset, Start.
	2. A lever, or similar control, that brings into play a particular timbre on organs and harpsichords.
Stop Bit	In serial data transmission (particularly Asynchronous) the use of an extra bit to succeed the data bits and which serves to indicate to the receiving device that the flow of data has stopped.
Stringendo	Italian for gradually becoming faster and with increasing tension.
Striping	The initial process of recording timecode onto audio or video tape.
Studio	A preferably soundproof room, equipped with microphones, stands, screens, etc., usually linked to a control room by an appropriate array of cables, and set aside for the purpose of recording audio events within an acoustically controllable environment. By extension, an entire recording complex, including individual studios, offices, etc. *See also* Control Room, Machine Room.
Stylus	The needle, often diamond-tipped, mounted in a Cartridge[2] on the Tone Arm of a record deck. It tracks the groove of a record and its vibrations are converted into an audio signal.
Subcode	In digital audio systems, particularly CD and RDAT, additional data interleaved with the audio information which carries synchronization and user information, such as tags and comments. *See also* PQ Codes.
Subdominant	*See* Scale.

Sub ID#1 Sub ID#2

Two data bytes which follow the Universal System Exclusive data byte in a System Exclusive message to define the type of message. A Universal Real Time Sub ID#1 value of 1 indicates MTC and may be followed by a Sub ID#2 value of 1 (for a Full Message) or 2 (User Bits) or 15 (Set Up). A Universal Non-Real Time Sub ID#1 value of 5, on the other hand, indicates a Sample Dump and may be followed by a Sub ID#2 value of 1 for a Multiple Loop Points message or 2 for a Loop Points Request.

Subito

Italian for suddenly, as in *subito f* – suddenly loud.

Subject

A significant musical theme. *See* Fugue, Sonata Form.

Submediant

See Scale.

Subtractive

See Synthesis.

Sum

The addition of several signals or variants of the same signal. This is normally achieved at the inputs of an amplifier. A mixing desk can be seen as a type of summing amplifier.

Supercomputer

A computer whose speed of operation is close to the maximum possible: currently in the 400–800 MIPS range. The use of new technologies, such as parallel processing, are already beginning to extend this above 1 GIPS. *See* Computer.

Supertonic

See Scale.

Sustain

1. The central portion of a musical note, between its attack and release.

2. A pedal fitted to pianos (and percussion instruments such as the vibraphone) that is used to prevent notes being damped, thus lengthening their decay time and therefore not a true (i.e. limitless) sustain. A pedal offering a similar function is often available for synthesizers where, of course, an infinite sustain can be achieved on some voices.

3. One of the defined MIDI Controller Change messages with a status byte value in the range 176-191 and a first data byte of 64. It is a switch assigned to the parameter in a synthesizer which reproduces the function described in Sustain [2].

4. An artificial prolongation of a note on electric guitars by using controlled Feedback. Achieved by feeding the amplified signal to a loudspeaker close to the string, which then excites further vibration.

Sustain Level

In an Envelope Generator, the level of Sustain [1], which will be maintained until the note is released or a gate signal removed.

Swell Pedal

A foot-operated control for synthesizers and electric organs that adjusts volume, hence allowing the sound to "swell". Originally, a mechanical device on a pipe organ with similar purpose.

Swing

1. A term used in popular music, and particularly jazz, for the subtle adjustment of note placement within the overall rhythm to create a particular mood. An effect which cannot be adequately conveyed by notation and therefore a style of playing that classically-trained musicians find notoriously elusive. *See also* Feel.

2. A development in jazz arising during the '30s, particularly featuring big band arrangements. Because these needed fairly comprehensive notation, opportunities for improvisation tended to be restricted to a few star soloists, such as Louis Armstrong and Count Basie.

Switched Controller

A type of Controller Change message, with a status byte value in the range 176–191, and a first data byte value in the range 64-90. It is used to introduce some kind of change between only two conditions: for example, Sustain pedal on or off. *See also* MIDI Controllers [2].

Sync

See Synchronization

Sync Head

In a multi-track tape recorder, the use of the record head to replay material from other tracks to be heard by the musicians while they simultaneously record a new track. This is essential for accurate synchronization, as the extra few milliseconds afforded by its position will compensate for the inevitable delay if the signal was taken from the main replay head, which is some millimetres downstream in the tape path. The replay quality is obviously less good when using the record head for a function for which it is not primarily engineered. Thus, it is important that the machine returns to monitoring from the main replay head during mixdown.

Synchronization

1. The process of time-locking a number of normally independent and free-running systems. Where one of these is a tape recorder, the term "tape sync" is used: one track of the tape is used to carry a Timecode signal which is used to provide timing for other devices.

2. In a synthesizer with two or more oscillators, the ability to lock the frequency of one oscillator (the slave) to another (the master). This has the effect of stopping any Beating which might otherwise occur. If the master's frequency is adjusted, both oscillators will change frequency. If the slave's frequency is adjusted higher than that of the master, there will be no actual change in frequency, but an alteration in the harmonic partials leading to a different timbre in the composite sound. This is most effective if the frequency of the slave is modulated constantly, perhaps with an envelope generator, producing a distinctive "wailing" sound.

Synclavier

The tradename of one of the earliest commercially available computer music instruments. It was first produced by the American company, New England Digital, in the late '70s as a digital synthesizer implementing a version of John Chowning's FM Synthesis. Sequencing and monophonic sampling facilities (at the then remarkable sampling rate of 50 kHz) were soon added. The sampler was expanded into a full hard disk recording unit which they called Direct-to-Disk, a phrase which has since entered the language. Towards the end of its development the Synclavier was an integrated system with 96 voices, sequencing, and multi-track hard disk recording, aimed at post-production and other professional users. Sometimes mentioned in the same breath as the Fairlight, although it is fair to say that NED's considerable research and development budget always seemed to keep it ahead of its Australian rival.

Syncopation

In music, the placing of accents on normally unaccented parts of the bar. The effect is usually to anticipate the main beats – a technique widely used in popular music and jazz.

Syncope

A term used to refer to the unnecessary proliferation of tied notes that can occur when a notation module in a sequencer program reflects every rhythmic nuance of the performance data. The problem can often be ameliorated by an option which quantizes just the appearance of the notation.

Sync Pulses

The output of a clock used to keep devices, such as tape and video recorders, in synchronization

Synthesis

The process of electronically creating sounds on a synthesizer. The word synthesis has the implication of combining separate elements into a new whole and is ideally a creative process – it should therefore not necessarily be taken to mean "synthetic" as a synonym for artificial. There are two principal methods of synthesis. Additive, in which separate sound components (particularly sinewaves) are added together to make a composite sound – a process that has only become practical with the advent of digital technology. Subtractive synthesis,on the other hand, removes sinewave components or partials from a complex waveform using a variety of filters. Most analogue synthesizers operate in this way and many modern synths incorporate both processes. Some devices also make use of Samples, which can be manipulated alongside synthesized sounds, although the process of sampling is actually concerned with digitally re-creating real sounds rather than imitating them or creating new ones.

Synthesizer

An electronic device for Synthesis. A wide definition would include virtually all electronic musical instruments, such as electronic organs, keyboards, samplers and drum machines, although it would probably not extend to every electronic device that can produce a sound. The term more specifically refers to programmable devices on which the user can manufacture or edit sounds, thus excluding, for example, cheap Electric Keyboards. Synthesizers, particularly if provided with MIDI, need not have a keyboard and most need to be connected to amplification equipment if they are to be heard. *See also* Master Keyboard, Tone Module.

Sys Ex

Acronym from SYStem EXclusive. *See* System Exclusive Messages.

System Common Messages

A classification of MIDI messages with status byte values in the range 241-246 (although not all in the range are defined), which contain instructions for all devices in a MIDI network, irrespective of Channel[2]. These include Song Position Pointer, Song Select and Tune Request.

System Exclusive Messages

A type of MIDI message, often called Sys Ex, containing information that is, in almost all cases, specific to the equipment of one manufacturer. Typically used to send voice data and parameter settings (even the entire user-programmable contents of the device) between synths of the same type. Also used to exchange data between synths, sequencers and Librarian programs. A typical Sys Ex message will start with a status byte of 240 to indicate Start of Exclusive (SOX), up to three data bytes giving the manufacturer and device ID numbers, and then an indication of the amount of data to follow. Next comes the actual Sys Ex data, in any format defined by the manufacturer. Finally, the whole message is terminated by a checksum and a status byte of 247 to indicate End of Exclusive (EOX). The only Sys Ex messages that are not exclusive to one manufacturer have the specific ID numbers 125, 126 and 127: *see* Universal System Exclusive.

System Messages

A general term for MIDI messages with status bytes values of 240 and above, intended for all devices on a MIDI network, irrespective of Channel[2]. It includes System Common, System Exclusive and System Real Time. It should be pointed out, however, that most manufacturers arrange their Sys Ex data so that it will only be received by one device in a network.

System Real Time Messages

A classification of MIDI messages with status byte values in the range 248–255, (although not all in this range are defined), which are used to synchronize the starting, running and stopping of drum machines and sequencers, and other functions. *See also* Active Sensing, Continue, MIDI Clock, Reset, Start, Stop.

System Reset

A System Real Time message with a status byte value of 255 which causes a MIDI device to reset to its default condition: i.e. its settings when first powered up. This will usually involve silencing all voices, resetting the display to the opening page, etc. In the early days of MIDI, due to a misunderstanding of the intention for this message, some manufacturers made their devices transmit a reset message if one was received. A few of these in a network could clearly lead to a chain reaction of gadgets resetting themselves for ever. *See also* Active Sensing, Continue, MIDI Clock Start, Stop.

Systems Music

See Minimalism.

Tail

Additional information which follows a block of data either on disk or for the purposes of data transfer between devices. The tail usually serves as a "full stop" to the data that precedes it. Commonly encountered in MIDI System Exclusive transfers. For example, in Yamaha System Exclusive transfers, the last two bytes are tail information, in the form of a Checksum (which allows a transmission error to be detected) and the EOX status byte.

Take

A colloquial term for a single, continuous recording made in a studio. This may be of a complete work, but is more often a short section. Each take is identified on tape (either verbally or electronically) and the most successful ones will later be edited together to provide the best possible recording. Also used as a verb: e.g. "let's take that again".

Tala

Also variously Taal, Thal, Tal, etc. The system of rhythmic or metrical cycles common in Indian art music. Tala are different ways of dividing a unit of time into a number of percussive beats (usually between six and sixteen) articulated in different patterns (e.g. ten beats may be phrased 2+3+2+3 or 7+1+2), which are then repeated cyclically. The percussion may be supplied by hand claps or drums such as the Tabla. Skilled exponents are able to improvise permutations of these highly systematized patterns over many cycles.

Talkback

A facility on a mixing desk which allows an engineer or producer to talk to a performer in the studio over headphones or a loudspeaker, to give instructions, identify Takes, etc.

Tape

Recording medium consisting of a magnetic coating applied to a plastic substrate. It is supplied in standardized widths on spools or cassettes for different purposes. In audio recording, ¼" is appropriate for stereo. Compact cassettes use ⅛" while anything up to 2" is required for multitrack recorders. Video recording uses ½", 1" or 2" tape. For data recording various sorts of specialized spools and cartridges are used. *See also* Chromium Dioxide, Ferric Oxide, Metal, Tape Type.

Tape Bias

In analogue tape recording, the use of a high frequency (50 kHz or more) signal while recording, to predispose the magnetic surface of the tape to conform to the audio signal. Usually generated by a bias oscillator, and filtered out on replay.

Tape Counter

A mechanical or electronic display of the relative amount of tape that has passed through the transport of a tape recorder. In professional systems using Timecode, it may show the absolute time value recorded at any given point on the tape.

Tape Echo

An early method of producing echo effects by means of a tape loop: *see* Loop [1].

Tape Head

A transducer used in a tape machine to convert electrical energy into patterns of magnetism on magnetic tape, or vice versa. *See also* Erase [1], Record Head, Replay Head, Sync Head.

Tapeless Studio

A studio designed for music production in the digital domain, which uses hard disks rather than tape as the primary recording medium. Integrated systems based on Apple MacIntosh computers, such as those produced by Digidesign, are an example of this approach. In a more amateur and limited sense, a synthesizer-sequencer workstation could be regarded as a tapeless studio.

Tape Loop

See Loop [1].

Tape Recorder

A device used to record a signal onto tape, also known as a Tape Machine. It consists of a tape transport (motor, spools, pulleys and guides) and electronics (motor control, record/playback amplifiers, noise reduction, etc.). A number of types are available, using either open reel or cassette tape: *see* Half Track, Multi-track, Portastudio, Quarter Track, Two Track.

Tape Returns

The inputs on a mixing desk that allow signals from a tape recorder to be monitored, mixed, etc.

Tape Speed

Speed at which the tape passes the record and playback heads on a tape recorder. Standard speeds are 76 cms/s (30 ips), 38 cm/s (15 ips) or 19 cm/s (7½ ips) for professional equipment, while domestic cassette machines run at 4.75 cm/s (1⅞ ips). In general, faster speeds produce better quality recordings.

Tape Sync

See Synchronization [1].

Tape Type

The categorization of recording tape (mainly cassette) according to its magnetic coating. Type I is Ferric Oxide, Type II is Chromium Dioxide and Type IV is Metal (Type III is discontinued).

Tautology

See Tautology.

Techno

A form of popular music derived from Disco, but with a distinctly electronic sound. Its exponents favour the thin and tinny sounds of early '80s synthesizers and drum machines.

Telharmonium	Also called Dynamophone, possibly the first and probably the largest electric keyboard instrument ever invented (its final version weighed over 200 tons). Only three were ever made, at approximately six year intervals starting in 1900. These were based on a tone-wheel principle developed in America by Dr. Thaddeus Cahill in the 1890s. It is interesting primarily because it was a predecessor of the more famous and much smaller Hammond organ. It was also at the centre of the world's first music "broadcasting" service (c. 1906) which was available only to telephone subscribers in New York City. Nowadays only ever mentioned in dictionaries such as this, when the author wishes to demonstrate how eclectic and wide ranging his research has been.
Tempo	The speed of the pulse of a piece of music. Either precisely indicated in MM or BPM, or more vaguely suggested by words such as "fast" or *allegro*. *See also* A Tempo.
Tempo Primo	Instruction to return to the speed shown at the beginning.
Tenor	From the Latin *tenere,* meaning "to hold". Originally, a vocal part with sustained notes in church music. Now used for the male voice which has a range from about C below middle C, upwards for as much as two octaves (on a good day). By extension, instruments which operate in a similar range may also be prefixed by the term: e.g. tenor saxophone. The tenor Clef, used principally by cellos, bassoons and trombones when in the tenor register, has middle C on the fourth line from the bottom of the stave. The term Counter Tenor is used to specify a male voice singing in the alto range. *See also* Alto, Baritone, Bass, Soprano, Treble, Voice [2].
Tent	An enclosed area of dead acoustic in a studio, formed from a number of screens.
Tenuto	An indication that a note should be held, shown in notation by a short, heavy line on the note.
Terminal	**1.** A point on a piece of equipment that allows a wire or cable to be connected, usually on a temporary or semi-temporary basis. **2.** In a computer system, particularly a mainframe, a remote keyboard and monitor and sometimes printer, which allows a user of the system to communicate with the computer. It is an input/output or IO device.
Ternary Form	A musical form in three sections, of which the last is a repeat (or modified repeat) of the first, sometimes represented as ABA since the middle section is usually contrasting in content and key. The first section generally finishes in the same key as it began, making ternary form distinct from the otherwise similar rounded Binary Form, in which the sections are less clearly delineated. The form was used in early operatic arias, in dance music and in short 19th century piano pieces.
Test Tape	A pre-recorded tape having test tones of known frequency, amplitude and flux density, which can be used to align a tape recorder for optimum performance.
THD	*See* Total Harmonic Distortion.
Thérémin	An electronic musical instrument, invented in Russia by Lev Termen (of French descent and known also as Léon Thérémin) about 1920. Pitch was determined by moving the right hand in proximity to a vertical antenna, while volume was controlled by the left hand's position in relation to a metal loop. It used the principle of heterodyning, in which one fixed radio-frequency oscillator was modulated by the output of another whose frequency was controlled by the capacitance of the air between the right hand and the antenna. Audio range frequencies were then produced by the sum and difference signals from this modulation – a principle to be exploited much later in FM Synthesis. The instrument was monophonic and almost uncontrollably microtonal. Later versions had different types of control to simplify performance, but never with the aftertouch capability that helped secure the success of the similar Ondes Martenot. Few composers of importance took the instrument seriously, although RCA Victor built a version of it combined with a gramophone, and issued records of backings against which enthusiasts could perform thérémin solos for which sheet music was also supplied.
Third	The interval between a note and the one three scale steps above or below it: three semitones (minor third) or four semitones (major third).
Thrash Metal	A form of popular music derived from Heavy Metal, although faster in speed. It can be seen as the return of Punk Rock to its roots.
Three-Head	A tape recorder with separate record, replay and erase heads.
Threshold	The specific point in a range at which some process or effect occurs. In an audio signal, it is the lower limit in the dynamic range above which a device, such as a Compressor, Limiter or Noise Gate, will come into operation.
Threshold of Hearing	The lowest amplitude at which a sound becomes audible. It is the zero reference of 0 dB SPL.
Threshold of Pain	The highest amplitude of a sound beyond which it is experienced as pain: about 140 dB SPL.
Tie Line	A permanent but undedicated connection between two points some distance apart: e.g. between a terminal box in the studio and the patchbay in the control room.

Timbre

The quality of a sound determined by the structure of its Partials: i.e. the relative frequencies and amplitudes of the various sinewaves which collectively make up that particular sound. It is roughly synonymous with "tone". It is this quality which allows you to distinguish between a flute and an oboe playing the same pitch at the same volume. *See also* Multi-timbral, Sound.

Timecode

An audio signal which encodes details of absolute time and other information in a form which can be recorded onto tape, usually for synchronizing the tape recorder with other equipment such as sequencers and video recorders. *See also* EBU, FSK, LTC, SMPTE, VITC.

Time Signature

The indication at the beginning of a piece of music, or individual section, usually in the form of two numbers. The lower of these determines which note duration represents the basic pulse, while the upper shows how many notes of this duration will occur in each bar. Thus, in $\frac{3}{4}$ time there are three quarter-note (crotchet) beats per bar. In "simple" times, such as $\frac{2}{4}$, $\frac{3}{4}$ and $\frac{4}{4}$, each beat is normally halved, quartered, etc., to form shorter note lengths. In "compound" times, such as $\frac{6}{8}$, $\frac{9}{8}$ and $\frac{12}{8}$, the basic pulse is grouped into threes, to form dotted notes. In faster tempos, musicians often find it more convenient to regard these dotted notes as the actual pulse. The time-signature **C** ("common time") indicates $\frac{4}{4}$ time, while **₵** ("cut C") indicates the generally faster $\frac{2}{2}$ time.

Toasting

A tradition of poetic oratory among Afro-Caribbeans and Afro-Americans, which takes the various forms of verbal sparring matches, boastful chants and (latterly) political and social comment. Most closely associated with Reggae and its DJs. *See also* Rapping.

Tonal Music

Music which is centred on a particular key and which exploits the hierarchical properties of related keys (particularly the Tonic – Dominant relationship). The concept of tonality had appeared by 1600 and dominated music during the classical era, but was gradually eroded by the increasing use of Chromatic harmony during the late 19th century. During the 20th century, art music has explored other forms of hierarchical relationships or has attempted to dispense with hierarchy altogether. However, tonal harmony has remained fundamental to most popular music styles. *See also* Atonal, Circle of Fifths, Key, Scale, Serialism.

Tone

1. A synonym for Timbre (e.g. "an instrument with a mellow tone").

2. An interval of two semitones, such as the step from C to D.

3. A synonym for (and an anagram of) note: *see also* Line-Up Tone, Serialism.

Tone Arm

The assembly on record decks which supports the Pick Up[2], allowing it to track across the record.

Tone Generator

A precisely calibrated oscillator, mainly used to generate Line-Up Tones. *See also* Tone Module.

Tone Module

A synthesizer without a keyboard which generates sounds in response to MIDI data from a Sequencer, Master Keyboard or other MIDI Controller[1]. Such devices will often be packaged in a standard 19" rack-mounted case, and may be multi-timbral. Often used to expand an existing MIDI system. Also variously called an Expander, Rack Module, Sound Module, Tone Generator.

Tonic

The "home" or key note: *see* Scale.

TOS

See Operating System.

Total Harmonic Distortion

A measure of the distortion to all the Partials in an audio signal, expressed as a negative number of decibels, caused by devices such as amplifiers. Sometimes abbreviated to THD.

Touch Sensitivity

See Velocity Sensitivity.

Track

1. One of the invisible "lanes" along a magnetic tape which is formed by recording an audio signal onto it.

2. In a MIDI sequencer, the area of memory into which events can be recorded or stored, and which is analogous in function to Track[1]. Typically, each track will contain performance data for a single line of the musical texture. Most sequencers offer many more tracks than tape recorders as well as much more flexibility in their use.

3. A section on a record, CD, cassette, etc., containing a discrete portion of the recording. By extension, in popular music the compositions themselves are often called tracks.

4. On printed circuit boards, the conducting areas for linking components.

Track Bouncing

The process of mixing down and re-recording material from a number of existing tracks to one or two (for stereo) free tracks on a multi-track tape recorder. This is usually done so that the original tracks may be over-recorded with new material, and has the effect of increasing the total number of available tracks, although there may be some loss of quality in the signal. Thus, using an eight-track recorder it would be possible to mix tracks 1 to 6 to stereo and re-record them onto tracks 7 and 8: tracks 1 to 6 could then be reused. Sometimes called ping pong recording or bumping.

Tracker Ball

A computer control which performs similar functions to a Mouse. Unlike the latter, the ball is moved by the hand while its casing remains stationary. *See* Mouse[1].

Tracking Error

1. An error which can occur in disk drives when the read/write head cannot be placed accurately over the data blocks. Also, a similar error in CD player mechanisms.

2. The problem caused by the inability of a pivoted Tone Arm to keep to the constant radial angle which was maintained by the cutter of a record groove during manufacture.

Track Laying

The process of recording audio signals to a track or a number of tracks on a multi-track tape recorder, either simultaneously or sequentially, prior to mixdown.

Tranquillo

Italian for quietly, tranquilly.

Transducer

A device which converts the form of a signal, usually from mechanical to electrical or vice versa. Thus microphones, loudspeakers, pick-ups and tape heads are transducers.

Transfer Rate

See Data Rate.

Transfer Suite

The facility where film location sound recordings are transferred to sprocketed magnetic tape. The soundtrack and the film can then be mechanically synchronized

Transformer

An electromagnetic device consisting of coils of wire wrapped around a magnetic material. This has the property of transferring an alternating current by induction from one coil (the primary) to another (the secondary) – there may be more than one secondary coil in a transformer. The amount of current (and, by extension, voltage) transferred can be increased or reduced by altering the ratio of the number of turns of wire in the primary and secondary coils. If the number of turns is equal and the transformer is 100% efficient (unlikely), the current in both coils will be equal. Transformers with equal coils are used to isolate equipment as there is no direct electrical connection – only the magnetic one. Transformers with unequal coils are used to convert voltage levels, with a corresponding change in current capability (power transformers), to match impedances (matching transformers) or provide a Balanced Line input.

Transformerless Input

On an audio device, an input which does not use a transformer for impedance matching. Such inputs will make use of semiconductors such as transistors, and may often be described as "active inputs". Their main advantage is a saving in size, although manufacturers also argue that they give better performance than transformers: this need not necessarily be true.

Transient

The short burst of Partials at the beginning of a sound. These are psychoacoustically significant as this information is used by the brain to identify and categorize sounds of different types.

Transistor

A type of semiconductor device generally having three terminals called emitter, collector and base, which has the property of letting current flow in one direction only, under the control of a biasing voltage present at the base. It can be thought of as an electrically-operated switch. Transistors are divided into two broad types: NPN and PNP, this describes the method of manufacture, but more importantly defines the direction of current flow. In NPN transistors current flow is conventionally from collector to emitter, while for PNP transistors the reverse is true. Transistors are principally used where a gain increase is required, such as in amplifiers.

Transmitter

Equipment for converting an audio and/or video signal into a modulated carrier wave which can be radiated by an aerial. By extension, any device generating output which is sent electronically to another location. *See also* AM, FM, Relay Station.

Transport Control

In its most basic form, the play, rewind, fast forward, stop and pause buttons and the Varispeed control on a tape recorder, i.e. the features which control the movement of the tape. These controls may be duplicated on a remote unit – essential if the tape recorder is housed in a separate Machine Room. More elaborate remote controls may include an Autolocator.

Transpose

The process of writing or playing music at a different pitch or key to the original. Some wind instruments (such as clarinets and trumpets) do not sound at the pitch that their written notation suggests: composers and arrangers therefore have to transpose their music to compensate for this. Synthesizers, sequencers, etc., often provide a facility for automatic transposition.

Transposer

See Pitch Shifter.

Treble

1. Audio frequencies above about 1 kHz.

2. A high voice or musical part equivalent to soprano, particularly a vocal part sung by a boy. By extension, instruments which operate in a similar range may also be prefixed by the term: e.g. treble recorder. The treble or G clef is the one whose script-like G is centred around the second line up from the bottom of the stave. *See also* Alto, Baritone, Bass, Soprano, Tenor.

Tre Corde

Three strings. Usually used in piano music to indicate the release of the left or "soft" pedal. This has the effect of returning the action to its normal position so that the three strings available (on most notes) are struck. *See also* Una Corda.

Tremolo

1. Strictly, a rapid fluctuation in the amplitude of a sound (a rapid fluctuation in frequency is called Vibrato). A small amount of tremolo is a natural part of the technique of singers and wind players. The effect is reproduced on the pipe organ by the stop (called a tremulant) which introduces rapid fluctuations in the wind supply, and on synthesizers by electronic means.

2. Originally one of the defined MIDI Controller Change messages with a status byte value in the range 176-191 and a first data byte of 92. It is assigned to the parameter in a synthesizer which alters the depth of the effect described in Tremolo[1]. More recently this message has been reassigned as one of five generalized Effects Depth messages. *See* Effects Control.

3. Italian for trembling. A rapid reiteration of one or more notes, especially on string instruments.

Triad

A three-note chord that is formed from any note of the scale, plus the note a third above it and the note a third above that. The lowest note is called the root in this basic arrangement (known as the root position), and the letter name of the root is used to identify the entire triad (e.g. triad of C). In practice, the notes may be arranged in any order, although if the lowest note is no longer the root, the triad is

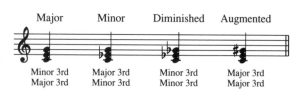

said to be inverted. As either of the thirds can be either major or minor, four different types of triad are possible, as shown in the illustration. The most common are major triads (lower interval a major third) and minor triads (lower interval a minor third). It is important to note that these terms refer to intervallic structure and not to key – major triads occur in minor keys, and vice-versa. *See also* Inversion, Root.

Triangle Wave

A geometrical waveform, triangular in shape, which comprises the same sequence of only odd-numbered harmonic partials as the Square Wave. However, the amplitude of each harmonic is the reciprocal of the square of its number (i.e. the 3rd harmonic is $\frac{1}{9}$ the amplitude of the first). So, the sound is much weaker and more mellow. *See also* Pulse Wave, Ramp Wave, Sine Wave, Square Wave, Waveform.

Trigger

A pulsed voltage of very short duration (typically less than a few milliseconds) which is used to instigate an event or process in an electronic device. On a synthesizer, this may be used to start the envelope generator, which will then progress through its attack, decay and release phases. However, there will be no sustain, as the pulse will have already gone before the sustain phase is reached. This, in contrast to the effect of a Gate signal, will invariably result in a percussive envelope: indeed, the most commonly encountered form of trigger is that generated by drum pads for electronic percussion devices.

Trill

See Ornamentation.

Trim

On a Mixing Desk, a rotary gain control on each Channel[1] for adjusting the incoming signal so that its peak level is achieved when the channel fader is set to 0 dB(v).

Triplet

Three notes (or rests) executed in the time normally taken by two of the same value.

Tritone

An interval of three tones (e.g. F to B).

Trojan Horse

See Virus.

Troppo

Italian for "too much", as in *allegro ma non troppo* – fast, but not too fast.

Tube

See Valve.

Tune Request

A System Common message with a status byte value of 246, which will instruct a MIDI device to re-tune its oscillators. This was useful in the days when oscillators were analogue and prone to pitch drift, but is seldom required now. *See also* Single Note Retuning, Bulk Tuning Message.

Tuning

1. The process of adjusting the pitch of all or some notes on a musical instrument, in order to conform with the pitch of other instruments and/or Concert Pitch. *See also* Beating, Equal Temperament.

2. The process of adjusting the frequency of a radio or TV receiver to lock onto a transmitted signal. *See also* Carrier[1].

Tuplet

A generic term used by some sequencers for any non-standard subdivision of a beat or beats, derived from the suffix of quintuplet, septuplet, etc, but also encompassing Duplet and Triplet.

Turntable

A synonym for record player: specifically, the rotating platform on which the record rests.

Tweeter

See Loudspeaker.

Twentieth Century

See Musical Periods.

Two Track

A tape machine which records onto two tape tracks, used primarily for stereo mastering.

U
See Rack Mount.

UART
Acronym from Universal Asynchronous Receiver Transmitter. An integrated circuit that carries out the function of asynchronous, bi-directional communication between a microprocessor and a serial interface. In MIDI, it is a chip in the interface that forms part of the link between the processor and the MIDI sockets.

UKASCII
A variant of ASCII which is adapted to the requirements of UK English, and thus includes symbols such as the £ sign which are not part of the basic ASCII character set.

UKMA
Abbreviation of the UK MIDI Association. A body which provides a forum for discussion of all areas of MIDI, and communicates information about updates to the MIDI Specification together with technical help on its implementation.

Ultrasonic
Pertaining to sounds which are above normal human hearing, i.e. above about 20 kHz.

U-Matic
A video tape recorder format developed by Sony for professional use. This machine is also used in conjunction with a PCM 1610 or PCM 1630 encoder to record digital audio instead of video.

Una Corda
One string. Used in piano music to indicate the use of the left or "soft" pedal. This has the effect of shifting the action so that fewer strings per note than normal are struck by the hammers, producing a softer sound. On upright pianos, a similar effect is achieved by moving all hammers closer to the strings. *See also* Tre Corda.

Unbalanced Line
A method of conveying an audio signal from one point to another using a cable having only one wire. In addition, there will usually be a Screen [2] wrapped around the wire to protect the signal from EMI [2]. This method is cheaper (but offers lower quality) than a Balanced Line, which is to be preferred, particularly where long distances are involved.

Under Modulation
A situation which occurs when the amplitude of a signal falls well below the optimum level in a recording or broadcasting system, causing it to be masked by noise. In digital systems, under modulation can lead to distortion. *See also* Over Modulation.

Unidirectional Microphone
See Cardioid Microphone.

Uninterruptible Power Supply
A type of power supply which can continue to provide electricity despite a momentary interruption, or even complete failure, of the mains supply. The unit contains trickle-charged batteries, along with an "invertor" circuit to produce an AC supply, so that computers (or even a recording studio) can be kept running long enough to be properly "shut down" without loss of data in event of a power failure. Then you light candles and sit in the gloom toasting marshmallows until the electricity company cures the fault.

Unison
Two notes, or musical lines, which have the same pitch. Also used less precisely to include a musical line played or sung in octaves.

Unity Gain
Said of a device such as an amplifier whose gain is 1: e.g. an input of 1V produces an output of 1V. In practice, the preservation of unity gain during all processes in the programme chain (with the exception of initial microphonic gain and final power amplifier gain) is considered the best way of minimising noise and distortion.

Universal System Exclusive
A part of System Exclusive which is intended for all equipment, irrespective of manufacturer. The message uses one of three particular ID numbers after the SOX status byte: 125 is for non-commercial or academic use; 126 is for non-real time use and includes messages for MTC Set Up, Sample Dump Standard, MIDI File Dump, Bulk Tuning and General MIDI; 127 is for real time use and includes MTC Full Message, User Bits, Show Control, Notation, Device Control, Machine Control, Single Note Retuning messages, Master Balance, Master Volume and Real Time MTC Cueing.

University Music Systems
Many academic establishments have developed their own technology systems for music production. These range from programming languages suited to the control of musical events, such as Music X, through to complete sound manipulation, synthesis and composition systems like the Composer's Desktop Project. They all have their strengths and weaknesses, although their supporters are often to keen to stress the former and neglect the latter, while simultaneously being very critical of other systems. The author is particularly saddened by the disdainful attitude adopted by many academics towards good ol' MIDI. It may have its limitations, but it is cheap and plentiful, it is used by the rest of the world for music production and you don't need a Master's degree to understand it. One wonders

if it is their lack of control over the development of MIDI that irritates them more than a genuine concern for its quality.

Upbeat
See Beat [1].

User Bits
1. A group of 32 bits within the 80-bit SMPTE message, which is available to users for their own purposes, such as recording tape identity numbers, dates, etc.

2. A Universal System Exclusive message of the Real Time type which implements the SMPTE message described in User Bits [1]. The 15-byte message consists of the SOX status byte, an ID number data byte of 127 indicating a Real Time Sys Ex message for the whole system, a sub-ID#1 with a value of 1 indicating an MTC message, a sub-ID#2 with a value of 2 indicating a User Bits message, eight bytes which describe the SMPTE user bits, two bytes which describe the group flags, and the EOX status byte.

VA
An expression of the work which can be performed by an electrical device, but which does not take account of the inductance of the load. It is related to the Watt, in that it is also the product of potential difference (V) and current (A), but it ignores the power factor inherent in that unit.

Valve
An electronic device, consisting of various types of electrodes (anode, cathode, grid, etc.) and a heater element, contained in a vacuum. The simplest form, the diode, is used for Rectification. The triode is functionally similar to a Transistor. ICs have largely replaced both of these. The type still in common use is the cathode ray tube (CRT) found in TVs and computer monitors. All valves are called "tubes" in the USA.

Vamping
The act of improvising a musical accompaniment.

Vapourware
An ironic term to describe software (or features in software) promised by the manufacturer, but never actually implemented.

Variation Form
Also called "theme and variations". A musical form in which a theme is presented and then repeated in a succession of different guises. These may include retaining the harmonic structure (the sequence of chords) while elaborating or otherwise varying the melody, changing the time-signature and rhythmic framework, or using new harmonies (e.g. substituting minor for major). In general, the simpler the theme, the more potential it will have for variation.

Varispeed
A facility on a tape machine for altering tape speed by a small amount, to cause a specific amount of pitch change.

VCA
Abbreviation of Voltage Controlled Amplifier. A type of amplifier in which the gain is controlled remotely by a control signal or voltage. Sometimes found on synthesizers and samplers but, in sound recording, more commonly encountered in automation systems for mixing desks. The amplifier will usually be an analogue device. *See also* DCA.

VCF
Abbreviation of Voltage Controlled Filter. A type of filter in which the cut-off frequency is controlled remotely by a control signal or voltage. Sometimes found on synthesizers and samplers. The filter will usually be an analogue device. *See also* DCF.

VCO
Abbreviation of Voltage Controlled Oscillator. An oscillator in which the frequency is controlled remotely by a control signal or voltage. Usually found on analogue synthesizers. *See also* DCO.

VCR
Abbreviation of Video Cassette Recorder. A device for recording and replaying video signals on cassette tape. Sometimes simply called a "video". *See also* VTR.

VDU
See Monitor [3].

Vector Graphics
One of the two principle ways of generating graphics on a computer. Vector graphics produce higher quality images (but smaller files) than the alternative Bitmap method, as each element in the drawing or Font is stored as an equation. This will give, say, just the start point, angle, curvature and length of a line, allowing it to be regenerated without the need to store data about all the intervening points along its length. Vector graphics maintain their quality when scaled up in size, their final appearance being determined only by the Resolution of the printer used.

Velocity
The speed at which a key (or pad) is pressed or released on a MIDI Controller [1]. This information is encoded as the second of two data bytes in a Note On or Note Off message. Note On velocity data (attack velocity) is generally used to control the volume of a sound, but the synth may be programmed

to use this information for purposes such as controlling the profile of an envelope generator. Note Off velocity (release velocity) is almost always used to control the release time of an envelope generator and therefore the duration of the note after the key is released. A Note On message with a velocity value of 0 is interpreted as a Note Off message: *see* Running Status.

Velocity Curve
The relationship between the actual speed of a key press and the velocity value assigned to it in MIDI devices such as synthesizers. In early equipment, this tended to be a linear relationship (i.e. a unit increase in speed produced a unit increase in velocity value). On more recent devices, the relationship can also be scaled to produce different degrees of response at different key speeds. As velocity is most often used to control volume, this could mean a big change in volume at slow speeds, but less change at high, offering greater sensitivity for quiet playing. Some devices now have a range of velocity curves, or may even allow users to program their own.

Velocity of Sound
The speed at which sound waves propagate: the precise speed will depend on the density of the medium through which they travel. In air, at sea level pressure and at 0° C, this is about 331.7 m/s (1088 ft/s). At average room temperatures it is slightly faster, say 334m/s.

Velocity Sensitivity
The ability of a keyboard to register changes in Velocity. Also known as touch sensitivity. Although MIDI allows for 128 discrete steps, devices may implement a smaller number.

Verse
See Song Form.

VHF
Abbreviation of Very High Frequency. Electromagnetic waves with frequencies between 30 MHz and 300 MHz. The range from 88.1 to 108 MHz is used for radio broadcasting in most countries.

VHS
Abbreviation of Video Home System. A domestic standard cassette system for making analogue video recordings. The commercially more successful of two such systems which first appeared in the early '80s. The other, which has not persisted, was Sony's Betamax. Both formats have also been pressed into service as a medium for recording digital audio data. Betamax was used in Sony's F1 system, while VHS's improved successor, S-VHS, is used in the ADAT digital audio multi-track system.

Vibrato
A small and repeating fluctuation in pitch used by instrumentalists (particularly string players) and singers. With the exception of the clavichord, it is not possible on keyboard instruments. However, the effect can either be programmed into a synthesizer's voice, or triggered by controls such as Aftertouch or a Modulation Wheel: vibrato is actually the modulation of frequency and should not be confused with Tremolo[1], which is the modulation of amplitude.

Video
Related to visual images (pictures), sight or seeing, and particularly to video tape recording.

Video-8
A domestic video recording format, which uses 8mm tape in a small cassette. It was developed for use in hand-held cameras and other portable equipment, but has also been adopted for use in some digital audio systems, such as ADAM.

Virtual
In computing, said of a facility or quality that simulates something else. For example, in Virtual Memory, a section of the hard disk might be used by the computer's operating system as if it were part of the main memory when the available RAM is full. Virtual Reality describes a complex computer-generated "environment", using sound, graphics and electro-mechanical devices to simulate a real or imaginary situation. This could have a practical application, as with flight simulation, or be used for such exotic entertainment as playing cosmic hide-and-seek amongst the galaxies. Users typically interact with their chosen environment by wearing a helmet fitted with a display system, a microphone for verbal commands and clothing fitted with motion sensors. The opportunity to live-out the fantasies offered by such a system seems likely to spawn a whole new entertainment industry.

Virus
A form of computer software which is designed to make copies of itself in new locations within a computer (in RAM, hard disk, or floppy disks inserted subsequently). Most viruses have pernicious effects, ranging from mere disruption of the computer screen to wholesale erasure of data. The problem is most acute if a virus enters a computer which is part of a network, since the potential damage will be widespread. A Trojan Horse is a type of virus which is concealed within an otherwise useful and desirable application. Viruses may not be as widespread as media hyperbole suggests, but the consequences of data loss can be devastating and thus the use of anti-virus software is always prudent.

Vision Mixer
A device for mixing video signals from a number of sources. The relative amounts of the signals are controlled by faders, primarily for mixing the output of television cameras.

VITC
Acronym from Vertical Interval Time Code (pronounced "vitsy"). A method for recording timecode (SMPTE or EBU) onto video tape. Unlike LTC, data is recorded in the otherwise blank areas between video frames. It is therefore physically located in little packets rather than the continuous form of LTC, although the net effect is the same.

Vivace
Italian for lively, quickly.

VLSI
Abbreviation of Very Large Scale Integration. An integrated circuit which contains about 100,000 active elements. *See also* LSI, MSI, SSI.

Vocal Score
A notated form of vocal music in which any orchestral parts are condensed into a piano reduction.

Vocoder

Acronym from VOice enCODER. An electronic device developed at Bell Labs in the late '30s as an attempt to increase the number of voice channels that could be squeezed onto a telephone line. After the war, a version of this device came to the attention of composers of Electro-Acoustic music, who started using it to process music and speech simultaneously. Modern versions have two inputs: one for the carrier – most commonly a musical signal – and one for the modulator, typically speech. The effect is to combine the profile of speech with the pitch and tonal characteristics of music. Thus, a vocoder can make string sections and waterfalls seem to talk, or news readers sing, etc. The effect was very popular in the late 1970s with bands like the Electric Light Orchestra (Mr. Blue Sky) and Pink Floyd (Animals).

Voice

1. Strictly, one layer of a synthesizer's Polyphonic [2] capability. Thus, an instrument with, say, 8-voice polyphony, will not be able to generate more than 8 notes at a time. However, the term is now more commonly used as in Voice [2] below.

2. A particular timbre (sometimes called a program or patch) on a synth. *See* Patch.

3. The "instrument" for human speech or singing. There are four broad classes of voice based on pitch range: Soprano, Alto, Tenor and Bass, often abbreviated to SATB. Sub-divisions such as Mezzo Soprano and Baritone are often adopted by solo singers. *See also* Counter Tenor, Falsetto, Treble.

Voice Coil

The central part of a loudspeaker, consisting of a coil of wire mounted on a frame. Variations in the electrical signal passing through the coil cause it to be repulsed from, or attracted to, a fixed magnet, in proportion to the frequency and amplitude of the signal. The resulting motion is mechanically transmitted to an attached cone, whose piston effect excites the surrounding air to reproduce (at what is generally the end of the Programme Chain) recorded sound.

Voice Over

An audio track containing an announcement or narration to accompany a TV or film advertisement, recorded by a person who does not appear on camera. *See also* Post Sync.

Voicing

The distribution of notes in chordal music to produce a particular texture. By extension, the allocation of these notes to different instruments or voices.

Volt

The SI Unit of potential difference. *See* Electricity.

Voltage

See Electricity.

Volume

1. The degree of relative loudness or amplitude.

2. One of the defined MIDI Controller Change messages with a status byte value in the range 176–191 and a data byte value of 7. It is assigned to the parameter in a synthesizer which determines output volume. Sometimes called main volume, although it only operates on the channel [2] to which it is assigned. Not to be confused with Velocity.

VTR

Abbreviation of Video Tape Recorder. A device for recording and replaying video signals on tape (usually open reel as opposed to cassette). *See also* VCR.

VU Meter

Abbreviation of Volume Unit meter. An electromechanical meter used to indicate the amplitude of audio signals on equipment such as mixing desks and tape machines. As they are only accurate for steady-state signals such as line-up tones, they are less useful than PPMs and tend not to be fitted to modern equipment.

Wait

One of the characters transmitted for the purposes of Handshaking in a data transfer. The character is sent back to the transmitting device by the receiving device to indicate that the receiver wants the transmitter to pause. The transmission will continue when the receiver sends an Ack, or it will be stopped altogether if the receiver sends a Cancel. It also occurs as part of the Sample Dump Standard as a System Exclusive message of the Non-Real Time type with a Sub ID#1 value of 124.

Watt

1. The SI Unit of power, equal to 1 Joule per second. 745.70 Watts is 1 horse-power (a unit with surprisingly little application in music technology).

2. A unit of electrical power, indicating the amount of work deployable into a given load by an electrical device such as an amplifier or motor. It is strictly the product of the potential difference (V), current (A) and power factor (cos Φ). In practice the power factor is often ignored and the term is reduced to VA.

Waveform	A cyclic propagation of energy through a medium at a constant velocity, such as sound pressure waves through air, or a diagram of such oscillations. Also refers to the appearance of the oscillating voltages of signals on an oscilloscope. *See* Pulse Wave, Ramp Wave, Sine Wave, Square Wave, Triangle Wave.
Wavelength	The distance covered by one cycle of a waveform. In high frequency waves, there are more cycles in a given unit of time than there are in low frequency waves, this means they are closer together and consequently the wavelength of a high frequency is shorter than that of a low frequency. For sound waves, the wavelength in metres (λ) can be determined by dividing the velocity of sound (approx. 334 m/s) by the frequency in Hz. Thus, audio frequencies have wavelengths in the range from 16 metres to 16 millimetres.
Wavetable	In some digital synthesizers, an area of memory which contains data describing one cycle of each of a number of Waveforms that are the basis for many different synthesized sounds. This table is used to determine the shape of the wave to be output, and is scanned repeatedly to generate a constant tone, reproducing the effect of an analogue oscillator. Sequential scanning of different areas of the table will produce a varying tone.
Weber	The SI Unit of Flux Density.
White Label	A small-scale pressing of a record or CD, with an anonymous blank (hence, "white") label, used for market testing a track (especially dance music) on a limited audience before release. Also used by contracted artists to issue a track rejected by their own record company.
White Noise	A signal which contains all possible audio frequencies in equal average amplitudes, just as white light contains all of the colours in the visual spectrum. Useful for testing equipment.
WIMP	Acronym from Windows, Icons, Mouse Pointer. A generic term used to describe any graphic user interface which employs these features in its operating system. Some would also apply the term to the user of such an interface, but *see* Power User.
Window	In a computer, an area on the Monitor[3] which some programs provide for the user to view or manipulate a discrete section of data. Windows can generally be adjusted in size, moved around the screen, and opened or closed, using a Mouse. It is also sometimes possible to "paste" data from one program into a window of another.
Windows	A proprietary name of Microsoft for their WIMP operating system for IBM-compatible PCs.
Windshield	A cover fitted over a microphone to reduce the amount of noise generated by wind blowing past.
Wipe	Synonym for Erase.
Wire	Usually, an assembly of metal strands enclosed in an insulating sheath, but sometimes used to refer just to the metal strand or strands, used to convey an electrical signal between two points. Wire is a component part of any Cable.
Woofer	*See* Loudspeaker.
Wolf Note	A term used to describe the inaccuracy in pitch which can occur when an instrument such as a harpsichord, which has not been tuned to Equal Temperament, is played in a remote key. Also used for the undue stridency (or even the muffling) of a note on an instrument such as a cello, where the pitch of that note is arithmetically related to the Natural Frequency of the instrument.
Word	In computers and digital systems, the number of bits used by the system to define a numerical value or sample. This indicates the resolution of such a sample. An 8-bit word is 1 byte, a 12-bit word is 1.5 bytes, a 16-bit word is 2 bytes. However in general usage, a word is considered to be two bytes unless otherwise qualified. 32 bits is often called a "long word".
Word Processor	Commonly abbreviated to WP. A category of computer software which allows a user to generate, edit and print text-based documents. Originally intended for simple documents such as letters, these programs increasingly are incorporating the graphics and layout facilities of Desktop Publishing software. However, WP is normally optimized for the keying and altering of text, rather than to the fine detail of typography. Additional facilities, such as a spelling and a grammar checker, a dictionary and a thesaurus, may also be included in the package.
Workstation	A term to which manufacturers apply often contradictory meanings. In music technology, it is usually a synthesizer with on-board sequencer, drum sounds and effects unit. With reference to computers, it may refer to a powerful, self-contained system for individual use, but is equally used to describe just a simple Terminal[2] on a Network[2].
World Music	A term which is used, often rather patronizingly, by western musicians to refer to the vast range of music from other cultures. Although greater awareness of the huge wealth of world music can only be a good thing, the term itself is really too broad to be meaningful.
WORM	Write Once Read Many. Essentially any form of memory which allows information or data to be stored or saved once only, but the information can be read as many times as you like (until it wears out). Recordable CDs are an example of this, although the term generally refers to programmable ICs.

Wow

Unintentional changes in pitch caused by slow speed variation in tape recorders or record players. Such variations may be due to a worn or defective pinchwheel or capstan, faulty motors or unreliable Varispeed control electronics. *See also* Flutter.

WPC

Abbreviation of Watts per Channel. A unit intended to give an indication of the output of a power amplifier. It should be qualified by a load condition such as the impedance of a loudspeaker: e.g. 200 WPC/4Ω, otherwise it is meaningless.

XLR

A type of connector favoured for use with low level (microphone) signals. Sometimes also called "Cannons", they are most commonly encountered with three pins for use in Balanced Line systems. They are physically large and heavy-duty, and are fitted with a latch to prevent accidental disconnection.

Yodel

A singing style, popular amongst certain of the male population in alpine areas of Europe, featuring a rapid alternation of falsetto and normal tone. This is facilitated by the almost invariable use of the nonsense syllables "yo-del-o-del-o-del", hence its name. The rapidity of the alternations is considered an important criterion in the style, making it more akin to a sport than an art form. *See also* Falsetto.

Zero Level

A level of 0 dB(v). All measurements are made relative to this level, as it represents (in properly lined-up equipment) the optimal recording or broadcast level. Higher signal levels than this (positive numbers) indicate the possibility of Over Modulation, significantly lower levels than this (negative numbers) indicate the possibility of Under Modulation. *See also* Unity Gain.

Zero Return

A control on a tape recorder which will automatically stop the tape on rewind when the Tape Counter reaches zero.

Zone

An area on a Master Keyboard, usually a contiguous group of keys, which can have a specific set of functions or attributes. For example, if a master keyboard is controlling two MIDI devices, it would be desirable to split the keyboard into two zones, each with different MIDI channel, velocity and aftertouch, etc.

Zydeco

Essentially the Afro-American equivalent of Cajun music, indigenous to Louisiana, USA. The term may be derived from the French title of the dance "Les haricots sont pas salés", several versions of which were recorded in Zydeco style. The local Creole pronunciation of *les haricots* (" 'zarico") may have led to Zydeco. Essentially dance music, it is characterized by syncopation and two-step rhythms, and the alternation of sung and played verses. Zydeco tends to favour saxophone and piano accordion, rather than the violin and diatonic accordion of Cajun, and the percussion sometimes features a washboard played with thimbles. Rockin' Sidney, Stanley "Buckwheat" Dural Jr. and Queen Ida are the best known modern exponents.

#

Sometimes called hash, this symbol is used in the USA as the equivalent of the English abbreviation Nº for number. Thus Americans write "telephone # ", English write "telephone Nº ".

μ

Micro. Prefix meaning one millionth. Sub-multiple of SI Units. Also used as the symbol for the now obsolete unit of length, the Micron (one millionth of a metre).

Ω

Omega, the symbol for Ohm, the SI Unit of impedance, reactance and resistance.

Decimal – Binary – Hexadecimal Conversion Table

(The space in each 8-bit binary number is provided purely for ease of reading)

Dec	Binary	Hex	Dec	Binary	Hex	Dec	Binary	Hex	Dec	Binary	Hex
000	0000 0000	00	064	0100 0000	40	128	1000 0000	80	192	1100 0000	C0
001	0000 0001	01	065	0100 0001	41	129	1000 0001	81	193	1100 0001	C1
002	0000 0010	02	066	0100 0010	42	130	1000 0010	82	194	1100 0010	C2
003	0000 0011	03	067	0100 0011	43	131	1000 0011	83	195	1100 0011	C3
004	0000 0100	04	068	0100 0100	44	132	1000 0100	84	196	1100 0100	C4
005	0000 0101	05	069	0100 0101	45	133	1000 0101	85	197	1100 0101	C5
006	0000 1111	06	070	0100 0110	46	134	1000 0110	86	198	1100 0110	C6
007	0000 0111	07	071	0100 0111	47	135	1000 0111	87	199	1100 0111	C7
008	0000 1000	08	072	0100 1000	48	136	1000 1000	88	200	1100 1000	C8
009	0000 1001	09	073	0100 1001	49	137	1000 1001	89	201	1100 1001	C9
010	0000 1010	0A	074	0100 1010	4A	138	1000 1010	8A	202	1100 1010	CA
011	0000 1011	0B	075	0100 1011	4B	139	1000 1011	8B	203	1100 1011	CB
012	0000 1100	0C	076	0100 1100	4C	140	1000 1100	8C	204	1100 1100	CC
013	0000 1101	0D	077	0100 1101	4D	141	1000 1101	8D	205	1100 1101	CD
014	0000 1110	0E	078	0100 1110	4E	142	1000 1110	8E	206	1100 1110	CE
015	0000 1111	0F	079	0100 1111	4F	143	1000 1111	8F	207	1100 1111	CF
016	0001 0000	10	080	0101 0000	50	144	1001 0000	90	208	1101 0000	D0
017	0001 0001	11	081	0101 0001	51	145	1001 0001	91	209	1101 0001	D1
018	0001 0010	12	082	0101 0010	52	146	1001 0010	92	210	1101 0010	D2
019	0001 0011	13	083	0101 0011	53	147	1001 0011	93	211	1101 0011	D3
020	0001 0100	14	084	0101 0100	54	148	1001 0100	94	212	1101 0100	D4
021	0001 0101	15	085	0101 0101	55	149	1001 0101	95	213	1101 0101	D5
022	0001 0110	16	086	0101 0110	56	150	1001 0110	96	214	1101 0110	D6
023	0001 0111	17	087	0101 0111	57	151	1001 0111	97	215	1101 0111	D7
024	0001 1000	18	088	0101 1000	58	152	1001 1000	98	216	1101 1000	D8
025	0001 1001	19	089	0101 1001	59	153	1001 1001	99	217	1101 1001	D9
026	0001 1010	1A	090	0101 1010	5A	154	1001 1010	9A	218	1101 1010	DA
027	0001 1011	1B	091	0101 1011	5B	155	1001 1011	9B	219	1101 1011	DB
028	0001 1100	1C	092	0101 1100	5C	156	1001 1100	9C	220	1101 1100	DC
029	0001 1101	1D	093	0101 1101	5D	157	1001 1101	9D	221	1101 1101	DD
030	0001 1110	1E	094	0101 1110	5E	158	1001 1110	9E	222	1101 1110	DE
031	0001 1111	1F	095	0101 1111	5F	159	1001 1111	9F	223	1101 1111	DF
032	0010 0000	20	096	0110 0000	60	160	1010 0000	A0	224	1110 0000	E0
033	0010 0001	21	097	0110 0001	61	161	1010 0001	A1	225	1110 0001	E1
034	0010 0010	22	098	0110 0010	62	162	1010 0010	A2	226	1110 0010	E2
035	0010 0011	23	099	0110 0011	63	163	1010 0011	A3	227	1110 0011	E3
036	0010 0100	24	100	0110 0100	64	164	1010 0100	A4	228	1110 0100	E4
037	0010 0101	25	101	0110 0101	65	165	1010 0101	A5	229	1110 0101	E5
038	0010 0110	26	102	0110 0110	66	166	1010 0110	A6	230	1110 0110	E6
039	0010 0111	27	103	0110 0111	67	167	1010 0111	A7	231	1110 0111	E7
040	0010 1000	28	104	0110 1000	68	168	1010 1000	A8	232	1110 1000	E8
041	0010 1001	29	105	0110 1001	69	169	1010 1001	A9	233	1110 1001	E9
042	0010 1010	2A	106	0110 1010	6A	170	1010 1010	AA	234	1110 1010	EA
043	0010 1011	2B	107	0110 1011	6B	171	1010 1011	AB	235	1110 1011	EB
044	0010 1100	2C	108	0110 1100	6C	172	1010 1100	AC	236	1110 1100	EC
045	0010 1101	2D	109	0110 1101	6D	173	1010 1101	AD	237	1110 1101	ED
046	0010 1110	2E	110	0110 1110	6E	174	1010 1110	AE	238	1110 1110	EE
047	0010 1111	2F	111	0110 1111	6F	175	1010 1111	AF	239	1110 1111	EF
048	0011 0000	30	112	0111 0000	70	176	1011 0000	B0	240	1111 0000	F0
049	0011 0001	31	113	0111 0001	71	177	1011 0001	B1	241	1111 0001	F1
050	0011 0010	32	114	0111 0010	72	178	1011 0010	B2	242	1111 0010	F2
051	0011 0011	33	115	0111 0011	73	179	1011 0011	B3	243	1111 0011	F3
052	0011 0100	34	116	0111 0100	74	180	1011 0100	B4	244	1111 0100	F4
053	0011 0101	35	117	0111 0101	75	181	1011 0101	B5	245	1111 0101	F5
054	0011 0110	36	118	0111 0110	76	182	1011 0110	B6	246	1111 0110	F6
055	0011 0111	37	119	0111 0111	77	183	1011 0111	B7	247	1111 0111	F7
056	0011 1000	38	120	0111 1000	78	184	1011 1000	B8	248	1111 1000	F8
057	0011 1001	39	121	0111 1001	79	185	1011 1001	B9	249	1111 1001	F9
058	0011 1010	3A	122	0111 1010	7A	186	1011 1010	BA	250	1111 1010	FA
059	0011 1011	3B	123	0111 1011	7B	187	1011 1011	BB	251	1111 1011	FB
060	0011 1100	3C	124	0111 1100	7C	188	1011 1100	BC	252	1111 1100	FC
061	0011 1101	3D	125	0111 1101	7D	189	1011 1101	BD	253	1111 1101	FD
062	0011 1110	3E	126	0111 1110	7E	190	1011 1110	BE	254	1111 1110	FE
063	0011 1111	3F	127	0111 1111	7F	191	1011 1111	BF	255	1111 1111	FF

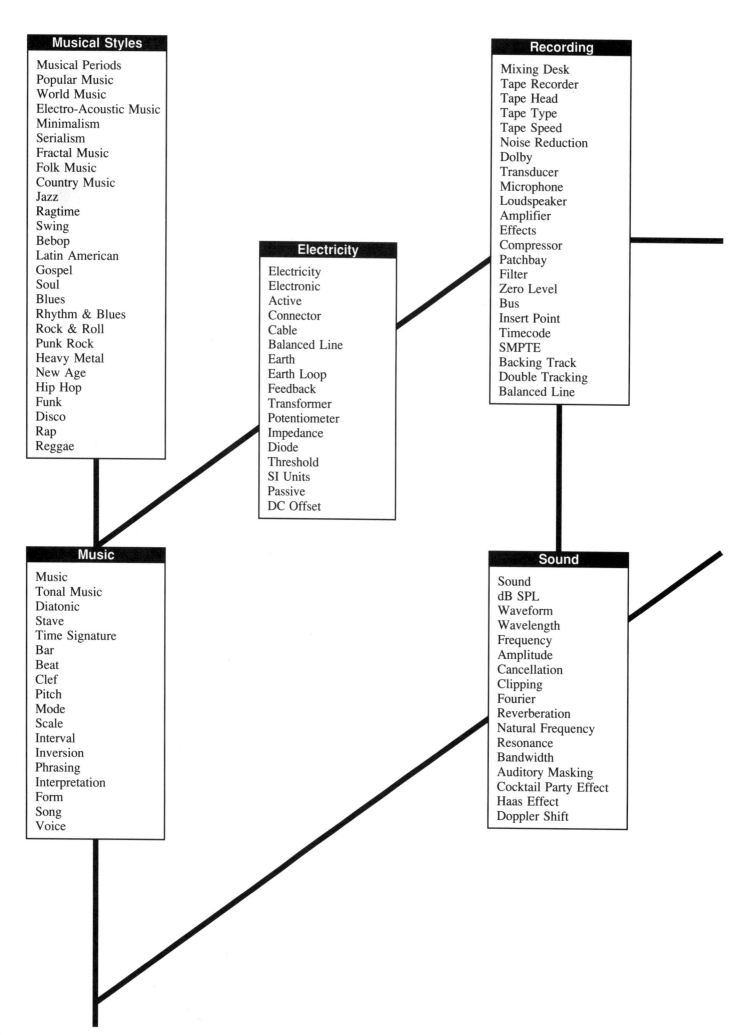

Musical Styles

Musical Periods
Popular Music
World Music
Electro-Acoustic Music
Minimalism
Serialism
Fractal Music
Folk Music
Country Music
Jazz
Ragtime
Swing
Bebop
Latin American
Gospel
Soul
Blues
Rhythm & Blues
Rock & Roll
Punk Rock
Heavy Metal
New Age
Hip Hop
Funk
Disco
Rap
Reggae

Recording

Mixing Desk
Tape Recorder
Tape Head
Tape Type
Tape Speed
Noise Reduction
Dolby
Transducer
Microphone
Loudspeaker
Amplifier
Effects
Compressor
Patchbay
Filter
Zero Level
Bus
Insert Point
Timecode
SMPTE
Backing Track
Double Tracking
Balanced Line

Electricity

Electricity
Electronic
Active
Connector
Cable
Balanced Line
Earth
Earth Loop
Feedback
Transformer
Potentiometer
Impedance
Diode
Threshold
SI Units
Passive
DC Offset

Music

Music
Tonal Music
Diatonic
Stave
Time Signature
Bar
Beat
Clef
Pitch
Mode
Scale
Interval
Inversion
Phrasing
Interpretation
Form
Song
Voice

Sound

Sound
dB SPL
Waveform
Wavelength
Frequency
Amplitude
Cancellation
Clipping
Fourier
Reverberation
Natural Frequency
Resonance
Bandwidth
Auditory Masking
Cocktail Party Effect
Haas Effect
Doppler Shift

The Studio Musician's
JARGONBUSTER

A Glossary of Music Technology and Recording

Digital Audio
Digital
Sample
Sampling Rate
PAM
PCM
Fourier
Quantization Error
Aliasing
Oversampling
CD
DASH
RDAT
DCC
MD
ADAM
ADAT
SDAT
SCMS

Synthesis
Synthesis
Modular Synthesizer
Monophonic
Polyphonic
Multi-Timbral
Patch
Aftertouch
Pitchbend
Modulation Wheel
FM Synthesis
Operator
Wavetable
Oscillator
LFO
Envelope Generator
VCA / DCA
VCF / DCF
VCO / DCO
Modulation
Ring Modulator
CV & Gate
S & S
Sampler

MIDI
MIDI
MIDI Socket
Daisy Chain
Star Network
MIDI Message
Data Byte
Status Byte
Hexadecimal
MIDI Controllers
Channel
Channel Voice
Reception Mode
Program Change
Note On / Note Off
Running Status
Active Sensing
System Exclusive Message
Universal System Exclusive
Sequencer
Velocity
Quantization
Real Time
Standard MIDI File
General MIDI
Sample Dump Standard

Computing
Computer
Computer Generations
Binary
Bit
Byte
Data
Data Compression
Instruction Set
Algorithm
Operating System
Machine Code
File
ASCII
Software
Database
Spreadsheet
Hard Disk
Floppy Disk
WIMP
Graphics
Hypertext
Interactive
Virtual
E-Mail
Hacking
Public Domain
Copy Protection
Bug
Virus
Memory
Integrated Circuit
ROM
RAM
Monitor
Mouse
Printer
Scanner

This "route map" shows the key entries for a number of important topics, many of which have further cross-references in the text. The coverage of the chart is not intended to give a comprehensive introduction to each subject: it gives only a selection of entries and it does not reveal the myriad of inter-connections between the varied disciplines of music, technology and recording. However, it is hoped that it will help provide a starting-point for readers wishing to use this book for the purpose of exploring areas that may be new to them.